Modernism and Its Media

NEW MODERNISMS SERIES

Bloomsbury's *New Modernisms* series introduces, explores, and extends the major topics and debates at the forefront of contemporary Modernist Studies.

Surveying new engagements with such topics as race, sexuality, technology, and material culture, and supported with authoritative further reading guides to the key works in contemporary scholarship, these books are essential guides for serious students and scholars of Modernism.

Published Titles

Modernism: Evolution of an Idea
Sean Latham and Gayle Rogers

Modernism and the Law
Robert Spoo

Modernism in a Global Context
Peter J. Kalliney

Modernism's Print Cultures
Faye Hammill and Mark Hussey

Modernism, Science, and Technology
Mark S. Morrisson

Modernism, Sex, and Gender
Celia Marshik and Allison Pease

Modernism, War, and Violence
Marina MacKay

Race and Modernisms
K. Merinda Simmons and James A. Crank

Modernism and Its Environments
Michael Rubenstein and Justin Neuman

Modernism and Its Media

Chris Forster

BLOOMSBURY ACADEMIC
LONDON • NEW YORK • OXFORD • NEW DELHI • SYDNEY

BLOOMSBURY ACADEMIC
Bloomsbury Publishing Plc
50 Bedford Square, London, WC1B 3DP, UK
1385 Broadway, New York, NY 10018, USA
29 Earlsfort Terrace, Dublin 2, Ireland

BLOOMSBURY, BLOOMSBURY ACADEMIC and the Diana logo
are trademarks of Bloomsbury Publishing Plc

First published in Great Britain 2022

Copyright © Chris Forster, 2022

Chris Forster has asserted his right under the Copyright, Designs
and Patents Act, 1988, to be identified as Author of this work.

For legal purposes the Acknowledgments on p. vi constitute
an extension of this copyright page.

Cover design: Eleanor Rose
Cover design by Daniel Benneworth-Gray
Cover Image: A radio is company for this girl in her boardinghouse room.
Photograph by Esther Bubley on assignment for the Office of War Information,
January 1943. FSA-OWI Collection / U.S. Library of Congress

All rights reserved. No part of this publication may be reproduced or transmitted
in any form or by any means, electronic or mechanical, including photocopying,
recording, or any information storage or retrieval system, without prior
permission in writing from the publishers.

Bloomsbury Publishing Plc does not have any control over, or responsibility for,
any third-party websites referred to or in this book. All internet addresses given
in this book were correct at the time of going to press. The author and publisher
regret any inconvenience caused if addresses have changed or sites have ceased
to exist, but can accept no responsibility for any such changes.

A catalogue record for this book is available from the British Library.

A catalog record for this book is available from the Library of Congress.

ISBN: HB: 978-1-3500-3315-3
PB: 978-1-3500-3314-6
ePDF: 978-1-3500-3317-7
eBook: 978-1-3500-3316-0

Series: New Modernisms

Typeset by Integra Software Services Pvt. Ltd.

To find out more about our authors and books visit www.bloomsbury.com and
sign up for our newsletters.

CONTENTS

Acknowledgments vi

Introduction: Art and Literature in an Age of Media 1

1 Modernism and Film 27

2 Purifying the Medium: Clement Greenberg and the Legacy of Medium Specificity 71

3 Rebalancing the Sensorium: The Media Ecology of Marshall McLuhan and the Toronto School 105

4 The Work of Modernism in the Age of Mass Media: The Frankfurt School 139

5 Friedrich Kittler and Media Archaeology: The End of the Book and the Birth of the Modernist Discourse Network 181

Conclusion: Digital Modernism 211

Works Cited 227
Index 244

ACKNOWLEDGMENTS

Foremost, I have to thank the series editors, Sean Latham and Gayle Rogers, for inviting me to contribute to this series. They have been unrelentingly supportive and patient.

My colleagues in the English Department at Syracuse University create a uniquely rich environment for anyone working at the intersections of media and literature. Graduate students in my "Modernism and Its Media" seminar have helped shape my thinking on these questions, as have students in my wider survey "Literature and Its Media." Susan Edmunds helpfully pointed me towards work on Hemingway and the telegraph. I especially want to thank my colleague Crystal Bartolovich, who provided invaluable feedback on my chapter on the Frankfurt School.

James Bridle's "Drone Shadow" (2013) appears courtesy of the artist.

Introduction: Art and Literature in an Age of Media

The latter part of the nineteenth and the first part of the twentieth century, those years most often called *modernist*, saw both widespread experimentation across the arts and the rapid development of new communication and media technologies. The first conventionally includes such disparate phenomena as fragmentation in poetry, stream of consciousness narration in fiction, atonal music, and a turn away from mimetic representation in the visual arts. The latter includes the development of photography, telegraphy, and the inventions of radio and film, to say nothing of less obvious, but perhaps equally consequential technological developments, such as the rotary press, the light bulb, half-tone printing, and even early computing technology.[1] What is the relationship between these two phenomena, and how should we understand it? That is the question which preoccupies this book.

We might define our key terms—modernism and modern media—*against* one another. The Marxist literary critic Raymond Williams writes that any explanation of modernism

> must start from the fact that the late nineteenth century was the occasion for the greatest changes ever seen in the media

---

[1] The foundations of computing technologies can be traced back at least as far as Charles Babbage and Ada Lovelace in the first half of the nineteenth century. Alan Turing's paper on the "halting problem" was first published in 1936, and Konrad Zuse began constructing the Z1, the first programmable computer, the same year.

of cultural production. Photography, cinema, radio, television, reproduction and recording all make their decisive advances during the period identified as Modernist, and it is in response to these that there arise what in the first instance were formed as defensive cultural groupings, rapidly if partially becoming competitively self-promoting.

(*Politics of Modernism* 33)

Modernism, in this view, reacts against the new technologies. The "cultural groupings," which would include movements such as the Futurists or Imagists, represent a defensive organization against rapid changes in "the public media." Discussing modernism and its media here means modernism as a reaction against modern media.

Alternatively, in earlier treatments of modernism, technology was often simply part of a wide-ranging description of *modernity*. What modernism shares with media is newness and novelty. Both *modernism* (say, T. S. Eliot's poetry) and technology are, in short, *modern*. In Malcolm Bradbury and James MacFarlane's influential *Modernism: A Guide to European Literature 1880–1930* (1978), technology is just one more item in a litany that includes Marx, Freud, Darwin, capitalism, and Heisenberg's uncertainty principle—all offering testimony of the "chaos" of modern existence.

> [Modernism] is the one art that responds to the scenario of our chaos. It is the art consequent on Heisenberg's 'Uncertainty principle,' of the destruction of civilization and reason in the First World War, of the world changed and reinterpreted by Marx, Freud, and Darwin, of capitalism and constant industrial acceleration, of existential exposure to meaninglessness or absurdity. It is the literature of technology. It is the art consequent on the dis-establishing of communal reality and conventional notions of causality, on the destruction of traditional notions of the wholeness of individual character, on the linguistic chaos that ensues when public notions of language have been discredited and when all realities have become subjective fictions. Modernism is then the art of modernization.
>
> (Bradbury and MacFarlane 27)

Modernism is the "art of modernization," which means, among other things, the "literature of technology." Technology here is a future-oriented force that breaks with the past and inaugurates the new as surely as the psychoanalysis of Freud or the physics of Heisenberg. Already we have here two diametrically opposed definitions: modernism as the literature *of* technology, or modernism as cultural defense *against* technology.

Rather than attempt broadly to determine the nature of modernism's relationship to technology, we might approach this relationship in more local ways. We might ask more specific questions about how modernism related to its media environment: What impact did different media have on writers, poets, and artists? Were artists intimidated by new media? How did new media change or shape the work of major modernist writers? Were modernist formal techniques taken up by the new media? How were particular media technologies—the telephone, the telegraph, or film—represented in the art, literature, and poetry of the period?[2] The literature *of* technology may suggest a literature that takes technology as its focus or subject matter, as works from Futurism to the novels of H. G. Wells did. Yet it may also suggest a new mode or type of literature, such as imagined by Bob Brown in his "readies,"[3] or uniquely modernist art forms, such as the "vortographs" that briefly interested Ezra Pound. Or the literature *of* technology may more simply mean a literature appropriate to a technologized age. For Bradbury and MacFarlane, modernism's relationship to its media is no different than its relationship to any other context. To Heisenberg and Freud, industrialization and capitalism, we might add other modernist contexts: feminism, suffrage, and changes in norms about sex and gender, evident in discourses such as sexology, First World War, radical politics.

Considered in this way, as one more historical context, developments in technology are likely to seem less important than, for instance, women's suffrage. The development of media technology surely pales in importance to the catastrophes of

---

[2]These questions are inspired by those Susan McCabe poses early in *Cinematic Modernism* (2005) about the relationship between film and poetry (2).
[3]See Brown's *The Readies* (1930) for his description of this modernized reading machine—which displays automatically moving horizontal strips of text—that, Brown suggests, could replace the book.

the first two world wars, social developments such as first-wave feminism, or the consequences of imperialism. Yet, media have a special relationship to art and culture. Media technologies are not, or are not *only*, a context that surrounds or shapes literature and culture. While at one level the new communications technologies of the early twentieth century are one more context that shaped the production and reception of modernism, at another level these technologies are a force compelling a moment of aesthetic self-recognition. For Williams, the changing media technological landscape is specifically relevant to the art and literature of the period because art and literature are themselves *media*, and so can be imagined in conflict or competition with these new technological upstarts. What happens to the novel after film becomes one of the chief sources of narrative? What happens to poetry after radio and recorded sound emerge as avenues for representing the lyric voice? What happens to painting after photography? Media change is not only something happening at the same time as modernism. It is something that happens *to* modernism. Not only do the invention of halftone printing and the development of radio, as Bradbury and McFarlane suggest, express (like so many other forces) the rapid change and novelty of modernity. Media are also a sort of aesthetic a priori or cultural infrastructure in which the arts are enmeshed. They are the very ground of those arts' being, and so changes to them are not simply events to be reflected or represented, absorbed or rejected, by art and literature; they change the nature of art itself. In this sense, the question of modernism and its media is nothing other than the question of modernism itself. To use an image from Edgar Allan Poe that Marshall McLuhan, often considered the founder of "media studies," was fond of invoking, in an era of rapid media change, the artist is tasked with trying to describe the whirlpool into which he has already been sucked. One might object that this is true of *all* those contexts mentioned above, that a British writer in the 1910s is just as surely absorbed in the maelstrom of imperialist culture. Yet media, in their materiality, are the very tools of expression, and so pose a more direct problem than those other cultural contexts, which we tend to imagine as somehow *saturating* the world of the artist or writer from the outside.

Such an intimate relationship between media history and literary history is evident in Ian Watt's *The Rise of the Novel* (1957). He traces the emergence of the novel to eighteenth-century journalism and the dominance of print as medium. "It was not until the rise of journalism that a new form of writing arose which was wholly dependent on printed performance, and the novel is perhaps the only literary genre which is essentially connected with the medium of print" (204). Watt suggests that print, in its uniformity and mass availability, enables a privacy of experience and identification that is central to the aesthetics of the novel. This sense of privacy and interiority reaches its climax, however, in a work of modernist fiction.[4] Watt writes, quoting Lewis Mumford's *Culture of Cities* (1938), "Perhaps the most representative and inclusive presentation of the problem in all its dubieties is to be found in the supreme culmination of the formal trend that [Samuel] Richardson initiated—James Joyce's *Ulysses*. No book has gone beyond it in the literal transcription of all the states of consciousness, regurgitating 'the contents of the newspaper and the advertisement, living in a hell of unfulfilled desires, vague wishes, enfeebling anxieties, morbid compulsions, and dreary vacuities'" (214). If the novel is inextricable from the rise of print in the eighteenth century, how can it continue as a form in the age of radio? How does one narrate the new world of instantaneous, electrical communication? Is *Ulysses* the last novel of the age of print? Is modernism a rearguard defensive action, of the sort Williams describes, against the encroachment of new media? Or is *Ulysses* perhaps the first novel of the age of new media, of what André Bazin in an essay translated as "In Defense of Mixed Cinema" (1951) imagines as an age of "films that dare to take their inspiration from a novel-like style one might describe as ultracinematographic" (Bazin, *What* 64)?

Despite the work of critics like Raymond Williams, and a few others, such questions have not always been central to accounts of modernism. Over the past two decades, however, critics have returned to these questions with a sense of increasing relevance. In part this reflects the emergence and centrality of the internet to our everyday lives. The experience of radical media change resensitized critics to the complexities and materialities of old media in contrast to new media. Justus Nieland summarizes this reemergent interest in media in modernist studies: "Positioning modernist aesthetics

---

[4]Watt would work with Jack Goody on *The Consequences of Literacy*, a work clearly in the tradition of the Toronto School of media studies discussed in Chapter 4.

within the dynamics of media change and competition, critics have recast modernist form as an event within a competitive media environment in which vanguard sensorial experiments become so many ways of making media a lifestyle, accommodating the challenge of technicity to the prestige and epistemic authority of the human" (234). Modernism, Nieland suggests, reflects the accommodation of new media into the arts at the level of the senses. Recent approaches to modernism return to, and enrich, the focus on media evident in the work of Williams and others.

This book attempts to make sense of these approaches by surveying some of the most important ways that critics and theorists have attempted to frame the relationship between modernism and its media environment. It traces modernism as a reaction to a history of media broadly centered around the turn of the twentieth century. How does modernism relate to its media? The answers to this question include the work of individual artists and writers who took up this question directly, but also a broader evaluation of these two key terms. Is modernism an embrace of media change or a rejection of it? There is a complication at the level, however, of theory: neither how we understand *modernism* nor how we define *media* are clearly given in advance.

Definitions

The term modernism is of course an object of debate and contestation. Sean Latham and Gayle Rogers, in the inaugural title in this series *Modernism: Evolution of an Idea* (2015), ask the question "what is modernism?" but conclude by admitting "We don't know" (206). The term itself represents less an object to be defined than a still ongoing set of debates. And these very debates and definitions intersect with the history of the media of the period. As we will see, different definitions of modernism respond differently to the question of media. Yet, the term "media" itself is no easier to define. Even in the most mundane of its meanings, as an adjective describing size, "medium" is defined only as a sort of in-betweenness, stuck in the middle of other things. A medium coffee differs purely in quantity from a large or small. This adjectival force of medium as "in between" carries over into the noun. In its definitions, the *Oxford English Dictionary* includes "intermediary," "intermediate agency, instrument, or channel; a means," "an intervening substance." It includes the "pervading or enveloping substance" in which an organism lives, like the agar in which bacteria are cultivated (or "cultured") in petri dishes. Remember as well the word's supernatural associations: a medium can also be a clairvoyant, a person who operates as an interface between this world and another, between the living and the dead.

The conventional assumption is often that a medium is *only* a means, an empty channel, itself unworthy of attention. We see this attitude when people describe a technology as a tool, which is itself neutral. It is not the tool that matters, this position says, but "how you use it." Such an attitude treats a medium or technology as an inessential bearer of other meanings and purposes. The definitions of medium—a channel, a mode, a means—share this sense of something that is not a primary concern, something that merely enables something else. The biologist's interest is in bacterial growth, not the agar where it takes place, just as surely as the visitor to a clairvoyant believes or hopes that the words they hear are communicated from elsewhere (they aren't simply visiting the clairvoyant for her or his company). However else they differ, the approaches to modernism and media surveyed here insist on the importance and meaningfulness of the medium. What they share, as versions of media studies, is attention to what is often ignored. They make opaque what is often taken to be transparent.

Beyond this focus on the "medium" as a category, however, the approaches discussed here are often quite different. Indeed, the term *medium* proves as slippery as modernism itself. In their introduction to *Critical Terms for Media Studies* (2010), W. J. T. Mitchell and Mark Hansen define media as a "deep, technoanthropological universal that has structured the history of humanity from its very origin" (viii–ix). For them, the term "media" is as important to the study of culture as the other major innovations of literary theory. Media, for Mitchell and Hansen, is a term akin to the Freudian unconscious, the Marxian mode of production, or Derrida's concept of writing as *écriture*. "In addition to naming individual mediums at concrete points within that history, 'media' in our view, also names a technical form or formal technics, indeed a general mediality that is constitutive of the human as a 'biotechnical' form of life" (x). Fundamentally "*media* names an ontological condition of humanization—the constitutive operation of exteriorization and invention" such that *media* is/are inextricable from "the form of life that is the human" (xiii, xiv). Media as ontologically intextricable from the human as such. Heavy stuff.

Lisa Gitelman, in *Always Already New: Media, History, and the Data of Culture* (2006), offers an equally rich definition of media, though one that avoids philosophical abstractions, and insists instead on historical specificity. Media are, she writes,

> socially realized structures of communication, where structures include both technological forms and their associated protocols, and where communication is a cultural practice, a ritualized collocation of different people on the same mental map, sharing or engaged with popular ontologies of representation. As such, media are unique and complicated historical subjects. Their histories must be social and cultural, not the stories of how one technology leads to another, or of isolated geniuses working their magic on the world.
>
> (*Always* 7)

In *The Audible Past: Cultural Origins of Sound Reproduction* (2003), Jonathan Sterne similarly tries to nail down a pragmatic definition of the term, suggesting that "a medium is therefore the social basis that allows a set of technologies to stand out as a unified thing with clearly defined functions" (182). Such definitions are not opposed to Mitchell and Hansen's "ontological condition of humanization," but they do operate at a different scale. Gitelman and Sterne deliberately avoid making media the chief agent of history by insisting on the thoroughly social, and utterly historical, agencies "behind" them. Media, alone, don't have wide-reaching effects because they are already "socially realized" cultural practices and historical subjects. Rather than agents themselves, Gitelman suggests, media "are more properly the results of social and economic forces, so that any technological logic they possess is only apparently intrinsic" (*Always* 10). Media include not simply technologies but the rules and protocols that enable those technologies to emerge *as technologies*. The gramophone does not simply emerge from nowhere and reshape cultural history. Its development was driven by economic incentives and a desire to create an essentially secretarial device (rather than one for music recording). The smartphone that seems, itself, to connect you to friends, information, and culture is made possible by decades of investment and other technologies, all of which were driven by particular interests and beliefs.

Though it insists on history, such a definition does little to delimit the history of *media* as a concept. John Guillory suggests in "Genesis of the Media Concept" (2010), however, that the "media concept" is of relatively recent pedigree. While the invention of printing prompted some attention to question of the medium, it is only in the modernist period that a fully developed concept of "media" emerges. While the traditional arts like literature and painting always relied upon some medium, before the nineteenth century those media did not need to be recognized as such. For most of their history, the fine arts "were not dominated by the concept of communication but by imitation or mimesis" (322).[5] The existing system of the "fine arts" sufficed; its conventions and media were accepted as self-evident. But, Guillory suggests, the materiality of works of art became more evident toward the end of the nineteenth century. "The emergence of the media concept in the later nineteenth century was a response to the proliferation of new technical media—such as the telegraph and phonograph—that could not be assimilated to the older system of the arts" (321). In this sense, the very concept of *media* is itself modernist, a self-conscious and reflexive response to technological acceleration. From this perspective, modernism and its media are twin sides of a single coin: each expresses the newly problematic status of art in the wake of a series of technological changes beginning in the second half of the nineteenth century, which, like so much else in the period, led to a questioning of previously self-evident ideas. Guillory explains, "It is much easier to see what a medium does— the possibilities inherent in the material form of an art—when the same expressive or communicative contents are transposed from one medium into another." That is, one notices the medium more when new media emerge to represent the "same" material—when a manuscript text is first available as a printed book, or when a novel is first adapted to film. This process of a single "content" moving from one medium to another is described by Jay David Bolter and

---

[5] "The very concept of media is thus both a new invention and a tool for excavating the deepest archaeological layers of human forms of life" (Mitchell and Hansen ix).

Richard Grusin as "remediation," in their 1999 book of that title. As Guillory notes, "Remediation makes the medium as such visible" (324). Such a recognition may even return us to the question of the definition of modernism itself. If, as Susan Stanford Friedman suggests in *Planetary Modernism* (2015), "modernism" represents a response to the advent of modernity, might not there be other modernisms, corresponding to moments of media modernity? A modernism of the invention of print? A modernism of the invention of writing itself? A photographic modernism? A radio broadcast modernism? A film modernism?

The Medium Is *a* Message: The Problem of Determinism

If our question concerns the relationship between modernism and media, might the answer simply be that modernism in the arts was *caused* by the broader shifts in technology occurring in the period? In *The Mechanic Muse* (1987), Hugh Kenner offers such a vision of modernism when he describes how new technologies became inextricable from everyday experience at the end of the nineteenth century. As he puts it, "New ways of writing, then, for new orders of experience" (*Mechanic Muse* 14). Modernism *reflects* the new experiences introduced by technological change. Such an account exemplifies a broader tendency to imagine culture as being *determined* by technology. This position—that literature, art, and culture are merely expressions of some deeper technological reality—is often described as *media* or *technological determinism*.

In the most strident versions of technological determinism, art and culture are mere epiphenomena. In those accounts, the true cause of key cultural and historical events is traced back to particular technological developments. A similar, and not unrelated, debate about agency exists in Marxist theory around the relationship between the economic "base," or mode of production, and the cultural "superstructure" (which might include not simply works of art and literature but also religion, politics, the law and culture in the broadest sense). What is called "vulgar Marxism" reduces Marx's thinking to a simplistic economic determinism. In such thinking, works of art or aspects of social organization are viewed as straightforward expressions of some "deeper" or "truer" reality.

The superstructure is simplistically determined by the base. Of course, few seek to deliberately practice such "vulgar determinism"; it is instead an accusation leveled against someone, or an error one commits, rather than a position one seeks to occupy.[6] A similar charge can be leveled against attempts to find the sources for cultural effects in media and technological causes. The idea that radio led to the rise of Hitler in Germany, or that video killed the radio star, offers typical examples of technological determinist claims. The printing press is probably the technology that has had the most effects traced to it: the Reformation, individualism, nationalism, the birth of science, and the development of the novel have all been traced to it.[7] Thinkers like Marshall McLuhan (discussed in greater detail in Chapter 3) and Friedrich Kittler (discussed in Chapter 5) are often accused of such a tendency toward oversimplification in attributing wide effects to media change alone.

McLuhan's famous, if somewhat enigmatic, declaration that "the medium is the message," in *Understanding Media* (1964), nicely summarizes the media determinist position. "The medium is the message" suggests ignoring *content* ("the message") to focus instead on technology ("the medium") as the deeper, truer reality. McLuhan himself offered many glosses on this statement. In one, he explains, "the personal and social consequences of any medium— that is, of any extension of ourselves—result from the new scale that is introduced into our affairs by each extension of ourselves, or by any new technology" (*Understanding* 7). Media restructure how

---

[6] As McKenzie Wark says in a brief 2014 essay, "If you want to show that your version of Marxism is better than somebody else's, the quickest way to do so is to call the other version vulgar. One's own version is nuanced, sophisticated, subtle, erudite, philosophically rich—all the things the vulgar is not."

[7] The most famous, and bombastic, account is McLuhan's, offered in *The Gutenberg Galaxy* (1962). Elizabeth Eisenstein's impressive *The Printing Press as an Agent of Change* (1979) offers the most famous, and scholarly version, of a McLuhanite thesis. (Eisenstein's *The Printing Revolution* offers a somewhat shorter version of the argument.) The French book historian Roger Chartier investigates the question of the book's role in history in his essay "Do Books Make Revolutions?" in *The Cultural Origins of the French Revolution* (1991). Like Chartier, Adrian Johns's *The Nature of the Book: Print and Knowledge in the Making* (1998) contests the equation of print, as a medium, with the fixity and stability that both McLuhan and Eisenstein attribute to it. Instead, Johns and Chartier balance the technological fact of print against the social conditions that shaped its meanings. Johns offers a clear and accessible account, if opinionated, account of the debate in "How to Acknowledge a Revolution" (2002).

channels of communication operate; any individual "message" only uses those channels. James W. Carey in a 2007 essay on McLuhan offers a particularly useful gloss on McLuhan's most famous slogan. "This is the sense in which the medium is the message: the complex of habits, dispositions, extensions, metaphorical and imaginative reproductions it creates and the secondary service background or industry it creates around it" (93). Or, as McLuhan put it in a 1977 television interview, "It doesn't much matter what you say on the telephone. The telephone as a service is a huge environment and that is the medium. And the environment affects everybody. What you say on the telephone affects very few. And the same with radio or any other medium. What you print is nothing compared to the effect of the printed word" ("National").

Such a focus on media technology may obscure the power that people have to shape and control technology and its effects. As one common objection puts it, it isn't the technology that is important—it's how you use it. To media determinists, such an objection overestimates human agency and ignores how profoundly technology reshapes human relations. McLuhan responds that the uses of technology are merely incidental to the more fundamental changes technology introduces. "Many people would be disposed to say that it was not the machine, but what one did with the machine, that was its meaning or message. In terms of the ways in which the machine altered our relations to one another and to ourselves, it mattered not in the least whether it turned out cornflakes or Cadillacs" (*Understanding* 7). Kenner defends McLuhan's focus on media as a corrective to our tendency to ignore our environment. He writes, "Our trouble—yours and mine—was insufficient attention to what we were doing. We smoked, but weren't interested in tobacco … We drove cars … but failed to reflect that our cars were driving us" ("Marshall" 295). For Kenner, "the medium is the message" is really a modernist technique of estrangement. It attempts to awaken our attention to the conditions under which we are living, conditions that might otherwise fade into the background.

More recently John Durham Peters, in *The Marvelous Clouds* (2015), has similarly noted that media determinism can usefully correct a bias toward voluntarism in our understandings of technology—that is, our tendency to overestimate human power and agency. Whatever the dangers of media determinism, Peters suggests we are more likely to ignore the particular powers and textures of media's materiality and to treat media as mere means.

"The agency of human beings," he writes, "is a question we should answer, not a fact we should assume." He continues,

> The fear of "technological determinism" serves to uphold a barrier between mind and matter, human and thing, animal and machine, art and nature—precisely the continuities across which the most interesting cultural histories of media are written. By isolating acute parts of our world as technology that we should control, it effaces the existential fact that we live environmentally, dependently, in apparatuses not of our own making, starting with the womb itself.
>
> (189)

Like McLuhan, Peters stresses the inhuman materialities that shape and control our existence, but he extends the scope of those forces beyond "technology" in any narrow sense (what McLuhan, above, calls "machinery") to all the "apparatuses not of our own making" that shape and contour our agency.

McLuhan's own tendency to make overbroad claims about the power and agency of media technology nevertheless illustrates the potential dangers of media determinism. His treatment of the Civil Rights movement in *Understanding Media* offers an illustrative example. There he seems to describe the American Civil Rights struggle as a consequence of electric media such as broadcast television.

> Electric speed in bringing all social and political functions together in a sudden implosion has heightened human awareness of responsibility to an intense degree. It is this implosive factor that alters the position of the Negro, the teen-ager, and some other groups. They can no longer be *contained*, in the political sense of limited association. They are now *involved* in our lives, as we in theirs, thanks to the electric media.
>
> (5, original italics)

At best, this account of the Civil Rights movement is partial by failing to identify the other, and surely more important, agents and historical actors motivating it. At worst, in so insistently stressing the role of television, McLuhan's description ignores the agency and activism of particular individuals, operating in particular contexts with specific goals, *against* other historical actors, and offers a description of the event that is so incomplete that it is simply false.

McLuhan's blindness to matters of race is characteristically expressed here by implicitly separating "our lives" from those he describes, as if his reader were necessarily white. McLuhan is right that broadcast television played an important role in the Civil Rights movement, yet errs in imagining it as simply an effect of broad television.

Avoiding an overly simplistic determinism involves asking not simply whether media affect culture but how they do so. In *Television: Technology and Cultural Form* (1974), Raymond Williams contrasts technological determinism with a position he calls "symptomatic technology." While determinism imagines technology evolving on its own, or perhaps as a simple, unidirectional expression of science (which is then granted the role of autonomous motor of history), and then having social consequences and effects, the symptomatic view sees technology as simply an expression of some other social force—say capitalism or industrialization. These positions both err, Williams suggests, by treating technology and society as if they were ever separable, and not always mixed together (*Television* 11–14). Neither position is satisfying for Williams. Refusing both the oversimplifications of the symptomatic and the deterministic accounts of how media operate, Williams balances a conventionally Marxist focus on large-scale historical forces against attention to material specificities that are the center of McLuhan's account. The result is that Williams, like Lisa Gitelman, offers not pronouncements on the nature media themselves, but specific histories of individual technologies as unique negotiations of these issues of determination and agency. One cannot answer, once and for all, the question of how media shape culture in the abstract. One can only offer particular histories of culture and technology's interactions; such histories acknowledge the material specificity of technologies while also revealing the power that individual intention and, crucially, financial investment, have in shaping how media are developed and used.[8]

---

[8]This focus on particularity and specificity may seem to anticipate the "Actor-Network-Theory" of thinkers like Bruno Latour, which has indeed proved influential for more recent accounts of media. Yet where actor-network-theory tends to dissolve agency across a non-hierarchical network of forces, from the raw material that enable a technology's production, to the companies that sell it, and the individuals who use it (sometimes for things quite unimagined by its producers), Williams preserved a sense of larger social forces that shape and ultimately determine technology's uses. While industrial capitalism, in Williams' account, cannot simply and directly reshape a technology like television to its immediate purposes, nor does a force like *capitalism* simply disappear from Williams' account (as it tends to, in actor-network-theory).

Mitchell and Hansen similarly offer a useful account of the complexities of agency and media's interactions. Responding to nineteenth-century critic William Hazlitt's suggestion that "The French Revolution might be described as a remote but inevitable result of the art of printing," Mitchell and Hansen ask, "'Is the printing press a necessary or sufficient condition for modern revolutions?' Probably the former, certainly not the latter" (xv). That is, such claims often have a grain of truth. It is indeed hard to imagine the Protestant Reformation as we understand it without the availability of scripture in the vernacular enabled by the printed books. Yet, the printing press *alone* does not explain much; nor does recognizing its role exhaust our understanding of the event. Mitchell and Hansen suggest a middle ground, defining media as a "three-way set of exchanges among the dimensions of individual subjectivity, collective activity, and technical capability" which allows them to avoid what they call "the seductive fallacy of technological determinism, which has haunted media studies from the outset" (xv).

We may worry whether any understanding of modernism as an expression of changes in media history will necessarily represent a sort of vulgar media determinism, evident in overhasty claims like realism is the literature of the age of photography, or abstraction in art expresses the spatial logic of modern telecommunications. McLuhan is fond of rattling off such claims: "The printed book had encouraged artists to reduce all forms of expression as much as possible to the single descriptive and narrative plane of the printed word. The advent of electric media released art from this straitjacket at once, creating the world of Paul Klee, Picasso, Braque, Eisenstein, the Marx Brothers, and James Joyce" (*Understanding* 54). When not simply wrong, such claims oversimplify causation, and, worse, offer *causation* as if it exhausted *explanation*. Despite such risks, however, McLuhan presides over much of this book precisely because his broad definition of media and his insistence that its effects are profound and often ignored are shared by most approaches to modernism and its media. The medium may not be *the* message, but it is surely *a* message; that is, even if we don't ultimately subscribe to a *determinist* position, often such claims helpfully clarify both what a "medium" is and how it might shape or otherwise affect culture.

The Specificity of Media

Many of the problems of technological determinism result from imbuing the abstract idea of *media* with too much power. The term may be too ungainly and abstract to usefully reflect history. Instead, why not discard it and attend to the specific histories of particular works and technologies? Gitelman writes that in studying media, "Specificity is key ... Media, it should be clear, are very particular sites for very particular, importantly social as well as historically and culturally specific experiences of meaning" (8). Any discussion of media and its cultural effects is doomed to fail if it builds its generalizations on sand. In studying *modernism* and its media, would it be possible to follow Gitelman's suggestion and focus our attention more narrowly, on Virginia Woolf's *The Waves* and filmic temporality, for instance, or how newspapers represented and responded to women's suffrage? Taking particularity seriously might require abandoning broad, sweeping McLuhanesque claims about "media" in favor of smaller, and more local observations, grounded in historically specific circumstances and better defined terms. Gitelman privileges the case study as offering an exemplary model of this sort of historicist media studies. Such inspiration might suggest structuring our analysis of modernism and its media around specific media technologies.[9] With such inspiration, one might offer chapters on the telephone, the typewriter, and the transistor radio.

That is not the approach of this book, however. This book focuses on the question of the medium (rather than particular media), and

---

[9]This has proven a productive route. Many books and collections are organized on precisely these grounds. Among them, on photography, are Michael North's *Camera Works*, Karen Jacob's *Eye's Mind: Literary Modernism and Visual Culture*, and Paul Hansom's collection *Literary Modernism and Photography*, as well as more recent work including *Still Modernism* and William Schaeffer's *Shadow Modernism: Photography, Writing, and Space in Shanghai, 1925–1937*; on film, Susan MacCabe's *Cinematic Modernism*, David Trotter's *Modernism and Cinema*, Sam Rohdie's *Film Modernism*; on radio, Debra Rae Cohen and Michael Coyle's collection *Broadcasting Modernism* and Timothy Campbell's *Wireless Writing in the Age of Marconi*, and Melissa Dinsman's *Modernism at the Microphone*, as well as studies grounded in specific national or international contexts, like Damien Keane's study of Ireland and radio, *Ireland and the Problem of Information: Irish Writing, Radio, Late Modernist Communication*, Emily Bloom's *The Wireless Past: Anglo-Irish Writers and the BBC, 1931–1968*. Some of these works will be discussed at greater length in later chapters.

takes theoretical answers to that question as its object. It risks a McLuhanite penchant for overbroad claims for a few reasons. As indispensable as case studies are, no medium achieves its meaning on its own. Gitelman's own study of early phonograph foils, for instance, reveals the extent to which their reception was shaped by other media. In the introduction to *New Media, 1740–1915* (2003), Gitelman and Geoffery Pingree write, "Print and nonprint media, evolve in mutual inextricability" (13). Similarly, even as N. Katherine Hayles in "Print is Flat, Code is Deep" (2004) advocates "media-specific analysis," which attends to how individual works exploit the specific characteristics of a medium, such a practice, as she describes it, remains essentially comparative across texts *and* media ("Print Is Flat" 69–70). More recently, in introducing *Comparative Textual Media* (2013), Hayles and Jessica Pressman have described an approach they call "comparative textual media," which similarly reveals how medium specificity is inextricable from a sense of *media* more broadly. To invoke a McLuhanism, the content of any medium turns out to be another medium. In this way, the notion of a single, independent medium may not really exist. Instead media form an environment or *ecology*, an idea first proposed by Marshall McLuhan and central to the work of Neil Postman.[10]

To better understand the necessity of this wider perspective, and the organization of the remaining chapters of this book, consider the case of photography. How should we understand its cultural consequences? Like many—perhaps all—media technologies, photography was not initially understood as a medium with aesthetic potential.[11] In the modernist period, the Photo-Secession

---

[10]The term receives a brief history in Thomas Gencarelli's account of Neil Postman's career in "Neil Postman and the Rise of Media Ecology." I first encountered the term "media ecology" in Mark Wollaeger's *Modernism, Media, and Propaganda* (xvii).

[11]The phonograph, was understood as a secretarial tool rather than a medium for music or recorded performance. Even writing seems to confirm this trend for media to emerge for utilitarian reasons, to be later repurposed for aesthetic ends. While the origin of writing remains a subject of debate, it is often suggested that writing evolved for essentially bureaucratic, rather than aesthetic reasons. For an accessible account of the invention of writing, see Denise Schmandt-Besserat's *How Writing Came About*. H. T. Wade-Gery's 1952 *The Poet of the Iliad*, is an example of the contrary claim—arguing that the alphabet was developed specifically to record Homeric epic.

movement, chiefly represented by Alfred Stieglitz and his journal *Camera Work* (1903–1917), sought to establish photography as a fine art by stressing the creativity of the photographer. The very thing that would later make the camera aesthetically interesting to so many others—the automaticity of its perception—posed a threat to its being recognized as art at all. Rather than what was novel and new about photography, the Photo-Secessionists, both in their work as photographers and in their discussions of photography, sought to establish continuities between photography and painting.

FIGURE 0.1 *Clarence H. White,* Spring *(1898), Art Institute of Chicago*

A photograph like Clarence H. White's *Spring* (1898), which appeared in Stieglitz's *Camera Notes*, exemplifies pictorialism (Figure 0.1). Its title and pose connect it to a long line of allegorical painting, and its peculiar "triptych" construction import the triptych panel structure typical of painting into a photograph. The content of photography, to adopt McLuhan's language, turns out to be painting. Understanding modernism and photography, here, also requires attention to painting.

Yet Stieglitz's was not the only way of understanding photography. André Bazin's question of cinema—"What is cinema?"—can be asked of each modernist medium: *what is* photography? For Stieglitz it is a painting with light. Yet, instead of Stieglitz's technologized paintbrush, might we understand the camera as an inhuman eye? A medium is never a self-evident thing, and so is open to multiple, competing understandings. Is a photograph a moment frozen in time, and so a melancholic testimony to ephemerality? Or is it a way of capturing, ordering, and rationalizing time by making the past material, durable, and so archivable and subject to study? And a medium's consequences are no more singular or certain. In addition to a medium for art, how does photography generate, or serve, politics? How do its representations shape understandings of war, race, or gender? Even if we do not treat photography in relation to painting, its meanings accrue in relation to other media and technologies.

Consider, for instance, Nancy Armstrong's ground-breaking account of the relationship between the novel and photography in *Fiction in the Age of Photography* (1999). Armstrong argues that photography, and the spread of photographic images in the Victorian period, changed how people understood what counted as *real*. Literary realism, including certain conventions of description that tend toward the visual, is not in some straightforward way a reflection of photography—it is not a simple matter of writers trying to write like cameras. Yet realism does reflect an equation of "seeing with knowing" that privileges visual information in a manner consistent with and reinforced by photography. "Realism," for Armstrong, thus names "the entire problematic in which a shared set of visual codes operated as an abstract standard by which to measure one verbal representation against another" (11). If realism knots together photography and fiction within a shared system for understanding and producing "the real," modernism, for

Armstrong, undoes (or at least loosens) this relationship. While the realist novel and the photograph had worked in tandem to create a shared picture of a world each represented, in the modernist period fiction and photography moved in opposite directions, away from any shared single image of the world. Modernist fiction turned inward; its focus on sexuality, Armstrong suggests, reflects fiction's turn away the visual. *Ulysses* and *Lady Chatterley's Lover* thus represent "the most fundamental element of human nature as fundamentally invisible," and so inaccessible to the camera (268). Armstrong offers an account of photography as a technology of the real and modernist fiction as a refusal of the camera.

Photography as a representation of the real, competing with other media laying claim to realism, is one way of understanding it. Michael North's *Camera Works* (2005), by contrast, focuses on photography as an inscriptive medium, a writing with light (*photography*). The importance of photography to the period, understood as a newly emerged mode of writing, is not limited to the visual arts or questions of *realism* in representation. Photography had ramifications across the arts and literature. North writes,

> Beginning with photography, then, the recording media pose a fundamental challenge to literature and the arts, confusing writing and images by confounding the seemingly elementary distinction between language and perception. Many of the most radical formal experiments of the twentieth century can be traced back to the new association of word and image suggested by the photograph. In fact, it would not be too far wrong to say that modernism itself, as a pan-artistic movement, begins with the critical interrogation of the relationship between text and image, brought equally into literature and the visual arts by mechanical recording.
>
> (11–12)

Photography, in North's description, muddles distinctions between *recording* and *representation*, between a record of reality and an imitation of it, and so upsets relations between word and image that help generate modernism itself. North here follows the art critic Rosalind Krauss who similarly argues, in essays collected in *The Originality of the Avant-Garde and Other Modernist Myths* (1985), that photography helped dissolve what André Breton described as a "dualism of perception and representation" (qtd. in Krauss, "Photographic" 94). Krauss notes that the surrealists were particularly fascinated by photography. This is surprising since surrealism's use of dreams and nonsense as material for art seems antithetical to the photographic image. Krauss writes, "we would expect Breton to despise photography. As the quintessentially realist medium," it would seem to offer the very antithesis of surrealism (97). Yet, understood as a type of writing, photography reveals the tension between word and image that North describes, or what Krauss calls the "syntax" and "spacing" of reality. For the surrealist, photography does not simply record the world as it exists, but shows that the world itself is already broken by the irrationalities that fascinated the surrealists. Photography reveals a "world infested by interpretation or signification, which is to say, reality distended by the gaps or blanks which are the formal precondition of the sign" (Krauss 107). In Krauss and North's analyses, photography's modernism lies in how it unsettles perception. Yet, like for Armstrong, photography is comprehensible only in relationship to some other medium—in this case, to writing and inscription.

More recently, Louise Hornby in *Still Modernism* (2017) and Alix Beeston in *In and Out of Sight* (2018) have offered accounts of modernism and photography in different terms. Hornby treats photography as an expression of *stillness*. Yet stillness is not simply some property of photography (though, of course, it is that), but the stillness of photography defines it as a medium only after the emergence of film. As Hornby shows, photography's lack of motion compared to film (re)defined it as a medium, and often marked it as unmodern, in comparison with the apparent dynamism and motion of cinema. Insomuch as *stillness* seems the very antithesis of modernity's constant blur of motion, it comes to change the way photography is understood in the period. The result, in Hornby's analysis, is that stillness continues to shape modernism, in ways that reflect "a gendered dynamic whereby stillness is feminized and motion essentialized as masculine" (8). Beeston similarly problematizes photographic stillness, drawing on scholarship on the relationship between film and still images, to analyze the neglected forms of composite and serial photography as a rich analogue for modernist prose. Forms like composite photography (which superimposes photographs over one another) and serial photography (which offers multiple related photographs in series) undermine the self-evident, testimonial character of the photograph by highlighting the gaps and intervals that make up the composite work. This composite character is equally present, Beeston argues, in the writing of Gertrude Stein, Jean Toomer, John Dos Passos, and F. Scott Fitzgerald. "Modernist writing is photographic in its connective and disconnective structuration, its tensile relation between the singular and the multiple, which extends into a dynamic interplay between coherence and incoherence, continuity and discontinuity, and movement and stasis" (11). For Beeston, as for Hornby, this composite relationship is gendered; it is often women who are placed in series, with complex and ambivalent results. Like Armstrong, Hornby and Beeston find in modernist fiction a relationship to photography that is not a direct emulation of photographic technique or subject matter, but a shared system of representations—representations of stillness and its attendant meanings (for Hornby) or seriality and composition (for Beeston).

This range of approaches, however, also shows the difficulty of organizing an examination of modernism and its media around specific media technologies. Individual media offer only a deceptive point of commonality, for the entirely McLuhanian reason that they do not exist in isolation but form an ecology or environment. The meanings of photography are thus less self-evident than we might have assumed. Beeston, Hornby, North, and Armstrong, who offer only a sampling of approaches, represent very different ways of understanding photography's identity, and the differences between their approaches are greater than the similarity of focusing on photography as a medium.

For this reason, with one exception, the following chapters are not organized around particular technologies but around specific theoretical traditions. That exception is the first chapter, focused on modernism and film. While no medium achieves its meaning except in relation to other media, film, as I argue in Chapter 1, is sui generis in the modernist period. It emerged in the modernist period as a major cultural and aesthetic form (perhaps *the* major aesthetic form of modernity), and so deserves special treatment. The chapter first considers the irresolvable paradox of "film modernism." How could a technology that is as new as film be *modernist*, if modernism involves a rejection of the past? At the moment when music, poetry, painting, and fiction were overturning tradition, film had no tradition to overturn. How does this sense of film as a medium out of step with its peers result in the work of filmmakers as various as Sergei Eisenstein, Orson Welles, and the French New Wave, all being, at various times, described as *modernist*? The chapter's second half then turns to the reaction of modernist writers, like James Joyce, T. S. Eliot, and Virginia Woolf, to film, to offer models of intermedial relations between film and literature. Did film offer modernist literature an example? A rival?

The remaining chapters take up influential theoretical approaches for exploring the relationship between modernism and its media. These are certainly not the only traditions one could imagine, but each has the advantage of offering a unique understanding of what a *medium* is, and a consequent way of imagining modernism in terms of its media. The second chapter focuses on Clement Greenberg's description of modernism as a quest to purify the medium. This idea is pervasive in midcentury discussions of modernist painting. In Greenberg "medium purity" becomes the defining feature of modernism, and separates it from the degraded mass cultural mode that Greenberg calls "kitsch." That idea is subsequently developed in the work of Michael Fried, Rosalind Krauss, and Stanley Cavell. The Greenbergian tradition ultimately offers an account of modernism as a mode that seeks to understand (through purification or acknowledgment) media as the condition of modern art.

Chapter 3 examines a tradition of thinking centered around Marshall McLuhan, the figure most clearly identified with *media studies* as a mode of inquiry; but it is also possible to see him as the founder of modernist studies. His trip, with Hugh Kenner, to visit Ezra Pound at St. Elizabeth's Hospital (where Pound was treated after being taken into custody by the US Military, for fascist radio broadcasts) helped shape Kenner's view of modernism in *The Pound Era* (1971). Or, as Jennifer Wicke pithily puts it, "McLuhan took Kenner to see Pound for a two-hour visit on June 4th, 1948. The rest is modernism" (Wicke, "Reading Modernism" 495). The Toronto School of media studies, of which McLuhan is the most famous member, broadened medium as a category to include every way in which humans have "extended themselves." Even speech (or orality) comes to appear as a medium in this account. The result is a sweeping, transhistorical account of media as a sort of prosthesis. Modernism, in this history, captures the moment when after a half-millennium of the book's preeminence as the technology of culture, electronic media enable a return to a more oral form of communication.

Chapter 4 then turns away from this North American group to the Frankfurt School and debates between Walter Benjamin and Theodor Adorno, concerning aura and the nature of mechanical reproduction. This tradition views media's importance less in relation to its materiality, than in how it enables mass reception. Media are important in this tradition not because of their intrinsic properties, but because of the historical forces that they are able to manifest. Benjamin expresses optimism about the potential of film to empower the masses, in part by viewing film and avant-garde art as, at least potentially, involved in a shared project to politicize art. Adorno and Horkheimer's *Dialectic of Enlightenment* (1944), by contrast, written out of the disaster of the Second World War, offers a far more pessimistic view of the effects of the mass media. Modernism, in this theorization, names that art which resists the encroachment of capitalism onto the realm of culture enabled by technologies of mass reproduction.

Chapter 5 examines an "archaeological" approach to media as well as the separate, but related, anti-humanist materialism of the German theorist Friedrich Kittler. To some extent the other approaches surveyed assume a sort of telos, or goal, to the history of media: Greenberg's history of art moves toward purification of the medium; the Toronto School, particularly in the work of Walter Ong, views media as enabling a fuller expression of human power; and the Frankfurt School sees media as ultimately an expression of a larger history of rationalization (or the force Adorno and Horkheimer call "Enlightenment"). For a media archaeological approach, such ideas of direction and progress distort media history and create the illusion that the present is the necessary outcome of the past. Media archaeology undoes this sense of progress by returning to the discarded, the unrealized, and the imperfect. Kittler transforms this focus on the particular materialities of media into the most stridently determinist version of media history we survey. For this tradition, unlike the others, modernism has no special status; it is as much a creation of the history of media as the rest of culture.

A brief conclusion turns to the way that the category of modernism is newly relevant in the context of digital culture. If modernism emerged in response to rapid technological changes around the turn of the twentieth century, can we understand the changes inaugurated by digital and information technology around the turn of the twenty-first century as a second modernism?

Among the understandings modernism and its media that I have artificially separated here, there is much overlap and similarity. McLuhan and Kittler, for instance, are frequently paired as media determinists. Greenberg and Adorno offer different, but not unrelated, flavors of elitism. Benjamin and McLuhan have been open to accusations of techno-boosterism. For purposes of illustration, in order to distinguish the approaches from one another, and to help explore the range of possibilities for relating modernism and media they offer, I will at times rely on ruthless oversimplification. I hope that such an account can clarify how theories of media offer an indispensable aid to still evolving understandings of modernism. I have tried to show the virtues of these approaches while remaining aware of their deficits and failings. Rather than answering how we should understand modernism's relationship to its media, these approaches help us to better ask the question. They enrich our vocabulary and deepen the questions we can ask if we wish to understand modernism's relation to its media.

1

Modernism and Film

In his 1835 *Lectures on Aesthetics*, Hegel identifies five arts: architecture, sculpture, painting, music, and poetry. In 1911, Ricciotto Canudo added one to Hegel's list: film. While "for thousands of years, in fact, no people have been capable of conceiving" a new art, with film a sixth art had emerged (Canudo 58).[1] Rudolf Arnheim, two decades later, was still announcing the arrival "[f]or the first time in history" of "a new art form" (qtd. in Marcus, *Tenth* 1). Such appeals to its novelty are central to the early reception of film. This novelty upsets Hegel's stable enumeration of the fundamental arts. With film a tenth muse joins the traditional nine of antiquity.[2] To its earliest critics, film is promising but inexperienced, full of potential but clumsy and undeveloped. Abel Gance, writing the year after Canudo, is excited not about what film *is* but what it could be. Film still "awaits its Corneille, its classic in a word." Both Gance and Canudo, writing early in the history of film, see their moment as one of birth. They describe an art form that has only just begun to emerge.

To others, this same novelty made film easy to dismiss. While complaints that film is simply devoid of aesthetic possibility now strike us as strange, they were not uncommon. Ezra Pound, in 1918, suggested that neither film nor photography could be great

---

[1] Dance is often added to Hegel's list, making film the *seventh* art. André Bazin, for instance, calls film "the seventh muse" (*What Is Cinema?* 60).
[2] Laura Marcus takes the title for her *The Tenth Muse* (2007) from Robert Sherwood, "The Tenth Muse," in *Life* Magazine (1921). Sherwood's essay is quoted in *The Origins of American Film Criticism, 1909–1939*, by Myron Lounsbury (qtd. in Marcus, *Tenth* xiii).

art because they are not creative, but mere slavish reproductions of the world ("Art Notes"). T. S. Eliot, in his essay on "Marie Lloyd" (1922), similarly complained that film is an empty, senseless form of mere entertainment rather than art—its novelty (in the sense of newness) made it a mere novelty (a trivial amusement). In film the "mind is lulled by continuous senseless music and continuous action too rapid for the brain to act upon," resulting only in "that same listless apathy with which the middle and upper classes regard any entertainment of the nature of art" (Eliot 174).[3]

Modernism and film emerge at roughly the same historical moment, and each declares itself an art of the new. Yet they offer different, and perhaps incompatible, visions of newness. The newness of modernism was one of break and rupture, carrying the negative force of a refusal. It was new because it rejected the past. This refusal may be mild, like Virginia Woolf's dissatisfaction with the contemporary novel as practiced by Wells, Galsworthy, and Bennett, expressed in "Modern Fiction" (1925). "Is life like this?" Woolf asks. "Must novels be like this?" (*Common* 154). Or this refusal may be as radical as F. T. Marinetti's proposal, in "The Founding Futurist Manifesto" (1909) to "set fire to the library shelves! Turn aside the canals to flood the museums!" (43). The novelty of film, however, is not a rejection of the old but a birth of the new, not a discarding of the past but an addition to the pantheon. While poetry must be, in Ezra Pound's oft-quoted slogan, *made* new, film simply *is* new. Early film had no burden to shake off. The result is what Peter Verstaten in a 2013 essay calls a "terminological deadlock" (219), a series of competing, uneven timelines of *when* (and even *if*) film had a modernist moment.

This chapter explores the vexing question of film's relationship to modernism in two ways. It first considers a range of answers to the question of film modernism. Is film a *modernist* medium? When was its modernist moment? As a completely new medium that emerges in the very heart of the modernist period, accounts of film's modernism produce competing and incompatible descriptions of precisely what film modernism would be. The chapter then zooms

---

[3]This quotation, from his essay on "Marie Lloyd," is perhaps too frequently used. David Trotter usefully complicates Eliot's relationship to film in a chapter of *Cinema and Modernism* (2007).

out to consider film's relationship to other modernist forms and media. How ought we understand film in relation to other art and media of the period?

The Birth of a New Art

The December 1895 exhibition of short films by August and Louis Lumière is often offered as the beginning of cinema history. The Lumière's invention, the cinematograph, was a device that could both capture a series of photographic images in rapid succession on a single roll of film, and later project those images onto a screen. Yet the cinematograph was in many ways a culmination of earlier visual technologies. The general idea of creating the appearance of motion through a rapid succession of images was being pursued in a number of ways. In the first half of the nineteenth century, devices like the phenakistiscope and the zoetrope had created the illusion of motion by spinning or rotating a series of still images, resulting in brief animations of horses running or men walking. Later in the nineteenth century Eadweard Muybridge and Étienne-Jules Marey each captured motion by taking a series of photographs in rapid succession, anticipating the operation of a film camera. With such precedents, by the end of the nineteenth century, many individuals were pursuing the goal of moving images. Muybridge developed a device he called a zoöpraxiscope (with which Thomas Edison was familiar) to project the images he had captured. The French artist Louis Le Prince had developed a single-lens camera capable of capturing multiple images in the late 1880s, but mysteriously disappeared before his innovation was developed further (Dixon and Foster 5). Max Skladanowsky had developed a camera and projector earlier in the same year as the Lumières. Thomas Edison, who developed his own projector after the Lumières, had publicly exhibited a device called the kinetoscope in 1893. Rather than projecting an image, the kinetoscope moved a strip of film in front of an eyepiece to create the illusion of movement. A similar device, the mutoscope, first appeared in 1894 and offered a similar experience to the kinetoscope with a more rudimentary mechanism, akin to a flip-book. So, although the Lumière brothers' 1895 exhibition offers a useful and recognizable landmark in the history of cinema, it is not a wholly unique or exhaustive point of origin. It represents the establishment of what would emerge as the typical mode of film as a medium—one with public, projected images, presented on the model of the theater (rather than a peep show).

Even accepting December 1895 as a beginning of film, what exactly has begun? The emergence of public, projected cinematic images, rather than peep-shows or other moving image technologies, established the basic framework for the movies, yet it remains to see what exactly this new medium is and what it can be used for. The skepticism about film's potential as art, evident in Pound's comments, was not uncommon and stems from a genuine uncertainty about what precisely this new medium could do. Even its inventors didn't know what to do with it. Louis Lumière had described the cinematograph as an "invention without a future" (qtd. in Dixon and Foster 7). Edison's initial failure to pursue film projection technology, of the sort developed by the Lumières, was a consequence of his belief that motion pictures would be a "passing fad" (Gomery 5). Edison had, however, seen the commercial (if not aesthetic) potential in film, and sold kinetoscopes for public viewing on the model of public exhibitions of phonographic recordings.

The faddish character of early film was evident both in the conditions under which early films were exhibited and in the films themselves. Starting in the first decade of the twentieth century, films were exhibited in storefronts. Charging a nickel for admission, viewers could enter these "nickelodeon" theaters and watch a selection of short films running one after another, in "continuous performance." Prior to the emergence of nickelodeons, however, the contexts in which one could see a movie were akin to carnival amusements, rather than to Hegel's system of the fine arts. Film found a home in traveling exhibitions (including circuses) and amusement parks. Such places would screen films, but also integrate them into attractions like "Hale's Tour Cars." By projecting a movie filmed from a real train inside a stationary train car, Hale's Tour Cars simulated rail travel (they were sometimes rocked side to side to heighten the effect). Here, the moving image becomes merely part of a fantasy of travel (Gomery 10). Films were added to vaudeville theater programs, screened alongside musical acts or feats of strength. Other moving image technologies from the same period, like the mutoscope and kinetoscope, were seen as cheap amusements, of dubious moral worth. Since these technologies did not project an image, but allowed a single viewer to peer through an eyepiece at a short movie, they encouraged a private, and almost voyeuristic, mode of viewing. The mutoscope lent itself to stripteases and similarly titillating subject matter, with titles like "A Peeping Tom" and "Maiden's Midnight Romp." The modernist writer John Rodker describes one such mutoscope in *Adolphe 1920* (1929), and Leopold Bloom in *Ulysses* (1922) recalls "A dream of wellfilled hose. Where was that? Ah, yes. Mutoscope pictures in Capel street: for men only. Peeping Tom. Willy's hat and what the girls did with it" (*Ulysses* 368). Allied with mutoscopes and kinetoscopes, screened with vaudeville performances, and exhibited in carnivals, early films might easily appear to be one more of these unpromising and dubious sorts of entertainment.

As an aesthetic matter, the earliest films themselves would also have done little to reveal the promise that would later emerge. Shaped by the technological constraints of early cinema technologies, these films were short, silent (though typically accompanied by live music or explanation), and colorless. The earliest films were "actualities," short documentaries which captured in a single shot some element of daily life. The Lumières 1895 exhibition featured ten actualities (each about a minute long) that included workers leaving a factory, a baby eating, and people playing at the beach. The interest in such films was far less *what* was filmed, than the curious technology that captured moving images. Edison's early films featured a similar set of activities, alongside elements drawn from vaudeville, like the bodybuilder Eugen Sandow or the sharpshooter Annie Oakley. George Méliès is often credited with inventing special effects. Before making films, Méliès was a magician, and his early films (from the late 1890s) depict him performing magic tricks. Overall, these earliest movies seemed to both glorify the technology of film as an amusement of its own (what is interesting is not the workers leaving a factory, but the fact they are recorded), and repeat the genres of amusements alongside which film was often exhibited (body builders, magic tricks). Faced with such programs, it would be counterintuitive, if not absurd, to compare film to the established arts of literature, painting, or even theater.

The perplexing novelty of this medium was evident even in mundane matters of ownership. Could a film be copyrighted? Was film amenable to existing rules for photographs, or was it different? And if so, who owned the copyright? Who was the author of a film—the camera operator? Starting in 1894, with his early short films, Edison deposited so-called "paper prints," which depicted each frame of a film, with the US copyright office in order to register copyright in his films (a tradition that continued until 1912). The 1903 case of *Edison v. Lubin* centered precisely on the question of whether films received copyright protection (Decherney). Such copying or "duping" was widespread and common (in part owing to the high prices Edison charged for his films). When Ernst Lubin copied and distributed Edison's 1902 film *Christening and Launching Kaiser Wilhelm's Yacht "Meteor"* (for which Edison had registered a copyright), had he violated US copyright law? Judge George Mifflin Dallas initially ruled that duping films was not a violation of copyright, because no existing law covered films—they were not (as Edison's lawyer had argued) simply a series of photographs. Judge Dallas's decision was overturned three months later, on appeal, but the debate reveals how uncertain film's identity as a medium was (Decherney 113–20). Answering the question of whether film could be copyrighted—with its implications about ownership and creativity—was ultimately a matter of addressing an even more basic question. What is a film? Is it simply a series of photographs? The novelty of film made its status as art uncertain and unclear. This novelty makes its relationship to modernism equally vexed.

The Problem of Modernist Film

The simultaneity of modernism and the emergence of film means that one can understand the idea of a uniquely *modernist film* in a variety of ways. Since modernist writers and artists were involved with film in a variety of ways (some of which will be discussed later in this chapter), we might understand modernist film as simply: films by modernists—movies made by writers and artists connected directly to avant-garde movements, pursuing their concerns in the new medium. The "modernism" of these films is borrowed from some other definition of modernism and projected on screen. By such a definition, a film like *The Cabinet of Dr. Caligari* (1920) might be considered modernist because of its expressionist set design. The modernist photographer Man Ray, while being a reluctant filmmaker (Hedges 99), made a number of films, including 1926's *Emak Bakia*, a work he subtitled a "cinepoeme." The work (less than fifteen minutes in length) refracts lights through prisms and shows silhouettes of pins and other objects exposed directly on the film. Man Ray himself described the work as "not an 'abstract' film nor a storyteller; its reasons for being are its inventions of light-forms and movements" ("Emak Bakia" 43). "In *Emak Bakia*," one critic writes, "Man Ray celebrates cinema as *machine célibataire*, or machine that, producing nothing, is 'pure invention'" (Hedges 100). The result is a film that looks like Man Ray's photographs set in motion. By this definition, modernist film would also include later works, like Samuel Beckett's sole experiment in the medium, *Film* (1965). Directed by Alan Schneider, *Film* is a short, silent, black-and-white meditation on perception and viewing. It carries themes and concerns from Beckett's fiction and drama into the new medium, and so might be called a modernist film (or at least as modernist as we're inclined to describe Beckett).

Films like *Ballet Mécanique* (1924) and the POOL group's *Borderline* (1930) offer other examples of what a distinctively modernist film might be. *Ballet Mécanique* began as a collaborative effort between the painter Fernand Léger, the musician George Antheil, Dudley Murphy, and Ezra Pound. The final film differed from its original plan (it lacked, for instance, George Antheil's music—which somewhat confusingly became a separate work with the same title). However, it captures the attempt to put avant-garde aesthetics into the new medium of film. Léger was a Cubist painter, and in *Ballet Mécanique* we see a Cubist's fascination with form and geometry. Before working on it, Léger had worked on Abel Gance's 1923 film epic *La Roue*, a long, erotically charged psychodrama about a railroad engineer who falls in love with his adopted daughter. While impressive in many regards, the film can be at times overwrought. Léger was fascinated by the film's representation of trains and machinery, however. The first part of the film opens on shots of single railway track passing before the camera, meeting and departing with other parts of track. After a few moments, Gance masks off the sides of the image to highlight the image of a single piece of rail track, moving inexorably before the camera. Later (as Sassif, the railroad engineer, attempts to kill the adopted daughter with whom he is love), the camera lingers on a dial indicating steam pressure. In a 1923 essay, Léger writes, "the machine becomes *the leading character, the leading actor*" (272). Léger saw in *La Roue* a film that had escaped the theater and its thrall to acting and performance. It had discovered a more purely visual language. "[Gance] is going to make you *see*" (273). Léger here echoes both Joseph Conrad (who described using "the power of the written word to make you hear, to make you feel—it is, before all, to make you *see*") and D. W. Griffith (who similarly cried "Above all ... I am trying to make you see").

A similar focus on the experience of seeing motivates *Ballet Mécanique*. The film offers no narrative, only a series of images. Some are created by prisms; some are simple shapes, or everyday objects filmed so closely that they are become strange and unfamiliar. By making the external world an object of visual attention, such shots force us to attend to elements of our experience we habitually ignore. "80 percent of the clients and objects that help us to live," Léger writes, "are only noticed by us in our everyday lives, while 20 percent are seen. From this, I deduce the cinematographic revolution is to *make us see everything that has been merely noticed.*" He elaborates, "The dog that goes by in the street is only noticed. Projected on the screen, it is seen, so much so that the whole audience reacts as if it discovered the dog" (273). Sequences of everyday actions—a smile, a woman on a swing, a woman walking up stairs—are similarly made strange by being repeated or filmed at odd angles. In one of the most famous sequences in Léger's film, a woman is seen from the top of a set of stairs, carrying a large bag on her right shoulder. As she nears the top of the stairs her head goes out of frame, but before she can finish her ascent the film jumps back to the beginning of the sequence. This sequence lasts less than two seconds, but the film loops it more than a dozen times when it first appears. Dudley Murphy explained the scene, writing "The scene in itself was banal, but by printing it 20 times and connecting the end of the scene with the beginning of her climb, it expressed the futility of life because she never got there" (qtd. in Freeman 31). One may also see it as another defamiliarization of sight, akin to the Russian Formalist Viktor Shklovsky's description of art as returning of reality to objects: "art exists that one may recover the sensation of life; it exists to make one feel things, to make the stone *stony*" (16). Yet, despite the considerable intrinsic value of all these films, defining film modernism as the films of modernists sidesteps the question that one really wishes answered—*what is* modernism on film? Rather than explore a modernism *of* film, it offers a restrictive, and essentially parasitic, definition of film modernism.

The most sustained and concerted interaction between early twentieth-century, avant-garde aesthetics, and film occurred in the Soviet Union in the aftermath of the Russian Revolution. Vladimir Lenin had insisted that "of all the arts for us the cinema is the most important" (qtd. in Taylor, "Ideology" 202). The Soviets took cinema seriously, establishing the world's first film school in Moscow in 1919 to train Russian filmmakers. Film had enormous potential as a vessel of propaganda, and its political use was hotly debated. Understanding its revolutionary potential was a key question in the period. The debates emerging out of Soviet cinema influenced Walter Benjamin (discussed in Chapter 4), who, like early Soviet filmmakers, saw revolutionary potential in this new medium. But how to best harness that potential? Should film be used for entertainment or education? Should films be fiction or documentary? Lenin suggested a balance between entertainment and education, allowing popular foreign (including American) films to be imported, so long as they were paired with educational films: "If you have a good newsreel, serious and educational pictures, then it doesn't matter if, to attract the public, you have some kind of useless picture of the more or less usual type" (qtd. in Kepley 72). While by the 1930s the rise of Stalin had effectively squashed it, Soviet film of the 1920s represents a remarkable burst of intense thinking about the nature of film, and embodies one influential understanding of modernist film. Central to the Soviet understanding of film in the 1920s, and the source of its modernism, was the idea of montage.

In the most general sense, montage is film editing. Originating in the French term *monter*, to assemble or put together, montage describes the combining of different shots—a process that originally involved the splicing together of lengths of film. The Soviet school elevated montage to a central place in their understanding of film. Soviet filmmakers were fascinated by D. W. Griffith's 1916 *Intolerance*, which cuts between four stories, from different places and time periods, to explore its central theme. Lev Kuleshov demonstrated the importance of montage by splicing together an image of an expressionless face (the actor Ivan Mosjoukine) with different images (e.g., a plate of food). The montage conferred different meanings (e.g., hunger) on the actor's expression depending on what it was spliced with. One could similarly splice together geographically disparate images to create the illusion of a place that existed nowhere on earth. For Kuleshov this process of combining images to create meaning is the essence of cinema: "Montage is to cinema what the composition of colours is to painting or a harmonic series of sounds is to music" (qtd. in Taylor, "Ideology" 202). As David Bordwell suggests, however, even if film represented a unique opportunity to use montage, the device itself had roots in other media. Indeed, the montage that Soviet film made central to its theory and practice in the 1920s shares much with modernist and avant-garde art of the period. "It is clear that the theory of montage, viewed most abstractly, can be applied outside film. The fundamental principles—assemblage of heterogeneous parts, juxtaposition of fragments, the demand for the audience to make conceptual connections, in all a radically new relation among parts of a whole—seem transferable to drama, music, literature, painting, and sculpture" (Bordwell, "Idea" 10). Montage in this sense is akin to the fragmentation of modernist poetry or the collage works of modernist artists. P. Adams Sitney, in *Modernist Montage: The Obscurity of Vision in Cinema and Literature* (1990), makes montage central to modernism broadly.

No single filmmaker is more associated with montage than Sergei Eisenstein. He uses such juxtapositional editing in his own films, and theorizes and elaborates its varieties in his essay (see "Methods of Montage" in *Film Form*). Eisenstein finds in the varieties of editing film's greatest power, for "the juxtaposition of two separate shots by splicing them together resembles not so much a simple sum of one shot plus another shot—as it does a *creation*" (*Film Sense* 7). Eisenstein's own work offers a rich variety of such creations. In the conclusion of his film *Strike* (1925), images of workers being murdered are juxtaposed with graphic footage of a cow being slaughtered to capture the violence and exploitation of capitalism (see Figure 1.1).

The edit is abrupt and would be confusing to a viewer who doesn't recognize the metaphor which motivates it. In *October* (1928), which depicts the 1917 Russian Revolution, similar juxtapositions are used (the leader of the provisional Russian government, Alexander Kerensky, is compared to a mechanical peacock), as well as a sequence showing the destruction of the statue of Tsar Alexander III in reverse, to capture a counterrevolutionary moment during the October Revolution. An image of soldiers' rifles raised to the air is

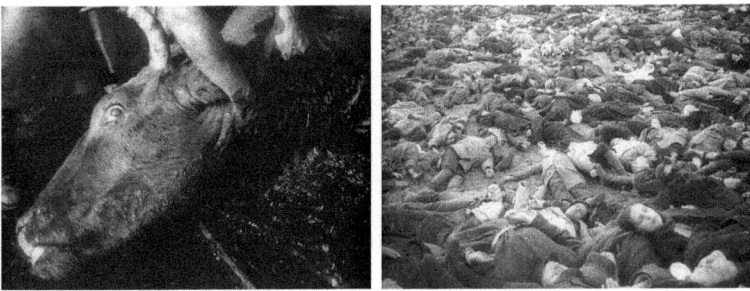

FIGURE 1.1 *Two frames from the concluding slaughter sequence of Eisenstein's* Strike *(1925).*

juxtaposed with sickles to suggest the continuity between different segments of the Russian working class. Eisenstein's films offer a unique mixture of politics, early film, and avant-garde aesthetics. To oversimplify, through Eisenstein, avant-garde ideas of montage akin to Soviet constructivism were combined with insights gleaned from watching D. W. Griffith's *Intolerance*, and embodied in films like *Strike* (1925) and *Battleship Potemkin* (1925). While criticized by some (particularly later, Stalinist Soviet filmmakers) as being difficult and inaccessible, Eisenstein's editing has proved remarkably influential, including in Hollywood (cf. Buck-Morss, *Dreamworld* 159). Indeed, Soviet montage represents both a uniquely filmic mode of modernism (in its elevation of juxtaposition above continuity, and active rather than passive reception) and a durable contribution to film's history that has shaped mainstream film.

Yet, even as Eisenstein shaped and affected mainstream Hollywood film, the dramatic montage of Soviet cinema was not its dominant note. Indeed, the history of mainstream film is often imagined as evolving away from the film as amusements of its first decades, and away from the dramatic experiments with montage evident in Eisenstein, toward "classical" Hollywood style. This idea is most rigorously described in David Bordwell's *On the History of Film Style* (1997) and is central to the narrative of Bordwell and Kristin Thompson's *Film Art* (1979 and later), which has served as a textbook in many film studies classes. Film exhibition shifted away from amusement parks and vaudeville stages, first to nickelodeon theaters, and then to purpose-built movie theaters (or "movie palaces"). The business consolidated into major studios. Aesthetically, a series of conventions developed which had the chief goal of establishing a coherent and intelligible sense of space and time. In the 1970s, Christian Metz influentially described these conventions as a sort of system or language. These conventions of film editing evolved to help make film more successful as a narrative medium by making editing itself less visible to an audience or viewer. Cross-cutting allowed filmmakers to show two simultaneous events (or a single event from two perspectives), while the conventions of so-called "continuity editing" freed the camera from the limited perspective of early films (which often deliberately adopted the framing of the theater stage), enabling a wider range of shot constructions (including close-ups). Filmmakers like Edwin S. Porter, and, most famously D. W. Griffith, developed such techniques that helped establish film as, foremost, a narrative medium. As a latecomer to the pageant of art forms—as tenth muse, or seventh art—histories of film have often relied on what Charles Musser calls in *Before the Nickoledeon* (1991) "some variation of a biological model of development. In its crudest form, this model suggests that the medium was born, grew up, learned to talk, and (having mastered the language of cinema) finally began to produce great works" (8).

This developmental narrative poses a problem for any understanding of a distinctively filmic modernism. For movies develop away from the juxtaposition and fragmentation evident in early films and in Soviet montage, toward what gets called by Bordwell and others "classical cinema." Yet while in other arts, modernism arrives after a period of stylistic stabilization, in the film it seems to be the reverse. Miriam Hansen summarizes this position (in the course of disagreeing with it), writing,

> The opposition between classicism and modernism has a venerable history in literature, art, and philosophy, with classicism linked to the model of tradition and modernism to the rhetoric of a break with precisely that tradition. In that general sense, there would be no problem with importing this opposition into the field of cinema and film history, with classical cinema falling on the side of tradition and alternative film practices on the side of modernism.

(62)

Before a modernist break, there must be a sense of tradition to break from. In many accounts, it is the classical Hollywood style, with its mode of continuity editing, associated in its earliest form with Griffith, which provides the tradition from which modernist film can break. While different accounts of film modernism isolate different moments in film history as the modernist break, each is later than most accounts of modernism in other arts because of film's comparative youth as a medium. As the other arts were breaking with tradition, film was still establishing it.

One sees this sense of film's belated modernism in André Bazin's comments, in 1950, that "it would seem as if the cinema was fifty years behind the novel" (*What Is Cinema?* 63). He notes (as does Virginia Woolf, in her essay "The Cinema") film's tendency to adapt nineteenth-century realist novels or syrupy, kitschy works, like Tennyson's poem "Enoch Arden" (adapted for film a number of times, including once by D. W. Griffith). Even when a film adapts a modern novel, it loses what makes it modern in the treatment; when a director adapts "*For Whom the Bell Tolls*, he treats it in the traditional style that suits each and every adventure story" (Bazin, *What* 63). Bazin here recounts the same developmental narrative Musser describes. For Bazin, the first three decades of film history were a matter of a medium discovering its possibilities and its practitioners mastering technique. Early filmmakers, Woolf had similarly written in her essay "The Cinema" (1926), are akin to a "savage tribe" that finds itself with a complex set of musical instruments, "fiddles, flutes, saxophones, trumpets, grand pianos," and begins eagerly hammering and thumping upon them, "without knowing a note of music" (186). Until around 1938, Bazin suggests, film developed its basic technology (lighting, sound, cameras) and established its fundamental techniques (editing, close-up, montage) (*What* 73). This early period is a mastering of the filmic apparatus.[4] During this period, Bazin describes an ongoing exchange between literary fiction and film, with film lagging behind. The novel absorbs techniques adapted from film, and even puts them to better use:

---

[4] In "The Evolution of the Language of Cinema," Bazin will describe film style with a geological metaphor: "By 1939 the cinema had arrived at what geographers call the equilibrium-profile of a river ... where the river flows effortlessly from its source to its mouth without further deepening of it" (*What* 31, qtd. in Morgan 13).

The novel it is that has made the subtlest use of montage, for example, and of the reversal of chronology. Above all it is the novel that has discovered the way to raise to the level of an authentic metaphysical significance an almost mirror-like objectivity. What camera has ever been as externally related to its object as the consciousness of the hero of Albert Camus' *L'Etranger*? The fact of the matter is that we do not know if [John Dos Passos's] *Manhattan Transfer* or [André Malraux's] *La Condition humaine* would have been very different without the cinema, but we are certain on the contrary that *Thomas Garner* [William K. Howard's *The Power and the Glory*] and [Orson Welles's] *Citizen Kane* would never have existed if it had not been for James Joyce and Dos Passos.

(Bazin, *What* 64)

Film techniques like flashbacks ("reversal of chronology"), editing ("montage"), and even the photographic character of the camera itself (with its "almost mirror-like objectivity") are all, Bazin suggests, put to better aesthetic ends in literature than film. It is only with films like 1933's *The Power and the Glory* (released under the title *Thomas Garner* in France)[5] and 1940's *Citizen Kane*, for Bazin, that film becomes as modern an art form as the novel. "We are witnessing, at the point at which the avant-garde has now arrived, the making of films that dare to take their inspiration from a novel-like style one might describe as ultracinematographic" (Bazin, *What* 64). Film's out-of-stepness with modernism is evident even in Bazin's appeal here to the avant-garde. The metaphor of aesthetic experimentation as an "avant-garde" comes from the military, where the avant-garde are the front-most division, who arrive before the rest of a military force. Yet film's avant-garde arrives late and develops an "ultracinematographic" style only by taking back from literature the devices that it had borrowed.

It is surprising to see a classic Hollywood film like *Citizen Kane* described as modernist. Conventional understandings of modernism, including that of the Frankfurt School (discussed in Chapter 4), typically contrast modernism with mass cultural forms (like film). Bazin's understanding of *Citizen Kane* treats modernism

---

[5]Bazin, "The Technique of *Citizen Kane*," 236n4.

as a sort of honorific. Rather than a rupture with the past, in Bazin's account, *Citizen Kane* is the film that, by finally mastering its medium, catches up with its modernist contemporaries in the other arts. In describing *Citizen Kane* in modernist terms, Bazin confounds conventional understandings of modernism by applying them to a popular text, and claims for *Citizen Kane* the prestige of modernism. And while unconventional, Bazin's comparison is not baseless. As he suggests, Welles's film, like novels by John Dos Passos or William Faulkner, develops its story through a nonlinear chronology, using overlapping flashbacks and what could easily be understood as multiple narrators. And while the film concludes with a swell of orchestral music typical of classical Hollywood film, *Citizen Kane* offers an unsettling ending. The film opens with the dying Kane's last word: "Rosebud," and journalists' quest to determine what the word means provides the film with its key motivation. As the film ends, it answers who (or rather *what*) "Rosebud" is cinematically, zooming in to focus on a sled that we have seen the young Kane use, at the precise moment that the sled, unnoticed, is burned. The film, through its zoom, grants the viewer what it denies the film's characters—who never learn the meaning of Kane's deathbed utterance. In a concluding speech, one character offers a sort of metacommentary on the film's narrative. Jerry Thompson, one of the reporters searching to discover what "Rosebud" means, insists that learning this piece of information is ultimately useless ("no word can explain a man's life" he says; it is merely "a piece in a jigsaw puzzle"). The film cinematically solves its mystery at the very moment it narratively suggests the answer is useless, and this tension remains unresolved at the film's conclusion. Critics like Bazin discover the film's modernism in such a refusal of closure.

One might equally, however, read the culmination of style expressed in *Citizen Kane* not as itself *modernist*, but as the very classicism and tradition that a filmic modernism must overturn. Modernism in film, in this understanding, only arrives later than the full maturity of the medium Bazin identifies—perhaps with the Italian neorealism exemplified by *Bicycle Thieves* (1949), or later still, in the films of the French New Wave (in the 1950s and 1960s). If modernism is about rupture of an established style, the jump cuts of Jean Luc Godard's 1960 *Breathless* rupture the rules of continuity editing that classical cinema labored to achieve.

While classical editing developed rules to make cuts between shots seem natural, indeed to almost be invisible, a jump cut appears jarring. In a jump cut the camera switches position enough to be perceptible, but rather than switching to a wholly new perspective, or corresponding to something in the film's events (the so-called "cut on action"), it breaks the artifice of continuity that classical cinema labored to create. An alternative theory of filmic modernism thus arrives at this moment—modernism is when the medium is sufficiently mature that filmmakers may break its hard-won rules for aesthetic ends.

By this definition "Modernism in the cinema, therefore, properly begins only around 1960, with the arrival on the scene of a film-making generation deeply versed in a classical tradition and equally convinced that they had to break with that tradition and—in the famous phrase of Ezra Pound, 'Make it New'" (Nowell-Smith xii). Here the French New Wave, with its intense fascination not only with film but with film history (evident in the journal *Cahiers du cinéma* with which the movement was closely associated), represents a coming-to-self-consciousness of film as a medium, the rules of which have sufficiently congealed that the breaking of them can represent a deliberate aesthetic choice rather than simple immaturity. John Orr's *Cinema and Modernity* (1993) elaborates this narrative of film modernism, locating the period between 1958 and 1978 as the moment when "we reach the true moment of the modern in Western cinema" (Orr 2). In this narrative, as in Bazin's, film catches up with James Joyce; it just does so a little bit later. The development of film follows the same path as the novel, just half a century behind. Orr is able to map a rather conventional account of modernism—as intense stylistic self-consciousness—onto film's different chronology, applying to a mass medium the levels of distinction that have evolved elsewhere.[6]

---

[6] In this Orr is largely congruent with Stanley Cavell's description of film. Cavell writes at a moment where he sees "traditional" film coming to an end. "The movie seems naturally to exist in a state in which its highest and its most ordinary instances attract the same audience (anyway until recently)" (*World* 5). While literature and music have seen their audiences split apart, Cavell imagines that (at least until the early 1970s) film had one audience. His *The World Viewed* is written, in part, out of a sense that traditional, non-self-conscious, *non-modernist*, film was coming to an end.

Other accounts of film's modernism, however, upset such conventional definitions. Walter Benjamin claims a fundamental similarity between film as a medium and progressive avant-garde art. While, he suggests, "the masses" often do not see the value of modernist, or, as Benjamin says, progressive, art, they can immediately see the value of a film. In traditional arts like painting, "The conventional is uncritically enjoyed, while the truly new is criticized with aversion." The modernist painting of Picasso, for instance, seems inaccessible to many. Picasso's newness elicits a hostile or skeptical response. Yet in cinema newness is celebrated by the masses. "*The extremely backward attitude toward a Picasso painting changes into a highly progressive reaction to a Chaplin film*" (Benjamin, "Work" 36). For Benjamin, this difference is ultimately not a function of the formal features of any particular painting or film, but is an effect of the collective mode of cinema spectatorship itself. It is not, as it is for Bazin, some particular film that is modernist, but film itself as medium.

Miriam Hansen's productive notion of film as a *vernacular* modernism, explained in "The Mass Production of the Senses" (1999), similarly identifies a mode of modernism that is not an effect of the particular stylistic properties of an individual work. Hansen's position exemplifies the New Modernist Studies more broadly, writing that "modernism encompasses a whole range of cultural and artistic practices that register, respond to, and reflect upon processes of modernization and the experience of modernity." Rather, therefore, than contrasting film and mass media with experimental works of art and literature, Hansen describes them all as part of a single "transformation of the conditions under which art is produced, transmitted, and consumed" (60). From that perspective, Hansen suggests "we consider the cinema as part of the historical formation of modernity" (62) and so describes film as a "vernacular" modernism, as opposed to more conventional or "high" modernisms. Film is no longer out of step with the modernism of art and literature because both are folded into what the Marxist critic Frederic Jameson might call "a singular modernity," a single, shared historical condition.

If Bazin's description of *Citizen Kane* relies on a conventional account of modernism, it also relies on a teleological account of film history. The modernism that Bazin identifies in *Citizen Kane* is arrived at by analogy to the history of the novel. Yet such a narrative oversimplifies the history of the novel which, after all, is not a simple march from realism to modernism. Rather than a linear teleology, the early history of the novel has a curious resonance with modernist formal experimentation. With its fragmented chronology, disregard of plot, and experimentation with print (e.g., all black pages), a work like Laurence Sterne's 1759 *Tristram Shandy* seems proto-modernist. This longer, more complicated history lets us see the realism/modernism dichotomy as a tension within the novel as a form, rather than a simple event in its history.

We might similarly complicate our understanding of film's modernism by more closely attending to its history, and its early history in particular. Tom Gunning, in "The Cinema of Attractions" (1986), offers an influential description of pre-narrative cinema (cinema before 1906) as a "cinema of attractions." Rather than viewing early films as imperfect, inchoate versions of the classical narrative cinema that would emerge from Hollywood, these films might be seen as harboring a potential of their own. Recognizing such work on its own terms reinserts a sort of proto-modernism into the history of film that avoids the teleological march described by Bazin and Orr. In the influential film theory of Christian Metz, *voyeurism* is the key metaphor for understanding a viewer's relationship to the screen. For Metz, the film spectator observes the action of a film from a position of invisibility, akin to that of a voyeur secretly observing others. Laura Mulvey's even more famous version of this argument contends that the voyeuristic gaze of film positions the spectator as a male. While such a theorization has proved both influential and contentious in film studies, Gunning, by contrast, describes the cinema of attractions as motivated by an *exhibitionist* tendency. Voyeuristic narrative uses editing and other formal elements to position the viewer as an unobserved voyeur, invisibly watching a narrative unfold, secure and unacknowledged behind an invisible fourth wall. The cinema of attractions, by contrast, is exhibitionist. It directly addresses the viewer in order to astound or impress; in a film like Méliès's 1898 *Four Troublesome Heads*, a magician (Méliès himself), addresses the viewer as he removes his head from his shoulders, places it upon a table, and a new head magically appears on his neck (all enabled through careful editing). Here the viewer is addressed directly, just as a magician addresses the audience of a performance. Such a movie, unlike Hollywood films, positions the viewer as an audience member, not an unobserved voyeur.

In Gunning's account, the exhibitionist character of the cinema of attractions connects it to the avant-garde. "[I]t was precisely the exhibitionist quality of turn-of-the-century popular art that made it attractive to the avant-garde—its freedom from the creation of a diegesis, its accent on direct stimulation" ("Cinema" 385). Figures like Eisenstein and the Futurist F. T. Marinetti were fascinated by popular attractions. In the cinema of attractions we have an alternative to mainstream Hollywood film that predates Hollywood film. Just as early novels (like *Tristram Shandy*) presage modernism by revealing an alternative to the later, dominant realism of the nineteenth century, so the cinema of attractions can retrospectively be understood as offering a range of avant-garde possibilities for film. Gunning cautions against romanticizing the cinema of attractions as a possibility snuffed out by mainstream Hollywood. It persists after the emergence of classical narrative film, but it "goes underground, both into certain avant-garde practices and as a component of narrative films, more evident in some genres (e.g., the musical) than in others" ("Cinema" 382). Gunning's description of the cinema of attractions undermines the progressive story of modernism as *either* a moment of maturity or a break with an established film tradition.

The ways a film can be modernist are various and not always reconcilable. One may be tempted simply to conclude that modernism in film simply means something different from modernism in literature or art. And yet even this seemingly reasonable conclusion risks an oversimplification of its own. For while it can be clarifying to understand that the features of Joyce's *Portrait of the Artist as Young Man* (1916) that may lead a critic to call it *modernist* (say, its development of a sense of interiority through the use of free indirect discourse) are perhaps unrelated to those features which lead a critic to call Godard's *Breathless* (1960) modernist (say, its jump cuts), these works did not evolve in a vacuum, strictly separate from one another. Allowing each art or medium to define its modernism for itself would impoverish the interactions between film and the rest of culture that were central to both avant-garde films like *Emak Bakia* or *Ballet Mécanique*, or even, in Bazin's description, *Citizen Kane*. And this very impossibility of keeping the term *modernist* clear and unambiguous itself reflects a real historical fact: that film is at once the *most modern* medium of the period and the newest, with the result that its interactions with modernism elsewhere are uneven, local, and inconsistent.

Modernists at the Movies

Jostling alongside the modernism *of* film is the relationship of film to modernism more broadly. As film emerged and ascended as the newest art, what were its consequences and implications for other art forms? Was it a model of newness to be emulated, or a competitor? And while film raised fundamental aesthetic questions about art, it also reshaped literature in more direct and material ways.

For one thing, the emerging movie industry gave many writers jobs. Novelists not only stood to benefit if their novels were adapted for screen, but many worked in Hollywood as screenwriters (or attempted to do so). William Faulkner did both. His 1932 story "Turnabout" was made into a film the following year, but he also shared writing credit for six films, including most prominently the 1946 noir classic *The Big Sleep* and 1944's adaptation of Ernest Hemingway's novel *To Have and Have Not*. John Matthews in "William Faulkner and the Culture Industry" (1995) notes that Faulkner's relationship to Hollywood was sometimes taken to exemplify a broader, uniquely modernist "myth of the artist corrupted by newly dominant commercial media like the movies and magazines" as a "counterpart to the nineteenth century's myth of the serious writer condemned to popular neglect" (51). However, more recent scholarship on Faulkner, including Stefan Solomon's *William Faulkner in Hollywood* (2017), like more recent scholarship across modernist studies, has insisted on tracing the continuities between Faulkner's work in these two areas. Solomon describes how Faulkner's fiction offers "a response (intended or otherwise) to a media ecology in which literature both resists and submits to cinema" (8). Tom Cerasulo in *Authors Out Here* (2010) similarly discusses the parallel cases of Nathanael West, Dorothy Parker, and F. Scott Fitzgerald—all writers who worked in Hollywood in the first half of the twentieth century. This experience reshaped the literary work of these writers, at the level of both content (West's *The Day of Locust* is set in Hollywood and was itself later adapted to film) and form. Aldous Huxley similarly would not only see his *Brave New World* adapted for film, but himself worked as a screenwriter in Hollywood. His novel *After Many a Summer Dies the Swan* (1939) draws on this experience.[7]

Recent scholarship has worked to excavate at greater length these continuities between modernism and film, sometimes at the level of the individual writer. Modernist writers who did not move to Hollywood nevertheless often directly responded to film in their writing. While James Joyce's efforts to adapt *Ulysses* for film with Sergei Eisenstein did not materialize (surely one of the great missed intermedial moments in modernist history), he was directly involved in establishing the first movie theater in Dublin, the Volta, in 1909 (McCourt, "Introduction" 1).[8] This fact has become a touchstone for much writing about Joyce and film. Anthony Paraskeva's *Samuel Beckett and Cinema* (2017) explores Beckett's relationship to film, but also Beckett's works for television and plays that, Paraskeva contends, were influenced by film.

But what do such individual cases add up to? What does Joyce's abortive business venture, Beckett's short-lived stint as a filmmaker, H.D.'s work as an actress, or Faulkner's ambivalent career as a screenwriter tell us about modernism and film? Behind the numerous cases of direct influence, either in the form of adaptation or of writers working directly in film lurks a more basic question. What should we make of the relationship of film to these "modernist" others? Did film offer a *model* for literature or a *competitor*? Did literature, art, or poetry achieve its modernism, and signal its modernity, by aping certain elements of film? Or did they reject film outright? Might we understand the rejection of conventional modes of representation across the arts a sort of allergic reaction to film as a superior method of *recording*? Alternately, if film and photography are superior means for accurately or "realistically" representing the world, do they free up art and literature for a vocation beyond mere recording? Put most simply, is modernism

---

[7]Huxley's relationship to film is discussed in Chapter 5 of Foltz's *The Novel After Film*.
[8]The volume *Roll Away the Reel World* (2010), edited by John McCourt, includes the most sustained recent examination of Joyce's involvement with the Volta Cinema.

an embrace of the new ways of seeing and representing that film helped introduce and explore, or is it instead a rejection of those very technologies? This question has persisted across theorizations of modernism, and remains a vital topic in contemporary modernist studies. Susan McCabe's *Cinematic Modernism* (2005), David Trotter's *Modernism and Cinema* (2007), Laura Marcus's *The Tenth Muse* (2007), Andrew Shail's *The Cinema and the Origin of Literary Modernism* (2012), and Jonathan Foltz's *The Novel After Film* (2018) set the parameters for examinations of modernist literature in relationship to film.

Emulation

Stylistic comparisons between modernist prose and film shaped the understanding of modernist fiction from the beginning. A broad claim about the "cinematic" quality of modernist writing is so ubiquitous as to be a cliché. Exactly *how* modernist writing and film are similar, however, is less clear, and the precise meaning of such comparisons is often quite varied. The multiple perspectives of the "Wandering Rocks" episode of *Ulysses*, or John Dos Passos's *U.S.A*, have been described as creating a sense of simultaneity akin to D. W. Griffith's early use of cross-cutting. Early reviews of Joyce's fiction appealed to film, though for very different reasons. While one invokes film to describe Joyce's "photographic realism, the sheer reporting in *Ulysses*" (qtd. in Deming 320), others find in film a way of describing Joyce's departure from conventional realist narrative. A review of *Portrait of the Artist as a Young Man*, for instance, complains about "[Joyce's] determination to produce kinematographic effects instead of a literary portrait" (qtd. in Deming 110). Another describes the style of *Ulysses* as emblematic of "the new fashionable kinematographic vein, very jerky and elliptical" (qtd. in Deming 194).[9] In exonerating *Ulysses*

---

[9]Keith Williams has thickened and enriched such comparisons by pursuing the representation of character development in *Portrait of the Artist as a Young Man* as a reflection of a wider cultural *cinematicity* evident in both the novel's representation of visual experience and in its episodic *bildungsroman* structure, which Williams describes as montage-like (Williams 98).

from the charge of obscenity, Judge John Woolsey adopts a similar comparison, describing the novel's style as "not unlike the results of a double or, if that is possible, a multiple exposure on a cinema film which give a clear foreground with a background visible but somewhat blurred and out of focus in various degrees" (Woolsey xi). To many readers Joyce's fiction was film-like or cinematic. Exactly what that meant, however, varied widely.

And it wasn't just Joyce. Winnifred Holtby, in the first book-length study of Woolf, describes the prose of Woolf's *Jacob's Room* (1922) as quintessentially cinematic. It is perhaps especially appropriate to describe as cinematic a novel that deals with the first war that was extensively filmed. *Jacob's Room* echoes the very structure of film; it captures fleeting glimpses of short everyday "scenes," and through these scenes it offers Jacob's presence through his absence. Holtby, though, means something narrower. The cinematic quality she identifies in *Jacob's Room* amounts to the claim that the novel offers a visual narrative in a set of episodes. Holtby contrasts the "cinematograph style" of *Jacob's Room* with the "orchestral effect" of Woolf's more mature fiction (136). Robert Humphrey in 1954 describes a different aspect of Woolf's prose as cinematic. The narrative perspective of her novels, he suggests, is camera-like, in its seemingly indiscriminate movement from character to character (qtd. in Shail 127). Such a camera-like perspective might be equally detected in the final section of Woolf's *To the Lighthouse* (1927), which "intercuts" back and forth between characters. Like the more experimental synchronization of "Wandering Rocks" in *Ulysses*, this is modernist narrative experimentation as the literary adoption of film editing. From the beginning, the novelty of film made it useful as a way of explaining or describing the novelty of modernist formal experimentation, even as the specific similarities that such analogy were meant to illuminate seem inconsistent or even divergent.

A more systematic approach to the comparison of modernist prose and film is evident in Alan Spiegel's *Fiction and the Cinema Eye: Visual Consciousness in Film and the Modern Novel* (1976). While Spiegel's critical vocabulary, and restrictive and largely canonical (and male) set of texts put it out of step with contemporary modernist studies, his exploration of "interior form" and "cinematographic form" as two strands of the modern novel, defined by their relationship to film, remains compelling. Spiegel describes two tendencies in modern fiction: a Flaubertian realism and the modernism of James, Conrad, and Joyce, distinguished by "a unified unobstructed, continuous field of vision and a blocked, truncated, and discontinuous field; between a large single vista and a multiplicity of peepholes; between scenography and cinematography" (65). It is a rich distinction, because it focuses on visual representation in fiction, without simply equating film with visuality. It seeks to distinguish in fiction instead a filmic kind of visuality. Spiegel sees a fundamental analogy between the inhuman filmic eye and a particular strand of modernist fiction exemplified by Joyce. He highlights a single sentence from *Ulysses* as exemplary. In the novel's first episode, Stephen stares out over Dublin Bay. "Across the threadbare cuffedge he saw the sea hailed as a great sweet mother by the wellfed voice beside him" (*Ulysses* 5). The narration here is not simply the objective realism of Flaubert (it does not just describe the scene), nor is it simply subjective vision that Spiegel associates with Woolf (this sentence is not chiefly about Stephen). It is, instead, unselective and undiscriminating in its representation of the world. It is camera-like. It offers not what a human would experience—a perspective motivated by human interests, ignoring some things and focusing on others—but simply re-presents a view on the world, as a camera would. "The camera, unlike the human eye, is unselective. It is, in a manner of speaking, an eye that has been severed from a brain ... It can only see whatever is to be seen—the accidental as well as the necessary, the ephemeral as well as the essential, the "cuffedge" as well as "the sea" (Speigel 66). This passage exemplifies for Spiegel "Joyce's characteristic coldness of vision" (67)—a coldness that is essentially camera-like. This cold, photographic vision is captured near the opening of Christopher Isherwood's *Goodbye to Berlin* (1939), "I am a camera with its shutter open, quite passive, recording, not thinking" (207).

In "New Media Modernism" (2015) Julian Murphet (whose work is discussed at greater length in Chapter 5) offers a particularly sophisticated updating of this argument, seeing in modernism something like the adoption of elements of new media generally into older literary forms. Modernism is a process of "testing the newly mechanized techniques of cinema and advertising for their aesthetic potentials and then transposing those back into the older arts" ("New Media" 213). In Hemingway's flat prose style, for instance, Murphet detects a consequence, and even a sort of emulation, of film. Others have traced Hemingway's characteristically laconic style to his training as a journalist, and perhaps even to the role of the telegraph. Milton Cohen, in *Hemingway's Laboratory* (2005), describes the "cablese" style in which telegrams were written. This short, clipped style was designed to "save newspapers money on expensive transatlantic cables that were billed by the word" (28). While Cohen avoids simply equating cablese (which Hemingway indeed had experience writing) and Hemingway's prose style, he suggests that "cablese did influence his creative prose, most obviously in requiring that superfluous modifiers be cut" (29). More generally, Cohen suggests, in Hemingway's short stories, "The story, in brief, should give the illusion of telling itself" (86), just as, we might add, a projector operates automatically. In Murphet's reading, this aping of the inhumanity of the projector is the central fact of Hemingway's style. Following Stanley Aronowitz's description of Hemingway, in *Dead Artists, Live Theories* (1994) as having "extirpated the 'extraneous' category of subjectivity" from his prose style (56), Murphet connects the affectlessness of Hemingway's prose to the inhumanity of the camera. While early film, in this account, was eager to overcome this sense of cold, machinic perception by adapting works of fiction and absorbing their sentimentality, modernist literature did precisely the opposite.

> Hemingway's prose style is an effort to incorporate, homeopathically, the ground tone of those mechanical means of production, without recycling any of the depleted Victorian feelings for which serious literature had no further use. The principal reason it had no use for them or the subject who was supposed to hold them together was that cinema had already arguably put an end to that entire humanist regime of sense and sensibility.
> (Murphet, "New Media" 214)

While Woolf's fiction offers a clear contrast with Hemingway's, critics have also seen evidence of film's impact on Woolf's style. Laura Marcus, for instance, describes the middle "Time Passes" section of *To the Lighthouse* as evidencing "an equivalent to the cinematic aesthetic in the novel ... produc[ing] a form of experimental cineplay, using visual images to express emotions and animating objects into non-human life" (*Virginia Woolf* 103).

Such an understanding of film as uniquely able to capture life in the passage of time itself resonates with Woolf's fiction and was not uncommon in descriptions of early film. Georges Méliès claims to have discovered his vocation in film after noticing the wind moving through leaves in the background of the short actuality film *Repas de Bébe*—one of the ten films screened by the Lumières in 1895 (Doane 177). D. W. Griffith, late in his career, similarly invoked such movement as what films still lacked. "What the modern movie lacks is beauty—the beauty of moving wind in the trees" (qtd. in Baumbach 107). Dorothy Richardson, in her first "Continuous Performance" article in *Close Up* (1927–1933), describes watching "a tide, frothing in over the small beach of a sandy cove ... foamy waves, to the sound of a slow waltz, without the disturbance of incident" (qtd. in Marcus, *Virginia Woolf* 39). Marcus notes the similar importance of images of waves, "The wave breaking on the shore was a highly significant image for early cinema" ("How Newness" 39). Such images of nonconscious, uncontrolled, or uncontrollable, movement reveal film, like photography, to be not an art of creation, *poesis*, or making, but an art of capture. Mary Anne Doane, in *The Emergence of Cinematic Time* (2002), makes this element of film—the way it captures unintended elements of reality, what Doane will broadly describe as the *contingent*—central to its function as a medium. For Doane film at once participates in this contingent, chance, element, and submits it to order and rationalization. It *captures* the contingent in all senses. In a fascinating 2018 essay, Jordan Schonig describes how images of waves, wind in trees, or smoke have become crucial to film history, because they "reveal cinema's ability to show the autonomy of the world unfold independently of authorial control" (31).

The revelation and illustration of the world's autonomy provide shared vocation for film and modernism. For Marcus, Woolf's "Time Passes" becomes filmic by adapting the plotless, empty beauty of unintended, purposeless motion to fiction, and David Trotter offers a very similar reading of "Time Passes." The inhumanity of the camera, or its automatism (a key term in Stanley Cavell's discussion of film and modernism, discussed in Chapter 2), is what Woolf's prose takes from film, and transforms into modernist fiction. Modernism in literature thus emulates the inhuman, automatic character of the camera. Automatism here does not mean simply a particularly inhuman type of vision (as it does for Spiegel), nor does it suggest the affectless prose of Hemingway as described by Murphet.[10] It means instead a particular attitude to the passage of time, and the revelatory power of such images of time merely passing, all made evident and aesthetically available to fiction through the film camera.

We might highlight not simply time, but the peculiarly melancholic fact that film's capture of the past necessarily excludes the present. Woolf's comments on cinema elsewhere focus less on time than on how film excludes viewers from the world it represents. In the essay "The Cinema" (1926), Woolf describes cinema as a window onto a world from which viewers are absent. Even, Woolf writes, "as we watch the antics of our kind," and respond, we are witnessing a world that has disappeared. The events we witness on the screen may have occurred more than a decade (or, now, a century) ago. Woolf's account of cinema here relies on descriptions of what sound like newsreels and early actuality films.[11] "We are beholding a world which has gone beneath the waves. Brides are emerging from the abbey—they are now mothers; ushers are ardent—they are now silent; mothers are tearful; guests are joyful; this has been won and that has been lost, and it is over and done with" (167). Woolf's description here highlights film's melancholic way of representing the world. Like photography and phonographic sound recording, film does not simply resemble what it represents. A photograph or film recording of a person does indeed, typically, *look like* that person (just as a phonographic recording of a voice does typically *sound like* a person's voice). This sort of resemblance it shares with painting. But unlike a painting, photographs and film images are *caused by* what they represent. A photograph or phonographic recording is the effect—the trace or inscription—of an event that was captured in a particular medium at a particular moment: grooves in a wax cylinder (caused by a stylus vibrating as its cuts into the wax) or the chemical effect of light on a photosensitive negative.

---

[10]Jordan Schonig extends the history of this phenomenon both backwards, to Kant and a concern with contingent forms, and forward to postcinematic digital representations of those same phenomena (wind in leaves, smoke) that represent a distinctly *cinematic* beauty in early film. Schonig links these together as "technologically distinct iterations of a more long-standing aesthetic concern" (33).
[11]Trotter attempts to reconstruct the source of the films Woolf references in "The Cinema" (*Cinematic* 167–8).

Such traces are more like a footprint than a painting—they are marks left in a particular substance at a particular moment. The (unaltered, unmanipulated) photograph testifies that at a particular moment light struck a photosensitive surface in just *this* way.[12] This is what is meant by the *indexicality* of film, and other such media. Woolf describes this indexicality as the loss of an object, in terms similar to Freud's description of melancholy. For Freud, when an individual loses something dear (the death of a loved one, for instance), they may pathologically preserve it, rather than simply mourn its loss. Freud describes a process of incorporation, whereby an individual unconsciously preserves something about a lost loved one (you might adopt a mannerism of a beloved parent, when they die, as a way of preserving their life). Film similarly incorporates an image and preserves it, though it does so technologically rather than psychically. Louise Hornby, in *Still Modernism* (2017), detects a similar melancholy in an impressive reading of photography and Woolf, writing that photography "glosses the elegiac form of her novels" (17). This elegiac note shared by the filmic character of Woolf's prose seems confirmed by the fact that Woolf herself described *To the Lighthouse* as an elegy (*Diary* III: 34). Here film and modernism are joined less by a style than a melancholic orientation to the world they describe.

A more common point of similarity between modernism and film is montage. The abrupt juxtapositions of T. S. Eliot's *The Waste Land* (1922) likewise seem to invite a comparison to cinematic montage. Consider just its opening.

> April is the cruellest month, breeding
> Lilacs out of the dead land, mixing
> Memory and desire, stirring
> Dull roots with spring rain.
> Winter kept us warm, covering
> Earth in forgetful snow, feeding
> A little life with dried tubers.
> Summer surprised us, coming over the Starnbergersee
> With a shower of rain; we stopped in the colonnade,

---

[12]The division of representation into iconic, symbolic, and indexical signs comes from C. S. Peirce. For a compelling introduction and overview of such questions of see Mitchell, "Representation," esp. 13–15.

And went on in sunlight, into the Hofgarten,
And drank coffee, and talked for an hour.
Bin gar keine Russin, stamm' aus Litauen, echt deutsch.
And when we were children, staying at the arch-duke's,
My cousin's, he took me out on a sled,
And I was frightened. He said, Marie,
Marie, hold on tight. And down we went.
In the mountains, there you feel free.
I read, much of the night, and go south in the winter.

(l.1–18)

In these lines "No single consciousness presides; no single voice dominates" (Levenson 172). The result is disjointed, even cacophonous. Yet readers have gained some clarity in imagining these lines as presenting a sort of Eisensteinian, intellectual montage. Colin MacCabe writes that, despite Eliot's stated hostility to the cinema (quoted at the start of this chapter), "there can be little doubt that it was the cinema that provided the major structural principle of *The Waste Land*," namely the "juxtaposition of scenes and images" (44). Those troubling first lines of the poem, with their incompatible, intersecting shifts—in tone (from the gnomic to the blasé), in diction (from the biblical to the conversational), in language (from English to German and back again), in person (from singular to plural), in perspective—all seem resolved if we imagine the poem not as the lyric expression of a speaker (or speakers), but as a description of a film, with edits at key points. Imagine three such cuts, after line 7, after line 12, and after line 17 (to separate the memory of freedom from the description of loneliness in the eighteenth line). Imagine the German line as voice-over, running over the edit. The poem is made intelligible by understanding its stylistic fragmentation as a version of a more recognizable film vernacular. The poet Louis MacNeice, in the essay "Eliot and the Adolescent" (1948), recalls feeling baffled when first reading *The Waste Land*, but notes that "the cinema technique of quick cutting, of surprise juxtapositions, of spotting the everyday detail and making it significant, this would naturally intrigue the novelty-mad adolescent and should, like even the most experimental films, soon become easy to grasp" (150; qtd. in Trotter, *Cinema* 2).

Susan McCabe adapts this trend, reading the fragmentary montage of the poem as a reflection of a wider social force. McCabe calls *The Waste Land* "the modern montage poem par excellence" (40). Like D. W. Griffith's 1916 film *Intolerance*, which intercuts between four historically disparate stories (all illustrating the titular theme), *The Waste Land* juggles multiple timelines, intercutting the present with a vast storehouse of literary tradition. McCabe's argument, however, does not simply analogize *The Waste Land* to montage but relies upon a third term to understand the formal similarity between Eliot's modernist poem and film as a medium. McCabe sees filmic and poetic modes of montage as grounded in contemporaneous understandings of the body, particularly around hysteria. Understandings of the hysterical body, in McCabe's account, undergird the similarities between film and modernism. "By layering and superimposing allusions, the text demands that the reader, akin to an hysteric medium, put together its frame-by-frame fragments, and then Penelope-like, the poem undoes or decomposes itself every reading" (McCabe 40).

Any equation of film and literary modernism at the level of style relies on such analogies. In place of such loose comparisons, David Trotter's *Cinema and Modernism* (2007) refuses film as an explanation of modernist style. He does not, however, deny commerce between film and modernist literature. Instead, he examines their relationship by looking at film in its historical specificity, identifying what he describes not as analogies between literature and film, but "parallels" (3). Rather than "montage" or other broad terms, Trotter's analysis draws on a more detailed account of the early history of film. This insistence on historical specificity reveals problems of chronology that often attend broad comparisons of film, as a medium, with modernism as an event in the arts. Consider again the case of *The Waste Land*. Experimental montage of the sort that seemed so clarifying for MacNeice in reading the poem, and that has been a cliché of descriptions of the poem's fragmented style, did not arrive in England until 1925, three years after the publication of Eliot's poem. Trotter follows Michael North in suggesting that a fascination with film montage among writers, evident for instance in the journal *transition*, was largely a phenomenon of the later 1920s. So, however the film was understood by subsequent readers (including MacNeice), Trotter argues that Eliot's poem could not have been written as a "montage" poem. It was simply written too early—and so some other explanation must exist for its fragmented style. In the case of the "Wandering

Rocks" episode of *Ulysses*, Trotter sees not montage or crosscutting, but an attempt to view the world as it would be seen by a machine, akin, in this case, to the actuality documentaries of early film. Because these short movies of daily life were often filmed in the cities where they were screened, they created the possibility of seeing yourself or someone you know in the movie—just as many of Joyce's Dublin acquaintances found versions of themselves in his novel. Joyce would have been familiar with such actualities, but would only become acquainted with the modernist editing of Eisenstein after *Ulysses* had been published. "Wanderings Rocks" (and, indeed, much of *Ulysses*), Trotter suggests, is much closer to film in its mechanical recording of the everyday than in its style's relationship to editing.

Trotter's larger point is that many understandings of the relationship between film and literature have been motivated by a rather loose and imprecise set of analogies. The idea of montage, so central to many accounts of modernism, oversimplifies the local and historically textured processes of film and literature's interaction in the modernist period. "Whatever its virtues, no account of modernist montage along these lines can tell us how and why works of literature conceived during the previous decade, works such as *Ulysses* and *The Waste Land*, came to be written as they were written" (Trotter, *Cinema* 3). Rather than broad, largely formal similarities built on analogy, Trotter insists that affinities with cinema must be grounded "on the basis of what a writer might conceivably have known about cinema as it was at the time of writing" (*Cinema* 2).[13]

Trotter's insistence on historical specificity exemplifies the archival turn motivating much of the New Modernist Studies. His treatment of film draws on the work of film studies scholars like Tom Gunning and Miriam Hansen (and reveals just how much the New Modernist Studies can benefit from additional engagement with film studies). Rather than analogies between film and

---

[13]Both Trotter and McCabe discuss the plan for a "ten-reel drama" Eliot sent to a friend in an October 1914 letter. One risk, it seems to me, of Trotter's insistence on biographical specificity—the requirement that one avoid generalizations about film by only discussing what we *know* an author knew of film—is that it grants an outsized attention and relevance to such relatively minor works (see Trotter, *Cinema* 137–40 and McCabe *Cinematic* 39).

literature, which typically focus on elements of form, Trotter looks to the history of film, and film culture, more broadly—elements of marketing, exhibition, and spectatorship that shaped people's understanding of film. Andrew Shail's *The Cinema and the Origins of Literary Modernism* (2012) reveals just how much of our sense of "film" is shaped by these larger factors. From such a perspective, however, Trotter, like Murphet and others, identifies film's neutrality as a medium, its sense of a world not *represented* but *recorded*, as its chief influence on modernist literature. "It was not cinema which made literary modernism, but cinema's example" (Trotter 9), which is to say, modernist literature is joined to film not through a shared formal language (montage, point of view, visuality) but through a shared fascination with *neutral perception*. Somewhat peculiarly, Trotter (drawing on Garrett Stewart) sees this neutrality in relation to *The Waste Land*'s prosody—its verse form. Rather than in montage or juxtaposition, Trotter discovers the presence of cinema in the "poetic automatisms of regular metre and rhyme" (Trotter, *Cinema* 146). He locates Eliot's cinematic modernism not in the fragmented opening of the poem, but as an expression of this metrical automaticity in a later passage in the poem's first section:

> Sighs, short and infrequent, were exhaled,
> And each man fixed his eyes before his feet.
> Flowed up the hill and down King William Street,
> To where Saint Mary Woolnoth kept the hours
> With a dead sound on the final stroke of nine.
>
> (l.64–68)

Like Holtby, Spiegel, MacCabe, and others, Trotter too locates modernism in relationship to film. Trotter's attempt to establish the relationship between modernism and film on grounds other than analogy enables him to see rich connections between the early history of film and modernism. Yet, in eschewing broad comparisons between film and modernism (on the grounds of *montage* or similar formal elements), and insisting instead on more specific relationships between literature and film history, he may at times miss the forest for the trees. Spiegel put aside such worries with a general appeal to culture as a sort of all-pervading climate. "By the time Joyce was writing *Ulysses*," Spiegel suggests, "a novelist need never have gone to a movie to know what was meant by one … Any artist could be influenced by film and know all about it simply by being alive and visually alert in the modern world" (xiii). Indeed, while Gertrude Stein seems to have been uninterested in any particular movie, she insists "what I was doing in the Making of Americans, I was doing what the cinema was doing" (Stein, "Portraits" 294). This question of scale and specificity continues to attend any attempt to relate modernist culture to film.

Competition

Whether through analogies, parallels, or archives, most work on modernism and film has insisted on some fundamental link between cinema and literature. Yet, one might just as simply reject the premise of film and literature having any influence on one another. Comparisons of film and prose style are of limited value not (as Trotter suggests) because they are unspecific, or even anachronistic, but because of a fundamental difference between the forms. We might reconsider the ease with which we equate, for instance, Joyce's "Wandering Rocks" with film editing. While the episode's narrative attention indeed shifts to different locations, representing events in each that we are to understand occur simultaneously, the novel does so in a rather unfilmic way. The heart of cross-cutting involves moving back and forth, typically between two locales (say, a family in distress, and the hero rushing to save them), to create a sense of simultaneity and, typically, suspense. "Wandering Rocks," by contrast, merely wanders. It lacks the clear back and forth rhythm of cross cutting. Moreover, it "cuts" between not two or three events or locales, but a cinematically unmanageable eighteen. Simultaneity in the episode is indicated through the episode's interpolation of short fragments from one section into another. These fragmentary intrusions are very different from cinematic cuts, and yet they are the clearest way in which the episode establishes a sense of simultaneity.

Such an observation may lead one to simply discount any meaningful influence between film and literature in the period. Maria DiBattista, in "This Is Not a Movie: *Ulysses* and Cinema" (2006), insists on a sort of absolute separation between a novel like *Ulysses* and a film. While acknowledging Eisenstein's enthusiasm for *Ulysses*, DiBattista shares Joyce's own skepticism about the adaptability of *Ulysses* to the screen.[14] Like Clement Greenberg (discussed in the next chapter) DiBattista takes inspiration from the eighteenth-century philosopher Gotthold Lessing's *Laocoon* (1766), which describes a unique logic proper to each art form. Such a view necessarily separates film and literature, as offering two fundamentally irreconcilable approaches to the world. DiBattista suggests that film is uniquely suited to the visual and fiction to interiority. "For literature, banishment from a paradise of images is compensated for by depth, by access to an interior where the fateful, not the fortuitous, dwells" (DiBattista 232). For DiBattista, these realms—the paradise of images and the interior realm—reflect the intrinsic properties of two different media, working out their own logics independently. In short, perhaps there is no important relationship between film and modernism within the other arts.

Yet, it is equally possible to see the very distinction DiBattista highlights not as an unchangeable reflection of the intrinsic properties of literature and film, but as itself a product of media history. Reflecting on James Joyce from the perspective of the early 1970s, the experimental writer B. S. Johnson stresses the differences and discontinuities with film as being the origin of modernism. For Johnson however, unlike Trotter or McCabe, film relates to modernist literature not through its similarities (whether parallels or analogies), but as its opposite. Film, Johnson suggests, simply does certain things better than prose, and Joyce's modernism follows from his recognition of these differences.

> Joyce saw very early on that film must usurp some of the prerogatives which until then had belonged almost exclusively to the novelist. Film could tell a story more directly, in less time

---

[14]While critics are fond of citing this abortive collaboration between Joyce and Eisenstein, Joyce appears to have been lukewarm, at best, at the prospect of a filmed *Ulysses*. Richard Ellmann writes, "Officially [Joyce] discountenanced the idea (though he had once endorsed it), on the ground that the book could not be made into a film with artistic propriety. But he allowed Paul Léon to keep the matter going, talked to Eisenstein about it, and did not discourage Stuart Gilbert from trying his hand at scenarios for *Ulysses* and *Anna Livia Plurabelle*" (Ellmann 654). After Joyce's death *Ulysses* was indeed adapted to the screen, most directly in Joseph Strick's 1967 *Ulysses* and Sean Walsh's 2003 *Bloom*.

and with more concrete detail than a novel; certain aspects of character could be more easily delineated and kept constantly before the audience (for example, physical characteristics like a limp, a scar, a particular ugliness or beauty); no novelist's description of a battle squadron at sea in a gale could really hope to compete with that in a well-shot film; and why should anyone who simply wanted to be told a story spend all his spare time for a week or weeks reading a book when he could experience the same thing in a version in some ways superior at his local cinema in only one evening?

(150)

Johnson describes film as taking over some of the uses that once belonged to literature. Modernism is the result. In this model, rather than an analogy or parallel, film offers to modernist literature a rival. This rivalry does not doom prose to obsolescence, but frees it to pursue its truest ambition. Prose, in the age of film, can explore deep psychological interiority and the possibilities of the book as medium. Film, in short, frees other media for new, modernist, uses. Just as, Johnson suggests, in the eighteenth century the emergence of the novel freed poetry to abandon narrative and instead pursue a sort of pure lyricism, so the emergence of film frees prose fiction to pursue new ends. "[T]he novel may not only survive but evolve to greater achievements by concentrating on those things it can still do best: the precise use of language, exploitation of the technological fact of the book, and explication of thought" (Johnson 152). We can see Johnson's "precise use of language" in imagist poetry or the austere prose style of naturalist fiction (including perhaps Joyce's *Dubliners*). The "exploitation of the technological fact of the book" is clearly evident in Johnson's own late modernist novels: in *Christie Malry's Own Double-Entry* (1973) the narrator tracks the debits and credits of his life as a double-entry account book, and *The Unfortunates* (1969) is written in twenty-seven unbound sections, presented in a box, to be read in whatever order the reader decides. This vein of print experimentation continues in artist books, as well as in more popular novels like Mark Danielewski's *House of Leaves* (2000). But it is the "explication of thought" that offers the most recognizably modernist element of Johnson's description. In short, we get movies for *seeing*, and books for *thinking*.

Andrew Shail's *The Cinema and the Origins of Literary Modernism* (2012) offers one of the most compelling versions of the argument that film and modernist literature relate not through similarity but through rivalry. Like Nancy Armstrong's in *Fiction in the Age of Photography* (1999) (discussed in the introduction), Shail sees modernism's inward turn as a reaction against the visuality of film. Shail traces, in one chapter, a dialectical relationship between literary and filmic modes of narration. Like Trotter's, this history of film and literary modernism avoids analogy, and draws on the film history of Tom Gunning and others to flesh out the early film culture that most immediately affected modernist literature. The evolution toward narrative, and away from the cinema of attractions, Shail suggests, shaped literary impressionism. Prior to the emergence of the conventions of narrative cinema, early films needed to be somehow explained to their viewers. This explanation could be offered by a live showman, who would offer explanatory commentary alongside the film, or could be offered through intertitles. Narrative cinema, what Gunning calls a cinema of "narrative integration," was attempting to communicate a sense of the film telling its story autonomously. Shail explains,

> In 1907 some American producers were still providing intertitles for every shot, a consequence of a still widespread perception that the images were illustrations for a pre-existing textual 'track.' In the turn to narrative integration, two growing ideas—that intertitles contravened an illusion of reality and that cinema's events should be able to self-narrate—led to the emergence in 1911 of a new ambition to abandon the expository intertitle.
>
> (51)

By attending to the wider realm of what Shail calls film culture—looking not simply at the films themselves, but their marketing, production, and reception—Shail traces the emergence and development of a specifically filmic narrative mode. This attention to film culture and the social contexts surrounding film as a form is exemplary of the New Modernist Studies. Shail's attention to these contexts reveals how the marketing of movies changed. Now movies were advertised not chiefly through a focus on spectacle, but by appealing to how a film accurately represented reality. Such a reorientation in how film, as a medium, was understood reflects changes in its place in a modernist media ecology. As filmmakers strove to eliminate metalanguage and commentary, movies began to look less like a carnival spectacle and more like a featureless window on reality.

In the face of this new, filmic narrative mode, even the most "transparent" realist prose, in comparison to film, seems hopelessly mired in the very metalanguage and commentary that film defines itself against. While realist narrative had already attempted to purge metalanguage and commentary from prose, when compared to a movie the realist novel can only look like one long, imageless intertitle. As Shail puts it, "Even though literary realist metalanguage dematerialised itself in relation to instances of object language, it could not be *as* dematerialised as the narrator-less narrational process which the public were encountering in cinema." Under those conditions "The narrative dynamic of a form that narrated itself [i.e. film] yet which was also merely 'happenings'—'cinema-as-narrator' *and* 'cinema-as-events'—rendered literary metalanguage highly tangible" (75). The inescapable tangibility of literature's linguistic basis, Shail suggests, produced literary impressionism in reaction. Exemplified by the fiction of Joseph Conrad and Ford Madox Ford, among others, and given an influential theorization by Ian Watt in terms of "delayed decoding" in *Conrad in the Nineteenth Century* (1979),[15] literary impressionism discards realism's attempt to simply show the world as it is, and deliberately highlights experiences of perception and subjectivity. It represents the world as it appears—describing not the world itself, but our impression of it. Film's attempt to expunge metalanguage "forced aesthetic practitioners to regard all literary metalanguage, *even* that of literary impressionism, as highly material" (Shail 91–2). Shail's focus on this materialized metalanguage enriches his account of impressionism; rather than simply recounting a focus on subjective experience shared by Ford and Conrad, Shail contrasts the work of these writers. Ford and Conrad, Shail contends, offer two different responses to this materialization of literary metalanguage. More broadly, however the rematerialization of literary language opens the path to the modernism of Joyce, Woolf, and others.

---

[15] See Watt, *Conrad in the Nineteenth Century* (174–5).

Jonathan Foltz's *The Novel After Film* (2018) also describes the modernist novel as shaped by competition with film, though in a very specific way. The competition Foltz describes is not a formal competition for objectivity or realism, but a competition at the level of address. Film's enormous success and huge audiences, Foltz suggests, led to a longing for its influence, its importance, and its cultural centrality among novelists. The result, Foltz writes, is that "the primary 'competition' for the novel after film is not film itself but rather the dignified idea of the 'novel'" (14). Ideas like character, point of view, and irony, Foltz suggest, undergo a change as the modernist novel seeks to modernize itself. Such a perspective might equally be read as a similarity with film. Yet it is a similarity not at the level of form or style, and a comparison that, like Shail's, attends to the wider social context in which films were viewed and understood.

These accounts offer a model for media interaction that will reappear under different guises in later chapters, whether as increasing autonomization (each art pursues its own logic), as rebalancing (the emergence of one medium unsettles the existing ecology), or outright competition (one medium usurps the place of another). The movies in these accounts offer a rival to other modes of representing the world, and as such becomes a key, perhaps the key, generating cause of modernism.

The "Modernity Thesis"

In addition to the models of emulation and rivalry discussed above, film and modernism may be understood as fellow-travelers. Rather than relating directly to one another, both express some shared modern condition. In the indispensable *On the History of Film Style* (1997), David Bordwell calls such accounts "the modernity thesis" (141–46). Echoing Virginia Woolf's too-often quoted suggestion that "on or about December 1910, human character changed," Bordwell describes such accounts of film as postulating "that at some point between 1850 and 1920, perception within European societies changed" (Bordwell 141–2). While such a description may seem to simply shift the burden of explanation away from one term (modernism) to another (modernity), the modernity thesis stresses a broader category that creates a new period that brings with it a new "mode of perception," of which film is simply one expression. Such a perspective builds on Walter Benjamin's insistence, in "The Work of Art in the Age of Its Technological Reproducibility" (1936), that "Just as the entire mode of existence of human collectives changes over long historical periods, so too does their mode of perception" ("Work of Art" 23). As the senses are reshaped by their environment, culture is reshaped in turn. Miriam Hansen's inclusion of film as a "vernacular modernism," discussed above, is an instance of the modernity thesis. Hansen's enlarged definition of modernism draws on a Benjaminian account of the senses changing in response to modernity.

How does film express modernity? Often, following theorists like Benjamin and Georg Simmel, whose essay "Metropolis and Mental Life" (1903) offers another important early theorization of the modernity thesis, modernity is described in terms of shock and dislocation. For Benjamin, film montage, with its rapid shifts of attention, offers the same experience of shock evident elsewhere in industrialized modernity. Streets crowded with cars, factories cacophonous with machinery, are echoed by the rapidly moving, industrialized technology of the camera itself. "For Benjamin, the shock experience of film makes it adequate to its age, unlike other aesthetic forms" (Doane, *Emergence* 15). Film's abrupt changes, its shocks, offer a training for modernity. Early film theorist Ricciotto Canudo, in "The Birth of a Sixth Art" (1911), similarly connected film to the wider environment of technological modernity. "Our age," he writes, "has destroyed most earnestly, with a thousand extremely complex means, the love of restfulness, symbolized by the smoking of a patriarchal pipe at the domestic hearth." Film is the art appropriate to this moment of destroyed traditions. "The cinematograph can satisfy the most impatient racer. The motorist who has just finished the craziest of races and becomes a spectator at one of these shows will certainly not feel a sense of slowness; images of life will flicker in front of him with the speed of the distances covered" (Canudo 60). Canudo's image of the motor racer, and connection of it to film, is echoed in Enda Duffy's *The Speed Handbook* (2009), which views such appeals to velocity and flickering intensity as central to the experience of modernism. A similar, though differently gendered, idea appears in Mary Richardson's writing on the cinema, which appeared in the

British film journal *Close Up*. Laura Marcus writes, Richardson's "film writings conjure up a community of spectators, often female, becoming educated for modernity by 'the movies'" ("How Newness Enters the World" 40).

Whatever we make of the strong claim that modernity altered the human senses,[16] it seems indisputable, as Ben Singer writes in *Melodrama and Modernity* (2001), that many of film's earliest viewers "described cinema as a medium of powerful fleeting impressions, kinetic speed, novel sights, superabundant juxtaposition, and visceral stimulation, and therefore as a medium in which people perceived a striking resemblance to modern urban experience" (130). Many experienced film as produced by, enmeshed in, and expressive of the technological modernity of the early twentieth century. This wider definition of film's relationship to modernism certainly might include the avant-garde films discussed above, but it might also include a wider range of film experience, including mainstream films that capture some sense of modernity—the melodramas discussed by Singer, or perhaps a film like Chaplin's *Modern Times* (1936). This mixing of attention to film, art, and literature as expressions of a shared social/historical condition exemplifies the eclectic revisioning of modernism by the New Modernist Studies. It offers what Rita Felski calls, in "Modernist Studies and Cultural Studies" (2003), a "cross-pollination of cultural studies with recent histories and theories of modernity" (504).

Modernity can also be described in terms other than the shock that is central to accounts of modern experience like Simmel's and Benjamin's. Like Benjamin, Jonathan Crary's *Techniques of the Observer: On Vision and Modernity in the Nineteenth Century* (1990) offers a history of the senses. Crary describes a history of vision in which modernity represents a transition away from an understanding of vision abstractly modeled on the camera obscura to one grounded in the physiology of perception. Rather than the shock of technology or the experience of the city, Crary focuses on a Foucauldian shift at the level of how the perceiving individual is imagined. Once, the observer was imagined as simply

---

[16]David Bordwell, for instance, is skeptical of the strong, Benjaminian version of the "modernity thesis" that claims the human senses have actually changed (*History* 143–7). Singer has an excellent discussion of the modernity thesis in Chapter 4 of *Melodrama and Modernity*.

a location, an empty place where an objective process of perception occurred. But in the modern period, with increased attention to perception as a physiological process, including experiments on the "persistence of vision" (which will become the basis for moving picture technologies), vision is understood as somehow produced by the observer. "The corporeal subjectivity of the observer, which was a priori excluded from the concept of the camera obscura, suddenly becomes the site on which an observer is possible" (Crary 169). Unlike the abstract geometry of vision offered by the camera obscura, nineteenth-century visual technologies, like thaumatropes and phenakistikopes—devices that simulate movement (either by switching between two images on a rapidly rotating disc, or by viewing multiple images on a spinning wheel behind a small slit)—were "bound up in *non-veridical* theories of vision that effectively annihilate a real world" (Crary 14). Any confidence that perception simply re-presents a pre-existing world is lost once one recognizes how perception is generated by the physiology of the observer. Understanding vision as a physiological process, Crary suggests, undermines "veridical" theories of vision—those accounts which describe vision as an unproblematic representation of a passively observed external world. And of course the most complete realization of these technologies, and of this uniquely modern understanding of vision, arrives with film. The realization that enables film to reproduce the illusion of the world by presenting images of it at twenty-four frames a second is inextricable from an understanding of perception that eliminates any absolute confidence that perception has unmediated access to the world.[17]

This reconceptualization of observation was part of a wider process that includes the emergence of both film and modernism. In Crary's account of modernity, photography must not be understood

---

[17]"Persistence of vision" as an explanation for film's illusion of motion has been the subject of some debate. See, for instance, Joseph Anderson and Barbara Anderson's "The Myth of Persistence of Vision Revisited." Yet, as Crary puts it, "The empirical truth of the notion of 'persistence of vision' as an explanation for the illusion of motion is irrelevant here. What is important are the conditions and circumstances that allowed it to operate as an explanation and the historical subject/observer that it presupposed" (110). Doane similarly asks, "The theory of persistence of vision may be 'wrong,' but the question remains—why was it so firmly ensconced, and why did it endure for so long?" (71).

chiefly in relation to painting or other elements of visual culture, but as part of this wider transformation. "To understand the 'photography effect' in the nineteenth century, one must see it as a crucial component of a new cultural economy of value and exchange, not as part of a continuous history of visual representation" (Crary 13). And modernism itself, in art and literature, reflects this same history. "It is not enough," Crary writes, "to attempt to describe a dialectical relation between the innovations of avant-garde artists and writers in the late nineteenth century and the concurrent 'realism' and positivism of scientific and popular culture. Rather, it is crucial to see both of these phenomena as overlapping components of a single social surface on which the modernization of vision had begun decades earlier" (5). Rather than a rupture, inaugurated in paintings by Edouard Manet or the impressionists, Crary sees a continuity at the level of the *observer*, which proceeds over a longer period. A technology like the stereoscope, for instance, can "indicate a greater break with a classical observer than that which occurs later in the century in the realm of painting. The stereoscope signals an eradication of 'the point of view' around which, for several centuries, meanings had been assigned reciprocally to an observer and the object of his or her vision" (Crary 128). The "decentered observer" Crary here identifies as a condition of modernity unites pre-film technologies like the stereoscope with "that which occurs later in the century in the realm of painting," that is, with modernism. Here it is neither rivalry nor emulation that explains modernism's relationship to film. Both modernism and the stereoscope reflect a single process: the destruction of a conventional understanding of a unified, coherent, and singular point of view.

Mary Anne Doane's *The Emergence of Cinematic Time* (2002) similarly describes film in relation to a wider notion of modernity, which informs both modernist art and the emergence of film. She defines modernity not by an epistemological shift in the understanding of perception (as Crary does), but as a rationalization of time and the responses this process of rationalization inspires. This rationalization of time is evident in Taylorist production, in the use of time cards to monitor work, in the establishment of time zones, and in the spread of pocket watches (4–5). Time, in modernity, is subject to measurement and analysis in the name of productivity and efficiency. It is carved into units (into hours, minutes, seconds) which can be counted and accounted, measured and made efficient. Yet, even as it is rationalized and organized, such schemes cannot eliminate the fact of unpredictability. The surprising, the unanticipatable—what Doane calls the *contingent*—persists, and must be factored into these systems. As Doane explains, "It is within the context of a modernity defined by rapid industrialization and the diffusion of new technologies as well as the rapid changes of urban life that contingency emerges as a site of awe and fear, constituted as both lure and threat" (Doane 13). Statistics offers one modern strategy for the management and control of uncertainty and contingency. Film and photography, Doane suggests, offer another. They emerge in relationship to a notion of contingency peculiar to modernity.

Cinema, Doane argues, is uniquely well suited to the management of contingency because it mediates between the rationalization of time that defines modernity and the inevitable contingencies that continue to resist it. In cinema, Doane writes, "The lure of contingency, the fascination of a present moment in which anything can happen, is safely deployed. The present—as the mark of contingency in time—is made tolerable, readable, archivable, and, not least, pleasurable" (107). By indexically capturing individual frames, and uniting them in a continuous (re)experiencing of the present, the modern tension between rationalization and contingency is "embodied or materialized in film form itself" (Doane 9). Each contingent frame is regularized by the fact of the camera and made subject to the rationalization of editing. At the level of its medium, film emerges as an expression, but also a participant, in a wider rethinking of time under modern conditions.

Both *Techniques of the Observer* and *The Emergence of Cinematic Time* offer rich accounts of film as inextricable from some larger history of modernity—a modernity defined by time in Doane's case and by theories of perception in Crary's.[18] These accounts also offer useful theorizations of media. For both Doane and Crary, media are not independent actors but are expressions of larger forces. And ultimately, for both Doane and Crary, it is at the level of the economic that modernity is most properly understood—in the

---

[18]In both Crary and Doane, that larger history of modernity is indebted to the work of Michel Foucault. For references to Foucault, see Crary 6n2, 22 and Doane 20–1.

rationalization of time for Doane and, for Crary, in "[t]he economic need for rapid coordination of eye and hand in performing repetitive actions" (Crary 85). Both Crary and Doane thus follow Walter Benjamin in understanding film as inextricable from a modernity that is intimately connected to commodity capitalism.

In surveying how critics and artists understood modernism's relationship to the new art of film, we have considered different types of relationship. To modernism, film has been imagined as model, as rival, and as fellow-traveler. This last model—exemplified here by Benjamin, Doane, and Crary—also illustrates the challenges and difficulties of treating a single medium alone. In these accounts, by treating modernism and film as expressions of a shared condition, both terms lose some of their coherence. Larger histories (of technology, of capitalism) shape this relationship and come to play a crucial role in the theorizations of modernism and its media that these critics offer. These accounts therefore reveal the challenge, and perhaps the impossibility, of understanding modernism's relationship to media by looking at individual media alone. Film's peculiar centrality to the twentieth century earned it a singular place in this book. In the following chapters other modern media technologies (e.g., radio, the typewriter) will appear, but they will no longer occupy center stage. Instead, our narrative will be framed by influential ways of theorizing media. These theorizations offer different accounts of modernism and its media because they make different assumptions about what media are, about the histories that shape their meanings, and how something called modernism emerges from these conditions.

2

Purifying the Medium: Clement Greenberg and the Legacy of Medium Specificity

One of the most influential accounts of modernism places media at its center. Strangely, it pays little attention to the explosion of industrialized, technological media that might be thought of as one of the chief hallmarks of modernity. Instead, it focuses on the media of the traditional arts and on the peculiar way that *modern* art seems obsessed by the materials out of which it is composed. Emerging out of art criticism and art history, this account describes the modernist work as eschewing "subject matter" or "content" in favor of purifying its relation to its own medium. This account of art is most often associated with the midcentury art critic Clement Greenberg, though it is elaborated and contested in the work of the other thinkers discussed in this chapter (Rosalind Krauss, Michael Fried, and Stanley Cavell). To its detractors it offers an empty formalism, which is elitist in its absolute separation of high art from the rest of mere "culture," and is dangerously blinkered in its disregard for history, context, and politics.

While Greenberg's account seems like a now rather conventional, formalist art history, it is also a media theory of modernism. Greenberg's description of the *opacity* of art in essays from the 1940s prefigures the role of "hypermediacy" in the media theory of Jay David Bolter and Richard Grusin in *Remediation* (1999). For Bolter and Grusin, linear perspective, which dominated Western art since the Renaissance, represents an attempt to hide or erase the fact of the medium and provide the viewer with an immediate experience.

"If executed properly, the surface of the painting dissolved and presented to the viewer the scene beyond" (Bolter and Grusin 25). Art before modernism effaced the medium, transforming the work into a sort of transparent window onto a represented world. Modernist art, by contrast, discards transparency as an ideal and foregrounds opaqueness or, in Bolter and Grusin's terms, its *hypermediacy*. "In modernist art," Bolter and Grusin write, "the logic of hypermediacy could express itself both as a fracturing of the space of the picture and as a hyperconscious recognition or acknowledgment of the medium" (38). Modernist art shares with digital media (including video games, hypertexts, and other "hypermedia") a refusal of transparency and a foregrounding of its own medium.

Yet, Greenberg's definition of medium is narrower and more restrictive than Bolter and Grusin's. The modernist work does not simply draw attention to the fact of mediation, but to the particular textures and limitations of its media. It is less the *fact* of mediation that the modernist work foregrounds than the particular character of its materiality. We might say that it is focused less on the qualities of a verb (a process of *mediating*) than on the characteristics of a noun (the materiality of the medium). Painting gives up perspective, illusionistic effects, and figuration not simply to foreground the fact that it is an illusion, but in a quest to establish its own conditions. In his later work, Greenberg invokes the critical philosophy of Immanuel Kant (1724–1804), with its search for the conditions of possibility of experience. Greenberg rereads art history as a similar quest to establish the "conditions of possibility" for each art form. These conditions, in Greenberg's theorization, are ultimately *media*. Painting becomes, in various ways, about paint and canvas—about the flatness and limitations of canvas, about color and line, about the verticality through which it faces us (in its placement on the wall, or on the easel). While some of his critics might see this as reducing art to lifeless formalism, Greenberg sees it as truer, purified means of expression, "the color, the verticality, the concentricity, and the interlocking are not there for their own sakes. They are there, first and foremost, for the sake of feeling, and as vehicles of feeling. And if these paintings fail as vehicles and expressions of feeling, they fail entirely" (*Collected* 4:153). Greenberg here echoes Pound: "Only emotion endures" (*Literary* 14).

Greenberg's formalism and elitism mark him decisively as a figure of the *old* modernist studies, against whom the New Modernist

Studies, thoroughly contextualist in its methods and omnivorous in its cultural tastes, defines itself. But in seeking to view such art through the category of *media* and in describing that category chiefly as a matter of *materiality*, his thinking inaugurates a lineage of theorizing modernism as an expression of its media environment. More narrowly, Greenberg's attempt to ground a theory of art in its medium inaugurates an understanding of modernism as a quest for the ontological grounding of art itself. This "quest" rhetoric is evident as well in the language of "discovery" and "experimentation" through which modernist art, in this tradition, is regularly figured.[1] And it culminates in a theorization of modernism that passes beyond the work, and its materiality, to the broader philosophical category of the work of art's *ontology* in the work of Stanley Cavell, and in more recent work by J. M. Bernstein.[2] Perhaps equally important, the logic of *purity* that Greenberg develops replays itself across the arts, even in places that Greenberg himself does not explore, including film and radio.

"Avant-Garde and Kitsch"

Like the relationship between modernism and its media, the relationship between modernism and "popular culture" or "mass culture," is one of the central theoretical questions of modernist studies. The relationship between works and their contexts is, of course, a key question across periods, but the revolution in communications technologies beginning in the nineteenth century restructured culture itself. This period saw the emergence of both experimental art and literature *and* a form of popular, industrialized culture. The relationship between art and "popular" culture, between high and low, has been at the center of modernist

---

[1] The language of *quest* is central to Greenberg's metaphors of modernism. Greenberg describes Picasso and Braque's "quest for a better way of transcribing the relations of volumes had been conceived of not as a scientific project but as a quest, ultimately, for a means of creating more firmly organized pictures" (*Collected* 2:273). He speaks of "the true object of Cézanne's quest" (*Collected* 3:88) and "the quest for the irreducible and primary elements of the art of painting in which Klee participated along with such other abstract painters as Kandinsky and Mondrian" (*Collected* 1:70).
[2] See Bernstein's essay "Late Style, First Art: The Fates and Politics of Modernism" (2018).

studies since its inception. Indeed, this relationship will be at the center of the fourth chapter on the Frankfurt School. Much criticism, prior to the New Modernist Studies, tended to stress the antagonism and antithesis between modernism and popular culture. Andreas Huyssen in *After the Great Divide* (1986), for instance, provides a key statement of this relationship, positing a sharp division between modernism and mass culture (which is later undone by postmodernism). Work like Jennifer Wicke's *Advertising Fictions* (1988), and the essays in the collection *Marketing Modernisms* (edited by Kevin Dettmar and Stephen Watt, 1996), worked to undo this sharp division by stressing the continuities between modernist works and the market. This trend within New Modernist Studies is well illustrated by David Chinitz's *T. S. Eliot and the Cultural Divide* (2003), which works in the exact opposite direction of Huyssen, showing the ways that T. S. Eliot's poetry was inflected and shaped by popular culture, rather than simply rejecting it. John Xiros Cooper, in "Modernism in the Age of Mass Culture and Consumption" (2010), offers a valuable review of this question.

This rich vein of scholarship on modernism and popular culture that has been part of the New Modernist Studies over the past two decades might be described as *undoing* the high/low dichotomy that Clement Greenberg helped cement. For Greenberg, art's turn to its own medium in the modernist period is imagined as a retreat from the forces of modernity. Art's antagonist, in this battle, is "Kitsch," Greenberg's term for popular culture. For Greenberg, kitsch looks like art, but in reality is a sort of pseudo-art. Huyssen offers a blunter definition, calling kitsch "cultural trash" (*After* ix). Greenberg's influential 1939 essay "Avant-Garde and Kitsch" opens with puzzlement precisely over the divided state of culture in modernity: "One and the same civilization produces simultaneously two such different things as a poem by T. S. Eliot and a Tin Pan Alley song, or a painting by Braque and a *Saturday Evening Post* cover" ("Avant-Garde" 3). How, Greenberg asks, do the new, challenging, experimental modes of art and literature relate to popular art and culture? How is *Ulysses* related to the now forgotten A. S. M. Hutchinson's *If Winter Comes* (the best-selling novel in the year *Ulysses* was published, according to *Publisher's Weekly*)? How are the paintings of Norman Rockwell related to those of Jackson Pollock?

What perspective of culture is large enough to enable us to situate them in an enlightening relation to each other? Does the fact that a disparity such as this within the frame of a single cultural tradition, is and has been taken for granted—does this fact indicate that the disparity is a part of the natural order of things? Or is it something entirely new, and particular to our age?
("Avant-Garde" 3)

To Greenberg, art and kitsch are two absolutely separate trends, and between them is no commonality but only what Huyssen famously calls a "great divide." Theodor Adorno and Max Horkheimer draw a similarly stark contrast between real art and "the culture industry," discussed in Chapter 4. Greenberg spends "Avant-Garde and Kitsch" trying to establish this difference as something at once intrinsic to works of art and produced by a particular moment of history. Such a disparity between the popular and the elite is a new development, particular to modernity.

Modernism, or what Greenberg calls the *avant-garde*, represents a turning inward of art in the face of kitsch. Here he invokes a recognizable description of modernity as a period when, in the words of the *Communist Manifesto* (1848), "all that is solid melts into air,"[3] where tradition and convention fall apart. Greenberg explains, "A society, as it becomes less and less able, in the course of its development, to justify the inevitability of its particular forms, breaks up the accepted notions upon which artists and writers must depend in large part for communication with their audiences. It becomes difficult to assume anything" ("Avant-Garde" 3–4). While the artist's role had once been dictated by the Church, or by a patron, or simply by a coherent bourgeois culture, by the middle of the nineteenth century (Greenberg will insist that it is contemporaneous with the socialist revolutions of 1848), the traditional bearings by which the artist understood the world had been lost. With its conventional justifications gone, art is sent "in search of the absolute" ("Avant-Garde" 5). Just as Stephen Dedalus in Joyce's *Portrait of the Artist as a Young Man* (1916)

---

[3]This description of modernity was sufficiently influential that it provides Marshall Berman with the title and key image of his 1982 *All That is Solid Melts Into Air: The Experience of Modernity.*

insists that the artist "like the God of creation, remains within or behind or beyond or above his handiwork, invisible, refined out of existence, indifferent, paring his fingernails" (219),[4] so, Greenberg suggests, "The avant-garde poet or artist tries in effect to imitate God by creating something valid solely on its own terms in the way nature itself is valid" ("Avant-Garde" 6). As the social grounding of the artist changes, as a consequence of "modernity" (here meaning some like a general fraying or evaporating of cultural coherence), so art itself is unyoked from the world, and freed from the task of imitating the world to pursue its own intrinsic values.

Art's evil twin, *kitsch*, emerges simultaneously, born of the same conditions. Kitsch is an inferior pseudo-art, or "ersatz culture." Like the avant-garde, kitsch too is a novel phenomenon, a "mass product of industrialism" ("Avant Garde" 12). It flattens cultural difference. It is neither genuine art nor folk culture but simply a commodity, produced for consumption by the newly industrialized working class. Kitsch is a by-product of urbanization and an expansion of literacy (in the service of new jobs, like clerks). While the peasant class of the past had traditional culture, this newly urban and literate working class needed a new form of entertainment.

> The peasants who settled in the cities as proletariat and petty bourgeois learned to read and write for the sake of efficiency, but they did not win the leisure and comfort necessary for the enjoyment of the city's traditional culture. Losing, nevertheless, their taste for the folk culture whose background was the countryside, and discovering a new capacity for boredom at the same time, the new urban masses set up a pressure on society to provide them with a kind of culture fit for their own consumption. To fill the demand of the new market, a new commodity was devised: ersatz culture, kitsch, destined for those who, insensible to the values of genuine culture, are hungry nevertheless for the diversion that only culture of some sort can provide.
>
> ("Avant-Garde" 10)

---

[4]Stephen here echoes Gustave Flaubert in an 1875 letter to George Sand, "my ideal of art demands that the artist reveal none of this, and that he appear in his work no more than God in nature" (2:227).

Kitsch raids the past for its materials, then simplifies and repackages them for easy consumption. It capitalizes on the real accomplishments of previous art, literally, in order to mass-reproduce them for profit.

This new product of industrialized modernity, for Greenberg, is intrinsically and essentially different from genuine art. The difference between modern art and kitsch is not a mere matter of habits or what Greenberg calls "conditioning." It is, instead, absolute, essential, and inescapable. The stark and unqualified character of this division between art and kitsch is where Greenberg most sharply differs from more recent criticism of modernism. Few would deny that Hollywood films and experimental novels, or Norman Rockwell *Saturday Evening Post* covers and Mark Rothko color field paintings, circulate in different ways, for different audiences, and elicit different modes of response. Yet these may be differences of degree, rather than kind. Following the work of French sociologist Pierre Bourdieu, in *Distinction* (1979; English translation, 1984), we might conclude these differences simply reflect differences in class structure that Greenberg otherwise seems so acutely aware of in "Avant-Garde and Kitsch." Moreover, recent critics often note that the continuities between the popular and the elite are often as striking as the differences. For instance, modernist poetry and fiction seems fascinated by popular culture, as Chinitz demonstrates in his study of T. S. Eliot's poetry, or as any reader of Joyce's *Ulysses* cannot help but notice. After all, the popular songs and advertising slogans of 1904 provide *Ulysses* with a sort of ongoing refrain. Edward Comentale's *Sweet Air: Modernism, Regionalism, and American Popular Song* (2013) inserts exactly the sort of the popular song that Greenberg disparages in "Avant-Garde and Kitsch" into modernist history. Or, one might stress the ways that "high" and "low" culture alike, while divergent in audience and circulation (or in subject matter and form), are nevertheless both responses to a single condition of modernity, a point that is thoroughly Greenbergian, but that seems to lose relevance for Greenberg *after* the split has occurred. As John Xiros Cooper and others note, modernism today is not at odds with popular culture but utterly integrated with it. From the design of Apple products (Cecire, "Apple's Modernism"), to the atonality of horror movie soundtracks, and poster reproductions of modernist painting (Cooper 310), modernism is not hostile to contemporary mass culture, but utterly dissolved into it. Cooper explains,

Fragmentary poetic forms, abstraction in the visual arts, fast-cutting montage techniques in film, the breakdown of traditional tonality in music in the era of dodecaphonic serialism, and the hard, gemlike flame of aesthetic epiphany defined the avant-garde culture of the early twentieth century. What was not noticed in those early days of modernism across the arts was how well these approaches harmonized with the unbounded, ruptured, non-linear nature of capitalist modernization. At its very core burned the intoxicating rapture of consumption.

(311)

For Cooper, whatever manifest differences exist between high and low, they equally testify to the shared, true ground of modernism: capitalism. Yet, to Greenberg, in 1939, it was the difference between modernism and kitsch, rather than their shared origin, that mattered. This difference, for Greenberg, gave modernist art an insurgent power to resist the market forces of capitalism.

Greenberg insists on absolute differences between art and kitsch at the level of aesthetic form. They represent two very different modes of aesthetic experience. Kitsch's meanings are "self-evident immediately and without any effort on the part of the spectator." Kitsch "pre-digests art for the spectator and spares him effort, provides him with a short cut to the pleasure of art that detours what is necessarily difficult in genuine art." To illustrate these differences, Greenberg imagines an untrained viewer ("an ignorant Russian peasant," "Avant-Garde" 14), who compares a kitsch painting and a painting by Picasso.

> ... the ultimate values which the cultivated spectator derives from Picasso are derived at a second remove, as the result of reflection upon the immediate impression left by the plastic values. It is only then that the recognizable, the miraculous and the sympathetic enter. They are not immediately or externally present in Picasso's painting, but must be projected into by the spectator sensitive enough to react sufficiently to plastic qualities.
>
> ("Avant-Garde" 14–15)

In his most succinct explanation, avant-garde art, like that of Picasso, offers *causes* that the viewer must confront and work through (or "digest") herself, while kitsch provides *effects*, available without any additional labor of understanding, predigested ("Avant-Garde" 15). This restrictive and elitist definition of modernism traces avant-garde art and kitsch to a common source, but insists that their subsequent separation is absolute. Once separate, the two never meet: one has genuine art *or* ersatz culture, the easy pleasures of representation *or* the difficult but rewarding values of mediation.

A Retreat to the Medium

Some theorists knot together a theory of media out of other strands of thought, building an approach to media out of materials ready to hand. Walter Benjamin (discussed in the fourth chapter) draws on a peculiar mix of Marxism and Jewish Mysticism. Marshall McLuhan's theory of media, discussed in the next chapter, is concocted equally of parts from Milman Parry and Harold Innis. Friedrich Kittler has been described as offering McLuhan-inflected version of Michel Foucault's historicism. Greenberg's "Avant-Garde and Kitsch" is different. While it is not unique in its concerns (the Frankfurt School and Andreas Huyssen offer similar analyses of the relationship between art and popular culture), its particular framing of this question provided the vocabulary in which an entire approach to modernism as a question of the *purity* of a medium would evolve. Greenberg's 1939 essay establishes a set of questions that other work, including Greenberg's own later essays, elaborate and complicate.

In Greenberg's later criticism, the relationship between the modernist work and its media is elaborated at great length as a quest for *purity*. Kitsch operates *immediately*, while the genuine work of art operates at a "second remove," requiring the viewer to understand its plastic values—its formal, and medial, identity. Indeed, Greenberg's hostility to figuration and representation in art is, in essence, a hostility to any perception of a work that is too immediate, that does not have to reflect on the mediating power of art's materiality. If kitsch offers easily consumable content, such that its medium provides no difficulty at all, then avant-garde art, in achieving autonomy and being loosed from mere representation or subject matter, has only the medium to rely on. "In turning his attention away from subject-matter or common experience, the poet or artist turns it in upon the medium of his own craft" ("Avant-Garde" 6).

For Greenberg the medium is not the message, so much as the source and bearer of aesthetic value. It is by foregrounding its own medium that a work of art can achieve the aesthetic difficulty and density that marks it as avant-garde, rather than mere kitsch. In arguing that each art has a medium-specific set of modes that are proper to it, Greenberg invokes Gotthold Lessing's 1767 essay, *Laocoon: An Essay on the Limits of Poetry and Painting*. For Greenberg, like Lessing, the success of an art requires recognizing its own medium specificity. Lessing argued that poetry had been seduced by the visual arts, and so indulged in a mode of painterly description at odds with its own, fundamentally narrative, mode. Since literature unfolds in time, it must aspire to different ends than painting, which unfolds in space. Against Horace's classical dictum that a single logic unites poetry and painting (*ut pictura poesis*—as in painting, so in poetry), Lessing insists that it is the difference between these arts that really ensures their success.

In "Towards a Newer Laocoon" (1940), published one year after "Avant-Garde and Kitsch," Greenberg radicalizes Lessing. For too long, Greenberg suggests, "literature" dominated the arts, with the result that drama, narrative, and ultimately even representation itself had distorted the other arts which all sought to ape the conditions of literature. Categories of illusion came to dominate across the arts. Such a state of affairs could only arise, Greenberg insists, at a relatively late stage in an art's development, when the means of an art were sufficiently advanced that *hiding* the art was even a possibility—*ars celare artem*, or art is a matter of concealing art, or, less paradoxically, art should appear natural ("Towards a Newer Laocoon" 43). Under such a standard, when literary "representation" defined the end goal of all art, the medium was at best a necessary evil. Ideally, under the regime of representation, Greenberg suggests, the medium "would disappear entirely to leave the experience of the spectator or reader identical with that of the artist" ("Towards a Newer Laocoon" 37). Such a perspective idealizes art as a sort of groundless representation. Art should be, in short, *immediate*. Greenberg returns to Lessing in order to restore the medium as a category for the understanding and analysis of art.

Painters are led astray by narrative, representation, and *content*. This was the failure of much art of the nineteenth century.

Greenberg, offering a typically sweeping value judgment, declares that such inattention to the medium led to "an all-time low" in art. "The name of this low is Vernet, Gérôme, Leighton, Watts, Moreau, Böcklin, the Pre-Raphaelites, etc., etc. That some of these painters had real talent only made their influence the more pernicious. It took talent—among other things—to lead art that far astray" ("Towards a Newer Laocoon" 38). The expressionist trend represented by Romanticism only further exacerbates this tendency by focusing on the genius of the artist. The result is a "denial of the medium" so complete and profound that the artist behaves as though he "were ashamed to admit he had actually painted his picture instead of dreaming it forth" ("Towards a Newer Laocoon" 39). Greenberg describes a confusion of the arts throughout the nineteenth century that only a return to the sort of separation that Lessing describes can solve.

Modernism reverses this trend. Gustave Courbert, the impressionists and, signally, Edouard Manet in Greenberg's account, all, in various ways, and almost certainly unconsciously, return to the medium rather than avoid it or hide it. As Michael Fried elaborates, following Greenberg, in the paintings of Manet all the practices developed by painting to hide its medium are slowly reversed and acknowledged as artifice. Manet uses a number of devices to acknowledge canvas, rather than render it an immediate, magical perspective on a represented scene. Manet's colors grow flat, rather than seeking to achieve illusionistic depth; the direct gaze of the female figure in Manet's *Olympia* (1863) defies conventions by acknowledging the viewer; more complicatedly, Manet recasts and dislocates genre conventions such as those of the nude in *Le Déjeuner sur l'herbe* (1863), discussed in the next section. Such work plays a crucial role in this history because it reverses the trend that Greenberg describes of trying to make the medium invisible.

Greenberg's wish for art to escape from the dominance of the category of representation here echoes an earlier narrative. Where, according to Greenberg, for centuries literature had dominated the arts, in a different tradition *music* assumed pride of place. Greenberg here follows earlier thinkers, like Walter Pater and Arthur Schopenhauer, in electing music, rather than literature, as the most important art form. In *The World as Will and Representation* (1819), the philosopher Arthur Schopenhauer granted music a special role because "music is by no means like the other arts, namely a copy of the Ideas, but a copy of the will itself" (I:257). At the close of the nineteenth century, in his study *The Renaissance: Studies in Art and Poetry* (1873), Walter Pater insisted that "All art constantly aspires towards the condition of music" (111).[5] Music's nonrepresentational character makes it a model for a very different sort of aesthetics than the one Greenberg identifies as being indebted to the literary, with its focus on narrative and representation. As Greenberg writes, "The effects of music are the effects, essentially, of pure form" ("Towards a Newer Laocoon" 41). Music did not simply provide a guide; it provided a deeper principle.

> Only by accepting the example and defining each of the other arts solely in the terms of the sense or faculty which perceived its effects and by excluding from each art whatever is intelligible in the terms of another sense or faculty would the non-musical arts attain the 'purity' and self-sufficiency which they desire; which they desire, that is, in so far as they were avant-garde.
> ("Towards a Newer Laocoon" 41)

The principle of avant-garde, or modernist art, becomes purification. The modernist work of art must expunge from itself everything that is not specific to its medium. "Purity in art consists in the acceptance, willing acceptance, of the limitations of the medium of the specific art" ("Towards a Newer Laocoon" 42). "There can be no art without resistance in the materials," William Morris had noted (qtd. in McGann 114). In Greenberg this principle is radicalized, and resistance in the materials becomes the grounding of art itself.

Painting since the mid-nineteenth century, or rather important painting—painting that is not kitsch—represents a "progressive surrender to the resistance of its medium; which resistance consists chiefly in the flat picture plane's denial of efforts to 'hole through' it for realistic perspectival space" ("Towards a Newer Laocoon" 43). Where the square canvas was once imagined as a transparent window onto what it represented, modernism restores to the canvas

---

[5]This oft-quoted line occurs in Pater's essay on "The School of Giorgione," the opening of which mentions Lessing's *Laocoon* and anticipates many of Greenberg's points.

its materiality and its opacity. So too across the arts, modernism "restore[s] the identity of an art" by "emphasiz[ing]" "the opacity of its medium" ("Towards a Newer Laocoon" 42). Poetry, for Greenberg, is not about love or daffodils, but about the "relations between words as personalities composed of sound, history and possibilities of meaning" ("Towards a Newer Laocoon" 42). Grammar and meaning become secondary concerns. Although Greenberg does not make this argument, we might read the allusive tendency in modernist poetry as another expression of this retreat of each art to its medium. Modernist allusion is an attempt to make poetry not out of expression or representation, but out of poetry itself. It aspires to the sort of purity Greenberg describes.

Of course, Greenberg's model seems to work far better in describing twentieth-century painting than it does in literature. Fiction goes entirely unmentioned in Greenberg's description. "Literature" operates in his rhetoric as a general term of opprobrium for that force which tempts painting away from its own proper modes, away from *opticality* to representation, away from stasis to narrative—"telling a story" is always a kitschy trap for art to fall into. Rockwell paintings always, for instance, tell a story, and so give in to the inferior pleasures of kitsch. Given the centrality of narrative to the novel as a form, and realism to its history, it seems intrinsically less capable of the sort of modernism that Greenberg describes, though one might try to argue that Beckett's trilogy of novels—*Molloy* (1951), *Malone Dies* (1951), and *The Unnameable* (1953)—pares back novelistic representation toward a sort of pure narration. In a different way, Gertrude Stein's *Making of Americans* (1925) might be understood as similarly jettisoning conventional notions of plot. Greenberg himself describes Joyce's *Ulysses* and *Finnegans Wake* (1935), approvingly, as "the reduction of experience to expression for the sake of expression" ("Avant-Garde" 7–8), a description at odds with the New Modernist Studies' elaboration of the political and historical contexts of Joyce's fiction, evident in work like Vincent Cheng's *Joyce, Race, and Empire* (1995). The dethroning of literature is not itself an argument *against* Greenberg's account of modernism. A shift in aesthetics may entail a reorganized hierarchy of arts and genres. In Greenberg's history *avant-garde* is both a descriptive and evaluative term, and some genres of art may necessarily be demoted. If the values and goals of literature had dominated the arts for centuries, in Greenberg's account its centrality must necessarily subside as it retreats to its own medium.

Autonomy and Its Politics

"Avant-Garde and Kitsch" and "Towards a Newer Laocoon" capture two tendencies in Greenberg's thinking at the end of the 1930s: "Avant-Garde and Kitsch" historicizes modernism as an expression of industrialized modernity, inexorably opposed to kitsch, itself another expression of that same modernity; "Towards a Newer Laocoon" grounds modernism in the formal specificity of the arts. Over Greenberg's career, it would increasingly be the narrative of "Towards a New Laocoon" that would grow more central to his thinking. Perhaps the canonical statement of Greenberg's insistence on medium purity comes two decades after these essays, in his 1960 essay "Modernist Painting." This shift in focus represents a formalist refocusing of Greenberg's theorizing, that turns away from the political dimension of his first essays. "Modernist Painting" lacks anything like the political declaration that ends "Avant-Garde and Kitsch": "Today we look to socialism *simply* for the preservation of whatever living culture we have right now" (21). Where the earlier essays grounded art within larger social and historical forces, "Modernist Painting" stresses a largely autonomous process of art's self-development. The Greenberg of the earlier essays is at once leftist in his political commitment to a revolution in the means of production, explicit in his socialism, and utterly elitist. T. J. Clark aptly describes the politics of this essay as a sort of "Eliotic Trotskyism" ("Clement" 143), a phrase that, W. J. T. Mitchell notes, "nicely captures the synthesis of a conservative elitism and left-wing radicalism" detectable in Greenberg's work (*Picture* 230).

If all approaches to modernism rely on some sort of history to define the modern, Greenberg's late writing expunges the concern with politics that motivated the history of his earlier essays. History becomes instead a history of art, loftily autonomous from social conditions. "Modernist Painting" replaces a history of urbanization and social change with a parade of great art works. While, as Clark notes, Greenberg's early essays are deeply political, this later essay evidences a Cold War shift. Any explicit reference to socialism has dropped out. The essay's own circumstances of composition reflect this change. "Modernist Painting" was first delivered as a radio lecture, part of a Voice of America series of broadcasts on American art, science, and culture. The lectures were broadcast around the world. Walter Nichols, of the USIA (United States Information Agency), described the lectures not as propaganda, but as meant to

> highlight current American trends and developments in the arts and sciences, and to gain added appreciation and respect for American intellectual achievement by displaying its best products. We believe that a program so conceived should also serve to stimulate among the intelligentsia behind the Iron Curtain an awareness of and interest in patterns of thought and creative endeavor differing substantially from those to which they are currently restricted.
> (qtd. in Francia 79)[6]

In short, Greenberg's later criticism, in response to the conditions of the Cold War, abandoned its explicitly socialist orientation, becoming instead a sort of depoliticized formalism. That depoliticized formalism, however, became itself politicized in the service of American Cold War politics, including McCarthyism and support from the CIA.

It is the later Greenberg who seems most clearly out of step with the New Modernist Studies. When critics distance themselves from Greenberg, it is this later, formalist Greenberg. For Fredric Jameson, in *A Singular Modernity* (2002), Greenberg is the "theoretician who more than any other can be credited as having invented the ideology of modernism full-blown and out of whole cloth" (169). This ideology, above all for Jameson, is an interpretation of modernist experimentation as expressing the autonomy of art. For Jameson, however, the later Greenberg is a natural outgrowth of the opposition between avant-garde and kitsch evident in the early essays. Greenberg's early "Marxian stance," Jameson writes,

---

[6]Francis Francina discusses at length the changes Greenberg made and the wider context in which "Modernist Painting" was produced.

posits an antagonism between modernism and the arts and its bourgeois context; and the levels within Marxism itself enable a slippage of the interpretation of that antagonism from an anti-capitalist position to an anti-bourgeois rhetoric. The latter, then, no longer grounded in an analysis of the socio-economic system, can easily deteriorate into social antipathies that no longer determine a politics at all, marking out an enclave position within bourgeois society which Greenberg's contemporary disciples have found themselves able to characterize as that of a "loyal opposition to the bourgeoisie."

(*Singular* 170)

That is, for Jameson, the heart of Greenberg's aesthetics is the separation of mass culture from art, of distinguishing the avant-garde from modernism; in so doing, it necessarily depoliticizes art, transforming it into what Jameson calls "an enclave position within bourgeois society." Greenberg's narrative of autonomy means that "politics itself, of whatever ideological persuasion, [becomes] what must be excised from the work of art in order for it to become something more purely aesthetic" (*Singular* 171). A modernist aesthetics of autonomy thus operates not, as we might assume, by separating art from everything that is non-art—from art, from politics, from history. Instead, Jameson contends, aesthetic autonomy is always a fission within the realm of culture, between "art" and some other cultural form—the very argument at the center of "Avant-Garde and Kitsch." "The autonomy of the aesthetic is not secured by separating the aesthetic from a real life ... Rather, it is achieved by a radical dissociation within the aesthetic itself: by the radical disjunction and separation of literature and art from culture" (176).

This separation is evident in much midcentury thinking about art. Susan Sontag in "Against Interpretation" (1964) sounds much like Greenberg in her hostility to "content" and repeats this separation: "What we decidedly do not need now is further to assimilate Art into Thought, or (worse yet) Art into Culture" (104). The New Criticism relied on a similar separation of a distinctly *literary* language from the rest of language and culture. This is evident in Cleanth Brooks's insistence on the paradox as the essential fact of literature in *The Well-Wrought Urn* (1947), or in the absolute separation of literature from both authorial intention and readerly feeling (the so-called intentional and affective fallacies), described by W. K. Wimsatt, and Monroe C. Beardsley, in *The Verbal Icon* (1954). Greenberg's role as ideologue of modernism captures trends across aesthetics thinking in the period.

The centrality of autonomy to such theorizations of modernism makes Greenberg's focus on *medium* all the more remarkable. Jameson notes the paradox of a theory of aesthetic autonomy being grounded in the least autonomous element of an art work—the medium on which it relies for its very being: "If the autonomy of art means some absolute spiritualization or sublimation beyond the figural, it can dialectically equally well be represented in terms of an absolute materiality" (*Singular* 173). Yet, this "absolute materiality" remains a largely unexamined abstraction in Greenberg's work. Even as the idea of the medium is central to Greenberg's analysis of modernist art, it remains an underexamined and taken-for-granted category. He accepts the traditional categories of the fine arts as the "media" of art without much questioning: sculpture, music, painting, and poetry. Film simply never arises as a question. The medium of painting seems a somewhat odd conjunction of qualities including color and opticality, but also canvas and pigment. These categories are a mix of formal characteristics and materialities. Greenberg's theorization avoids entirely the problem of medium determinism. The medium does not *determine* art; rather, art itself is an exploration of the medium. Indeed, Greenberg seems to allow art to determine the contours and definition of the medium. Greenberg's "medium" never exceeds the boundaries of the conventional arts. This approach, however, inaugurates a tradition of thinking about modernism as a relationship between art and its medium that, in the work of later critics, develops beyond the beaux arts limitations of Greenberg's initial theorization.

Art and/or Objects

The art critic and historian Michael Fried replaces Greenberg's focus on reduction and purity with an account of modern art as an exploration of the ways to *acknowledge* its own being as art. Such acknowledgment may include, but cannot be reduced to, the purifying of its materials. This recasting of Greenberg's concept of the medium enables two modes of aesthetic experience, which

Fried calls absorption and theatricality. Greenberg's concern with art's medium is transformed by Fried into something broader than materiality alone. Robert Pippin, in "Authenticity in Painting: Some Remarks on Michael Fried's Art History" (2005), explains that for Fried, "Paintings might be said to teach us how to appreciate their 'ontological status' and the historical fate of such embodied self-understanding. I think that it is the great achievement of Fried to have shown how profoundly important these ontological dimensions are in our appreciation of many modern paintings" (578). Pippin suggests that for Fried the problem of authenticity and art is inextricable from a broader socio-historical "question of modern forms of social dependence and therefore the conditions under which the appeal of an authentic life, one not mediated by the normalizing or conforming, expectation-generating gaze of others ... would rise to such prominence" (580). *Authenticity* as a criterion separates Fried from the formalism of the later Greenberg by regrounding the question of art in the social world; but it also separates Fried from the explicitly political Greenberg of the early essays. Rather than being either aesthetic or political, the question becomes fundamentally *ontological*, about the way art exists and how it achieves its being as art.

The problem of authenticity and modernism, of what Pippin calls "*the historical provocation for paintings of a certain sort,*" is neither an aesthetic nor a political problem. It is concerned not with "the solution of painting problems in a prior generation, nor with such things as the political misdistribution of power, an unequal social organization of labor, the status of a failed religion, nor with bad aesthetic theories or contingent interventions by creative geniuses (creating threats to be met)" (581). It is, instead, more fundamental and less historically specific, "a general ontological condition, brought to a crisis starting in Enlightenment modernity" (581). Rather than historicizing modernist art in relation to industrialization (as Greenberg does), Pippin describes Fried's historicization as a consequence of the Enlightenment. Such a lapsarian account of fall into inauthenticity resonates with other narratives of philosophical (rather than social or strictly historical) change. It is not far from accounts central to, for instance, Martin Heidegger in *Being and Time* (1926), that describe a sort of historical forgetting (which Heidegger traces to the origins of philosophy), which renders experience itself inauthentic. Stanley Cavell's account of the historical emergence of the modern problem of skepticism, discussed later in this chapter, is another such account. As with Greenberg, and many others, Fried theorizes modernism as the aesthetic response to *modernity,* which here is a chiefly epistemological condition. Fried recasts the historical emergence of the medium as a problem, and resource, for art, in philosophical terms (of acknowledgment, absorption, and theatricality). What had been in Greenberg an essentially social problem is in Fried foremost an epistemological problem.

Rather than a contrast between kitsch and art, this produces a distinction within the history of art, continuing into the present, between absorption and theatricality as modes of experiencing art that are shaped and reflected in art itself. Such a distinction recalls the distinction between the exhibitionist cinema of attractions and the subsequent voyeuristic cinema of classical Hollywood narrative film. Yet, while early film moves from the theatrical exhibitionism of the cinema of attractions into an absorptive, narrative mode, painting

FIGURE 2.1 *Édouard Manet,* Le Déjeuner sur l'herbe *(1862–63). Wikimedia Commons.*

seems to have moved in the opposite direction, from the absorption of the early nineteenth century to increasing theatricality. For Fried, theatricality becomes unavoidable in modernity. Acknowledging it, often through reference to the medium, becomes a way to escape theatricality.

Fried elaborates the emergence of modernism from a contrast between absorption and theatricality in his reading of Manet's *Le Déjeuner sur l'herb* (see Figure 2.1), in *Manet's Modernism, or, The Face of Painting in the 1860s* (1996). The painting features four figures, three seated at a sort of picnic while a fourth is visible in the background, bathing. Incongruously, one of the seated figures is nude. Fried sees in *Déjeuner* a painting that tackles all the major traditional genres of painting at the same time: it is a study of the nude, but it is also a portrait (indicated by the direct gaze of the seated female nude, but also by the identifiability of its chief subjects), a still-life (the basket and fruit visible in the foreground, on the lower left), a landscape, and even, Fried suggests, a sort of "parodic but not therefore unserious" religious painting, through what Fried detects as an allusion to the dove of the Holy Spirit in the bullfinch at the top of the center of the canvas (*Manet's Modernism* 174). In combining all the major genres of art painting, *Déjeuner* offers

> a deliberate attempt to bring together and in effect to fuse in a single large-scale work as many of the major genres of painting as he could encompass—to paint a picture in which the separate categories indeed make way for résumé, a word that means not just "summing up" but "epitome" and thus seems particularly appropriate to Manet's venture as I have described it.
> (*Manet's Modernism* 174)

In so doing, Manet attempts "to summon *all* the resources of painting, or at least as many of them as could be made viable at that juncture. Perhaps more than anything else—certainly far more than any desire for purity of medium based on exclusion and simplification—a desire for comprehensiveness, a pursuit of ... 'painting *altogether*,'" which Fried says, "was the hallmark of Manet's modernism" (*Manet's Modernism* 175). In *Déjeuner*, Manet offers a painting about painting, one that tackles all the genres in order to make a painting that is about the history and conventions through which paintings become understandable.

Such a reading of Manet differs from Greenberg's. For Greenberg, Manet, with his comparatively flat and unfinished use of color, represents the beginning of a process of reduction and purification—of a fleeing from pictorialism to flatness. Insomuch as Manet eschews illusionistic depth, even as he paints recognizable figures, he is already, in Greenberg's reading, on the path that leads to abstract expressionism. Yet, for Fried, the absence of half-tones in the colors of Manet's paintings creates not simply *flatness* but instantaneousness. By denying a sense of represented space, it creates "a means of enforcing a certain rapidity of perception with respect to both the depicted figures and, beyond them, the painting as a whole" (*Manet's Modernism* 294). The bullfinch frozen in motion at the top of the canvas suggests "a representational act so lightning fast in its attack ... as to perfectly capture a bird in midflight." The gaze of the seated nude figure, who stares out at the viewer, eliminates any pretension to absorption, and the painting offers a "subversion of narrative and dramatic intelligibility in the figure group as a whole" (*Manet's Modernism* 295). All these features mark this painting as modernist. The painting violates narrative and dramatic intelligibility in order to evoke the "instantaneousness of seeing, of visual perception, itself" (*Manet's Modernism* 296). This instantaneousness is crucial to Fried's vision of art. For the work of art is one where, as Fried states elsewhere, "*at every moment the work itself is wholly manifest.*" It offers a "continuous and entire *presentness*, amounting, as it were, to the perpetual creation of itself, that one experiences as a kind of *instantaneousness*, as though if only one were infinitely more acute, a single infinitely brief instant would be long enough to see everything, to experience the work in all its depth and fullness, to be forever convinced by it" (*Art and Objecthood* 167). It is the creation, or acknowledgment, of this sense of instantaneousness, rather than flatness or medium purity in the simple sense, that Fried sees in modernist art.

Fried recasts Greenberg's reading of Manet, seeing Manet not as the beginning of a process of formalist reduction and purification (as Greenberg did), but as the beginning of art's investigation of its own ontology. Rather than retreating to its medium, as if the purity of canvas or the simplicity of color could provide a stable source of meaning, modernist painting must explore and justify the conditions that make a painting a work of art. Modernism here is indeed a quest, but not for purification so much as for a definition of art that will continue to be convincing and satisfying in modernity. Paintings in the nineteenth century, Fried argues, typically sought to absorb their viewers—viewers were to get lost in the canvas they viewed. Achieving this absorption, however, grew harder and harder in modernity. Other painters of Manet's generation solicited their viewer's absorption by representing it on the canvas—painting individuals asleep, reading, or praying, and so maintaining a degree of voyeuristic illusion. Manet's innovation, and his modernism, were to defeat theatricality through theatrical means—to escape theatricality by acknowledging it. As Pippin writes, "there came to be no way to avoid or negate theatricality except by theatrical means, paradigmatically by those stunningly direct, bold looks at the beholder by the idiosyncratically nude females in Manet's *Olympia* and *Déjeuner sur l'herbe*, oddly and decisively reversing the relation of activity and passivity, subject and object" (579). Cavell, citing Fried, similarly explains, "Painting, in Manet, was *forced* to forego likeness exactly because of its own obsession with reality, because the illusions it had learned to create did not provide the conviction in reality, the connection with reality, that it craved" (21). Exactly why painting at some point in the nineteenth century suddenly loses its ability to absorb its views through the older, traditional means is not entirely clear. Fried, and Cavell and Pippin following him, insists simply that something has changed, some event, which severs illusion from conviction.

Fried's 1967 essay "Art and Objecthood" similarly revises the Greenbergian history of modernism. The essay takes as its antagonist the minimalist art of the 1960s, an art that Fried calls *literalist*. In "literalist art" the focus on medium has become so intense that art threatens to "degenerate" into mere objecthood (Fried, *Art and Objecthood* 164). "Art and Objecthood" offers a binarism as stark—if more subtle—as that between the avant-garde and kitsch. But Fried's binarism occurs within art, between modernism and minimalism. This distinction is no longer between easy kitsch, which arrives as predigested product for mass consumption, and difficult, challenging art, but between modernist art (his focus in the essay is chiefly on painting and sculpture) and objecthood. If the medium has guaranteed a source of authenticity for art, this authenticity must nevertheless still achieve itself in the properly modernist work of art—art must still find some grounds for transcending its medium, lest it become simply another *object*.

In Fried's vocabulary, art and objecthood, no less than avant-garde and kitsch, are diametrically opposed terms.

Minimalist art is art guilty of decaying into mere objecthood. Fried is responding most immediately to works like Donald Judd's *Untitled* (1966), a work of art consisting of four metal cubes aligned at the same height. The cubes have sides that are roughly three feet and are presented to the viewer in a symmetrical arrangement, elevated a little off the ground (hung on a wall). Each cube is identical, with four shiny metallic faces. The sides (that are almost not visible to the viewer looking at the work from the front) are an amber plexiglass, revealing to the viewer (who approaches them from the side) that the cubes are hollow. Such works are less art works than experiences; all aspects of the work, including the beholder's presence, contribute to its meaning. While a canvas, or even a traditional sculpture, is delimited, these works seem open and inexhaustible. The minimalist work is, above all, interesting. It inexhaustibly solicits the beholder's interest.

Such a description may sound laudatory. For Fried, however, such works undermine the specificity of art as such. In being inexhaustible they never achieve the "all at once" effect that Fried describes as the instantaneousness of the modernist work of art. Minimalism is a response to the same circumstances that produce properly modernist art, those very conditions described by Greenberg. But minimalism, in Fried's assessment, is a sort of failure to fully reckon with those circumstances:

> objecthood has become an issue for modernist painting only within the past several years ... [Formerly] The risk, even the possibility, of seeing works of art as nothing more than objects did not exist. That such a possibility began to present around 1960 was largely a result of developments within modernist painting. Roughly, the more nearly assimilable to objects certain advanced painting had come to seem, the more the entire history of painting since Manet could be understood—delusively, I believe—as consisting in the progressive (though ultimately inadequate) revelation of its essential objecthood.
>
> (*Art and Objecthood* 160)

This is the reading of Greenberg as *reductionist*, which Fried dismisses. If modernism is art concerned only with its own medium (Fried might say, drawing on Cavell, that art which acknowledges its own medium), minimalism represents a dangerous misunderstanding, or deviation, within this tradition. It threatens to lose its status as art in the medium and become instead a mere object. What, for genuinely modernist art (in Fried's sense) is a condition to overcome ("modernist art must defeat theatricality"), for minimalism is art itself—or rather that new practice which emerges since, Fried suggests, minimalism is not particularly keen on even maintaining the category of art as a useful or meaningful one. The medium, which in Greenberg had provided a refuge for art, in Fried has become a source of debate. The difference between minimalist art and the art the Fried identifies as genuinely modernist concerns how they understand this medium. Fried wishes to avoid (the art, in Fried's terms, must defeat) allowing art to be reduced to sheer objecthood.

The Post-Medium Condition

The idea that modernism is essentially a matter of art's relationship to its own medium is complicated and elaborated by a number of thinkers, theorists, and critics who followed Greenberg. Rosalind Krauss maintains the essential relationship between modern art and its media posited by Greenberg, but argues, in essays starting in the late 1970s, and collected in *Perpetual Inventory* (2010), that after modernism art has entered a "postmedium condition." If modernism is largely a process of reduction, of gradual purification of the medium—in painting, say, a drive toward categories like color, opticality, or flatness—it must at some point encounter a limit. If the radical shift within painting from Manet through Picasso, to Jackson Pollock or Helen Frankenthaler, is understood as a process of *purification*, of a slow revelation of the conditions of its own possibility, at some point those conditions may be fully and utterly revealed. At what point does the well run dry? Indeed, Greenberg's modernism might be critically read as an attempt to secure the authority of Western art one last time in modernism by cashing out the accrued cultural capital of the long history of Western painting. At the exact moment when art seems in crisis, perhaps even at an end, Greenberg's modernism sets itself the task of exposing the conditions of the media that made its history possible, so that it may, one last time, continue the tradition of high art.

If purification and reduction, as described by Greenberg, injects a *telos* into art history (with its ultimate trajectory, for Greenberg, in abstract expressionism and the painting of Jackson Pollock), does it not necessarily imply what Arthur Danto, in his 1964 essay "The Artworld," famously called the *end* of art? For Danto, the real revelation of art in the twentieth century was not a matter of media, of a Newer Laocoon, but of art *as* institution. This revelation is perhaps most clearly illustrated by Marcel Duchamp (a figure almost diametrically opposed to Greenberg), whose ready-mades made clear that art as a category was empty. Ready-mades were ordinary objects that were treated as art; the artist's role was simply the selection of the object. In 1917, for instance, Duchamp placed a urinal (signed "R. Mutt") on a pedestal and submitted it to the exhibition of the *Society of Independent Artists*, under the title *Fountain*. Krauss notes that the ready-made bypasses the problem of medium entirely, in order to address "art itself," rather than any particular, and medium-delimited, art form. "The readymade strategy overleaps the problem of the aesthetic medium with the single bound that takes it directly into the central question of aesthetics, by circumventing the 'trivial' issue of specific artistic practice" (*Perpetual* 48). Where Greenberg celebrated painting for achieving *opticality*, the ready-made escapes what Duchamp calls the merely "retinal." It is work that is *conceptual*. No fundamental property of the medium defines art, because *nothing* essentially defines art. *Anything* can be art. This realization, for Danto, ends modernism, which Danto suggests, "was too local and too materialist, concerned as it was with shape, surface, pigment, and the like as defining painting in its purity" (14). One might be able to simply discard *medium*, as a category, entirely. This condition is one which many celebrated. The sculptor Tony Smith famously recounts a revelatory experience driving on an unfinished portion of the New Jersey turnpike at night:

> This drive was a revealing experience. The road and much of the landscape was artificial, and yet it couldn't be called a work of art. On the other hand, it did something for me that art had

never done ... its effect was to liberate me from many of the views I had had about art ... Most painting looks pretty pictorial after that.

(qtd. in Fried *Art and Objecthood* 158)

The medium and its constraints could easily be imagined as a sort of prison from which art must escape, into a wider category like *concepts* or *experience*. Art becomes a matter of *installations* and *performances*, uncommitted to, and ungrounded in, any particular medium. It offers no longer self-contained, autonomous works that confront a viewer, but experiences in which a viewer participates in precisely the way Fried describes the experience of minimalist works.

But for Krauss, like Greenberg and Fried, "the abandonment of the specific medium spells death for serious art" (*Perpetual* xiii). She argues that there is indeed a way for art to move out of the impasse of reductionism while maintaining the essentially Greenbergian focus on medium which, in her view, is essential to any art worthy of the name. Krauss however talks not of a *medium*, which "in most readers' minds refers to the specific *material* support for a traditional aesthetic genre" but to a work's "technical support." Such a concept allows Krauss to move beyond the traditional arts and their media (paint, canvas, sculptural materials) on which Greenberg focused, and turn to newer, more recognizably technological forms. Krauss describes these new media as "the layered mechanisms of new technologies that make a simple, unitary identification of the work's physical support impossible" (*Perpetual* 37). Here *medium* marks the limit between modernism and postmodernism; postmodern art is, for Krauss, post-medium art.

In declaring a post-medium condition, Krauss nevertheless keeps faith with a focus on medium specificity; what media are appropriate to "art," however, is radically uncertain. Art's media cannot be taken for granted, they are no longer self-evident and given—no longer obviously painting or sculpture and their received histories. This opens art to a wider range of media, but also severs connection with the traditions of art history. Indeed, the post-medium condition represents something like the wholesale dissolution of any steady tradition; the artist has no tradition readily available, and so is in the position of somehow inventing her own medium. It is as such a process of invention that Krauss understands works like William Kentridge's animated drawings or James Coleman's "slide-tape" works. The slide tape is essentially a slide projector—it projects still, photographic images onto a screen and it can automatically advance through a set of images (sometimes with synchronized soundtrack). For years it had been used for corporate presentations (now superseded by PowerPoint), for advertisements, and for presentations in schools. Krauss stresses the medium's lack of traditional artistic meanings; it is, instead, inextricable from advertising culture, "part of the spectacle culture so widespread in the West—a public form of entertainment to distract commuters and relax shoppers" (*Perpetual* 52). Coleman's slide-tape works show dramatically staged, somewhat histrionically posed figures, and project them. What interests Krauss about these works (and the other artists she discusses) is that they invent a medium. Within the peculiar constraints of this discarded and obsolescent material support, an artist can essentially invent a new medium for art.

Like Fried, Krauss sees reduction and purification as dead ends. The alternative she proposes opens up the possibility of new media that can be explored and exploited to retain and even redeem the aesthetic that Greenberg described in relation to the traditional media of art. Krauss follows Walter Benjamin (discussed at length in Chapter 4), in seeing in the discarded technologies and detritus of modernity "instances in which the obsolescent could be said to have a redemptive role in relation to the very idea of the medium" ("Reinventing" 296). That is, art will find its new media in those material supports and technologies (like Coleman's projected slide tape) that have been discarded. Such works do not continue a tradition, so much as they exploit a medium for aesthetic ends. Imagine somehow finding a way to exploit Microsoft's PowerPoint for aesthetic ends. Indeed, the work of Young-Hae Chang Heavy Industries—an art group that uses the now obsolescent web animation technology Flash, as a medium for poetry, discussed in Jessica Pressman's *Digital Modernism* (2014)—might represent a more recent (re)invention of the medium. The essential relationship between modernist art and media is preserved in Krauss's thinking, by expanding media to include many elements of culture that Greenberg ignored or bracketed off as kitsch.

Cavell and the Search for New Automatisms

Like Fried and Krauss, Stanley Cavell follows Greenberg in imagining modernist art in relation to its medium. And like them he revises Greenberg, by refusing to see modernism as primarily a matter of art's reduction or purification of its medium. Cavell is not an art critic or an art historian, but a philosopher, following in the ordinary language tradition associated with the later work of Ludwig Wittgenstein. More surprising still, his theorization of modernism finds its most explicit statement in his book *The World Viewed: Reflections on the Ontology of Film* (1971), a book chiefly concerned with mainstream Hollywood movies. Yet Cavell's thinking about modernism here is fascinating and sophisticated, and continues the Greenbergian concern with media we have traced in this chapter. Moreover, both Krauss and Fried explicitly draw on Cavell's thinking for their own treatments of modernism. Krauss's vision of Coleman and other artists inventing new media echoes Cavell's claim in *The World Viewed* that "the task [of the artist] is no longer to produce another instance of an art but a new medium within it" (103).

If Pollock's "all-over line," as described by Greenberg, is key to his art, why? For Cavell, this particular practice, of dripping lines of paint across the entirety of canvas, and so painting all over, *discovers* something about painting itself. It reveals "not exactly that a painting is flat, but that its flatness, together with its being of a limited extent, means that it is *totally there*, wholly open to you, absolutely in front of your senses, of your eyes, as no other form of art is." The painting has a "[t]otal thereness" (109). It is this quality, far more than simply Greenbergian *flatness*, that is the real source of Pollock's modernism. In Cavell, like Fried, a Greenbergian focus on medium specificity is transformed from a quest to purify the medium to a quest to discover new automatisms that can respond to the conditions of modernity. Like Krauss, Cavell imagines the artist is capable of inventing new media and new opportunities for art. If what Pollock discovers is an automatism that reveals, or acknowledges, the "total thereness" of the painting as the ontological grounding of its confrontation with a viewer, this thereness represents a new automatism that offers a vein for the modernist artist to mine.

Discussing Morris Louis's "unfurled" paintings, in which stained colors seem to simply run down the canvas, Cavell writes, "In achieving these works without the trace of hands or wrists or arms, without muscle ... an automatism of canvas and paint ... is set in motion, admitting an overpowering beauty." There is no way of knowing in advance, Cavell insists, how productive or "successful" such a procedure, or automatism, will be. "One automatism may not be so deep or fertile as another, the vein may give out or not be worth working"(113). Such an understanding continues the Greenbergian figure of art as an exploration or quest, but sees it less as a series of distillations and purifications, and instead a process of experimentation—an attempt to discover an automatism that will produce a feeling of authenticity. Just as Greenberg suggested that modernist painting revealed what was always true painting—its flatness—Cavell describes the modernist painter as striving to discover something true about paintings as such. But the source and object of this discovery, in Cavell, is not the purity of the medium, but the automatisms which enable it. Cavell writes

> What does it mean to say that a painter discovers, by painting, something true of all paintings, something everybody has always known is true of paintings generally? Is it a case of something hidden in unconsciousness becoming conscious? It is like something hidden in consciousness declaring itself. The mode is revelation. I follow Michael Fried in speaking of this fact of modernist painting as an *acknowledging* of its conditions. Any painting might teach you what is true of all painting. A modernist painting teaches you this *by* acknowledgment—which means that responding to it must itself have the form of accepting it as a painting, or rejecting it.
>
> (109–10)

It is painting's *acknowledgment* of its conditions, rather than any direct appeal to its medium per se, that marks a painting as distinctly modernist. The discovery of automatisms, rather than a process of reduction or purification, is how modernist painting exists in Cavell's account. The power of modernist painting as described by both Cavell and Fried is revelatory. Modernist art in this sense responds to a predicament, rather than advances a cause. The motivating *telos* of Greenberg's narrative, the story of purification, of painting becoming ever more painterly, is here replaced by a history of attempts, none guaranteed, to simply find what works, what will satisfy the desire to "view the world itself" (102). And as a result, to speak of an "avant-garde," of an *advanced* position in this continuous process, makes no sense. "To speak now of modernism as the activity of an avant-garde is as empty as it is in thinking about modern politics or war, and as comforting: it implies a conflict between a coherent culture and declared and massed enemy" (110). The position Cavell critiques, of modernism "as the activity of an avant-garde," is surely Greenberg's—a coherent history of painting, of which modernism is the living embodiment (the "avant-garde" of Greenberg's 1939 essay), marshaled against a massed enemy, embodied in Greenberg's thinking as kitsch. It was that binarism, and that sense of embattlement and conflict, that made Greenbergian art history so uniquely available to be co-opted to Cold War thinking: a conflict between a "coherent [liberal, free market] culture" and a "massed [collectivist, Soviet] enemy." The story of art for Cavell, though, is different. It is not a conflict, but instead "an effort, along blocked paths and hysterical turnings, to hang on to a thread that leads from a lost center to a world lost" (110). The modernist artist is not a soldier at war with kitsch, but an experimenter trying to discover what *art* means in modernity.

A reasonable criticism of this manner of theorizing modernism is its tendency to abstraction and philosophizing. Cavell's description of artists "mining" automatisms might seem to only redescribe the problem of modernism, rather than provide a solution. When he suggests that "one automatism may not be so deep and fertile as another, the vein may give out or not be worth working" (113), one might see this as a viable alternative to both the teleological direction implied by Greenbergian purification and the sense of art's catastrophic postmodern end in Danto. One might also see it as rather vague. However one evaluates Cavell's account of art and modernism, we are certainly a long way from the question of the history of communications technologies. Yet, the Greenbergian tradition insists on an almost definitional relationship between modernism and its media. And within that tradition, Cavell's work is the most interested in film and television. Indeed, Cavell's attention to the history of art as a history of *automatisms* of necessity brings it into closer proximity with material that Greenberg largely ignores, including Hollywood film.

To understand the relationship between film and modernism in Cavell's thinking, it helps to return to Fried. Interestingly, the one experience that completely escapes theatricality for Fried is film. Because the audience is necessarily removed from the actor, film "by its very nature, escapes theater," and so "provides a welcome and absorbing refuge to sensibilities at war with theater and theatricality" (*Art and Objecthood* 164). The defeat of theater, which is central to Fried's account of modernist art, is intrinsic to the technology of movies. That does not mean, for Fried, that films are modernist. Indeed, for Fried, there *cannot* be modernist film because "the automatic, guaranteed character of the refuge—more accurately, the fact that what is provided is a refuge from theater and not a triumph over it, absorption not conviction—means that the cinema, even as its most experimental, is not a modernist art" (*Art and Objecthood* 164). Modernist art escapes the ever-present threat of theatricality in modernity by somehow passing through it, acknowledging it, and defeating it. Film, by contrast, for Fried in 1967, remains a naive medium, which can still *absorb* its viewers without the complications of theatricality—it operates with confidence in its tradition, as paintings before Manet did. This is not an accomplishment but simply a fact about film, which seems naturally to be something that modernist painting or sculpture must work to achieve. Those older forms can only escape theatricality by defeating it. "This helps explain," Fried writes, "why movies in general, including frankly appalling ones, are acceptable to modernist sensibility whereas all but the most successful painting, sculpture, music, and poetry is not" (*Art and Objecthood* 164). The burden of tradition and the historical challenge of modernity have yet to fall on the shoulders of the relatively young medium of film. Fried joins critics from the last chapter, like Shail and Trotter, in treating film as a medium out of step with modernism.

Cavell agrees with Fried about film's automatic defeat of theatricality. Much of *The World Viewed* is concerned with elaborating the peculiar character of film's ontology, where what Cavell calls a "view of the world" is present to a film's viewers, even as they are not present to it. Cavell lavishes attention on film, and on the products of Hollywood, granting it a seriousness that seems to never have occurred to Greenberg. Cavell answers the objection of readers that Hollywood films are unworthy of the attention and seriousness he grants them not by denying that some films are superficial, but by insisting they are no more superficial than other, more often recognized, art forms. To the complaint that Hollywood produces empty, commercially oriented products (a criticism of precisely the sort the Frankfurt School, discussed in Chapter 4, would offer), evident in their silly, saccharine happy endings, Cavell responds:

> All that the prevalence of the happy ending shows ... is that Hollywood did its best work in genres which call for happy endings. Of course it is arguable that the genres and conventions of Hollywood films are themselves the essential limitation. But to show that, you have to show either that there are no comparable limitations in other traditions ... Hollywood films are not everything; neither is American fiction at its greatest. But it is not clear to me that American films occupy a less honorable place among the films of the world than American fiction occupies in world literature.
>
> (174)

However great Cavell's admiration for Hollywood movies, however, these movies are not, in Cavell's telling, modernist.

Indeed, the reason that Cavell's "reflections on the ontology of film" end up elaborating a theory of modernism, almost by accident, is because Cavell sees film on the cusp of losing its power to compel an audience and escape theatricality. Cavell, writing in 1971, explains,

> Within the last decade film has been moving into the modernist environment inhabited for generations by the other major arts, within which each art has had to fight for its survival, to justify its existence in its own way. Of course, many films are still made within traditional genres—detective movies, romances, war films, etc. But there is no longer the same continuity between these movies and the films we take seriously.
>
> (60–1)

The tradition of thinking about art in relationship to its media that emerged in Greenberg, as an opposition between avant-garde and kitsch, is drawn into Hollywood film and transformed into an interior account of how the devices and automatism of Hollywood are losing their strength to compel—just as the automatisms of diatonic harmony in music, or representation in painting, likewise lost their power.

From Art to Technology

While differently explored by Greenberg, Krauss, Fried, and Cavell, the idea of the medium discussed in this chapter nevertheless remains largely a separate question from the wider question of technological media. Even in Krauss's discussion of post-medium condition and Cavell's discussion of film, it is the sense of automatism that drives the discussion. It is the artist, not the engineer who has agency here—questing, discovering, and inventing new possibilities for art. These are theories of the *aesthetic* before they are theories media. Provocatively, Jameson suggests that this tradition is itself a product of the arrival of mass communications media: "this operation takes place historically only at the very beginning of the television age, when what will later on be stigmatized as mass culture is in its infancy" (*Singular* 177). The Greenbergian theorization of media separates art from the rest of culture, a separation that Krauss and Cavell to some extent resist, though their central concerns remain essentially aesthetic.

Fried's reading recasts Greenbergian medium specificity in ontological terms. Like Greenberg's, Fried's account of art is formalist. Unlike Greenberg's, however, Fried's is not a reduction to medium. While he shares with Greenberg a language that positions the modernist artist as an explorer of the medium, what that artist seeks is different. Fried writes, "the modernist painter seeks to discover not the irreducible essence of all painting but rather those conventions which, at a particular moment in the history of the art, are capable of establishing his work's nontrivial identity as painting" ("How Modernism" 227). In an illuminating debate with T. J. Clark, precisely over the legacy of Greenberg, Fried argues that his view of art does not ignore history. He insists that his criticism does not seal art off from the rest of the world, that the very historicity of his analysis opens art onto its others; that his insistence on *conviction*, as the ground of modernist art, opens onto a "politics of conviction," which may include "the countless ways in which a person's deepest beliefs about art and even about the quality of specific works of art have been influenced, sometimes to the point of having been decisively shaped, by institutional factors that, traced to their limits, merge imperceptibly with the culture at large" ("How Modernism" 227). Yet, Fried's terms—conviction, absorption, authenticity—are not political in any conventional sense. To an unsympathetic reader, they sound somewhere between mystical and mystifying. And, of course, Fried himself invites a reader to equate art and religion with his closing declaration "Presentness is grace" (*Art and Objecthood* 168). Clark, however, seems unconvinced: "when it comes to ontology, all the nods to Merleau-Ponty cannot save Fried's prose from sounding like old-time religion" (Clark 86).

Against such "old-time religion," Clark insists, above all, on a social understanding of modernism. Against a formalism, however buttressed by appeals to ontology or even a "politics of conviction," Clark views modernism as inextricable from its social environment. He stresses the political dimension of Greenberg's early essays (essays like "Avant-Garde and Kitsch" and "Towards a New Laocoon"). What might a criticism look like that followed this insistence on the inextricably social dimension of modernist art? The Frankfurt School, the focus of Chapter 4, gives us some sense of such a perspective. While often insisting, as fiercely as Greenberg or Fried, on aesthetic form, they never abandoned the social as the ultimate horizon of meaning for modernist art. To so conceive of modernism, however, also requires a reorientation of one's understanding of the medium. No longer could be it simply the conventional materialities of the traditional arts (as it was for Greenberg) nor the ontological instaneousness of the fully present work (as it was for Fried). The role of mass communications technology, which lurks in the background of Greenberg's account of kitsch, blossoms into a central role in the theorization of modernism offered by the Frankfurt School. Before, however, turning to the Frankfurt School's historicization of technology, we will turn to another theorization—that of the Toronto School, which does not begin in art at all, but in those very media technologies that are only ever in the background of Greenberg's thinking.

3

Rebalancing the Sensorium: The Media Ecology of Marshall McLuhan and the Toronto School

While he is now chiefly remembered as a media theorist, or as one of the inventors of "media studies," the Canadian Marshall McLuhan was first an English professor. And he attributes his understanding of media directly to modernist writers and critics. "[I. A.] Richards, [F. R.] Leavis, [T. S.] Eliot and [Ezra] Pound and [James] Joyce in a few weeks opened the doors of perception on the poetic process, and its role in adjusting the reader to the contemporary world. My study of media began and remains rooted in the work of these men" (McLuhan, *Interior Landscape* xiii–xiv). Richards and Leavis are key midcentury critics of modernism, and Eliot, Pound, and Joyce offer us three quarters of the "men of 1914." Here is the old modernist studies. Yet what McLuhan learned from it is unique. Writing in 1960, McLuhan explains that

> [t]he so-called new criticism which followed after the new poetry which followed after the new developments in our Western world has most typically been engaged in explaining why works of art have no content and no subject matter. It was the new media themselves, from the telegraph (1830) onward which created the

situation which the poets and painters tried to explain to us by 'prophetic' new art forms.

(*Report* 4)

McLuhan here recasts the New Critical formalism of figures like I. A. Richards, with whom McLuhan had studied at Cambridge, as a response to the "new poetry," that is, to modernism. The formalism that was central to accounts of modernist painting discussed in the previous chapter, what McLuhan here calls art with "no content and no subject matter," is here read as an expression of the situation of the new media, "from the telegraph (1830) onward": modernist art as media prophecy.

This chapter shows how McLuhan, and related figures around the so-called Toronto School of media studies, developed a theorization of media which, at least according to McLuhan, was uniquely "modernist" in its orientation. First Eliot, and later Joyce, were major influences on McLuhan's thinking. He met, and corresponded with, Ezra Pound and Wyndham Lewis and saw his own work as continuing in the vein of modernist experimentation, urgently seeking to alert people to the unrecognized ways that media shaped modern life. It is a history and theory of media that understands technologies as capable of radically extending the human senses, but in ways so profound that they could easily overwhelm people. Modernism emerges as a strategy for managing this radical reorientation, with modernist writers and artists uniquely able to navigate it.

In the late 1960s and early 1970s, following the publication of *The Gutenberg Galaxy* (1962) and *Understanding Media* (1964), Marshall McLuhan was a pop culture celebrity.[1] Tom Wolfe, in a 1965 profile, captures the aura surrounding him. Business leaders sought out an English professor as the "oracle of the modern times" (15), able to predict which products would succeed in the markets shaped by new media. Offering prognostications that today seem alternately prescient ("Even shopping will done by TV," Wolfe 24) and foolish ("a city like New York is obsolete," Wolfe 25),

---

[1] Today, the most remembered testimony of this celebrity is his cameo in the 1977 film *Annie Hall*. John Durham Peters's essay, "'You mean my whole fallacy is wrong': On Technological Determinism," provides the most extensive discussion of this cameo.

McLuhan appeared regularly on TV and was interviewed by popular magazines. Artists and the 1960s counterculture proved just as fascinated by McLuhan as the executives who paid to have him flied in for consultation. Glenn Willmott calls McLuhan "the most powerful literary academic to have affected North American popular consciousness" (xi).

Yet, McLuhan's importance to modernist studies, or literary and cultural studies more broadly, has been at best oblique. His work has proved influential in departments of communications and media studies, but to students of art and literature McLuhan remains an unknown or marginal figure. The celebrity, jet-setting English professor described by Tom Wolfe earned the skepticism of later critics. Literary and cultural studies followed a very different path from the one McLuhan explored (with the odd consequence that, for a period, McLuhan's North American reception in literary theory came by way of Jean Baudrillard). McLuhan's critical vocabulary and his politics were out of step with developments in academic literary studies after the 1970s. So, after his burst of celebrity, his reputation waned to the point that Northrop Frye, in 1980, could write that McLuhan "was hysterically celebrated in the sixties and unreasonably neglected thereafter" (11). In 2000, with the popularization of the internet, the *New York Times* may have been premature in announcing that "Marshall McLuhan is Back From the Dustbin of History" (Stille). Yet the New Modernist Studies' expanded attention to modernism's media environment, as well as a broader interest in alternatives to post-structuralist accounts of signification across literary and cultural studies, make McLuhan an intriguing, if imperfect, figure for our own moment.

McLuhan's Modernist Style

McLuhan's critics might insist that he did not have a theory of media so much as a series of slogans or catch phrases (e.g., "the medium is the message," "the global village," or "hot and cool media"). And while McLuhan shared with a series of thinkers a broad history of media, discussed in the next section, as well as a humanistic vision of media as fundamentally prosthetic, his style of presenting that theory was untraditional and nonlinear. Instead of such *typographic* habits, McLuhan offers what he alternately calls "probes" or "mosaics." These anti-typographic structures, Mark Krupnick suggests in a 1998 essay, offer "an example of a familiar kind of modernist art object, a collage of brilliant fragments that have associative or analogical links but no strictly logical coherence" (118). McLuhan does not simply theorize modernism as a response to media (though he does that as well), but enacts a mode of modernist dislocation in his own work.

McLuhan's first book, *The Mechanical Bride* (1951), offers a series of more than fifty readings of elements of popular culture. Its concerns are similar to Roland Barthes's nearly contemporaneous *Mythologies* (1957), a key early example of the structuralist approach to culture. Barthes treats elements of contemporary culture (wrestling, an advertisement, some detail of a film) as modern myths and adapts Ferdinand de Saussure's semiotics to excavate the hidden significations of such myths. While Barthes's text has proved more influential, McLuhan similarly sees advertisements, comics, and other elements of contemporary culture as expressions of the "folklore of industrial man."[2] "[M]uch of the industrial world's entertainment and public expression," McLuhan writes, "is just as unconsciously expressive of its inner life. Our hit parade tunes and our jazz are quite as representative of our inner lives as any old ballad is of a past way of life" (*Mechanical Bride* 113). *The Mechanical Bride*, like *Mythologies*, attempts to reveal what is latent behind the manifestations of popular culture, discovering sexuality motivating the American vision of the automobile, or sadism in our attitudes to technology. In taking seriously the ephemeral elements of everyday culture, both Barthes and McLuhan are light-years away from Clement Greenberg (discussed in the previous chapter), who at the same time was developing his formalist account of modernist painting. Yet where Barthes's analyses, offered in the semiotic language of structuralism, remain key texts of literary theory, McLuhan's analyses are now not widely known and seem fragmentary and idiosyncratic.

The *Mechanical Bride* anticipates McLuhan's later work by offering a sort of intervention into the public culture of its time,

---

[2] Willmott similarly compares McLuhan and Barthes (22), as do Donald and Joan Theall, in "Marshall McLuhan and James Joyce" (47).

which attempts to train its reader to resist the media environment in which they find themselves. The book works to undo, or combat, the effects of advertising and popular culture. "Since so many minds are engaged in bringing about this condition of public helplessness, and since these programs of commercial education are so much more expensive and influential than the relatively puny offerings sponsored by schools and colleges it seemed fitting to devise a method for reversing the process." *The Mechanical Bride* offers itself as such a method by "us[ing] the new commercial education as a means to enlightening its intended prey" (*Mechanical Bride* v). (McLuhan would never again be so clearly hostile to advertising and American capitalism as he is here.) The result is a very strange book. It offers a series of "exhibits"—close readings of pieces of popular culture, including characters from comics (like Superman, and L'il Abner) and magazine advertisements. Yet they don't, McLuhan insists, offer "conclusions," but "mere points of departure." They do not "prove a case" but "reveal a complex situation" (*Mechanical Bride* v). This collage-like approach has itself been described as modernist. Somewhat like the mosaic structure of McLuhan's next book, *The Gutenberg Galaxy* (1962), it offers not a linear argument, but a series of discrete readings or perspectives. Later, McLuhan will call such offerings "probes," meant to provoke and inspire thought, rather than convince or fully describe.[3]

McLuhan presents *The Mechanical Bride* as "reversing" the propagandistic effects of advertising through an essentially modernist process.[4] In justifying the difficulty of modern poetry, Eliot famously wrote in his essay on the "Metaphysical Poets" (1921) that "Our civilization comprehends great variety and complexity, and this variety and complexity, playing upon a refined sensibility, must produce various and complex results. The poet must become more and more comprehensive, more allusive, more

---

[3]In a 1967 video, McLuhan explains, "I tend to use phrases, I tend to use observations, that tease people, that squeeze them, that push at them, that disturb them, because I am really exploring a situation. I am not trying to deliver some complete set of observations about anything" ("Probe").

[4]Willmott's *McLuhan, or Modernism in Reverse* makes this gesture of "reversal" central to McLuhan's work.

indirect, in order to force, to dislocate if necessary, language into his meaning" (65). McLuhan alludes to this project for modern poetry directly in explaining the goal of *The Mechanical Bride*. He quotes a "film expert" who explains that film has enormous commercial potential because it "suppl[ies] that spectator with a ready-made visual image before he has time to conjure up an interpretation of his own." *The Mechanical Bride*, McLuhan explains, "reverses that process by providing typical visual imagery of our environment and dislocating it into meaning by inspection" (*The Mechanical Bride* vi). Just as difficult poetry, Eliot insists, dislocates a language perverted by modernity into meaning, so McLuhan's exhibits resist kitsch-like consumption and so restore them to meaning.

Perhaps because McLuhan studied under I. A. Richards, it is not uncommon to see *The Mechanical Bride* linked to the New Criticism.[5] It treats popular culture with the same closeness of attention and dedicated explication the New Critics reserved for poetry. "The idea," of *The Mechanical Bride*, Mark Krupnick writes, "was to analyze ads as if they were poems" (110). Willmott similarly suggests that *The Mechanical Bride* "applies a modernist 'inclusive' language and form drawn from literary theory and art to the critique of commercial mass culture" (9). McLuhan himself connected his method not to the New Critics but to the symbolists. It is the American proto-symbolist, Edgar Allan Poe, who is quoted in the foreword to *The Mechanical Bride* and to whom McLuhan appealed throughout his career. Poe's story "A Descent into the Maelstrom" (1841) offers a description of what McLuhan takes to be the place of the artist/critic in modernity. The story describes an old man who takes the narrator to the top of precipice, from which they observe the formation of the Moskstraumen tidal whirlpool in Norway. After observing the whirlpool, the old man recounts to the narrator his own harrowing experience of nearly being drowned by the whirlpool. Trapped with his brother in a storm, and sucked into the whirpool's vortex, the sailor gives up all hope of survival, and instead chooses to amuse himself by observing the objects being drawn into the whirlpool. "I must have been delirious—for I even

---

[5]The title of McLuhan's most important work, *Understanding Media*, was meant to echo Brooks and Warren's *Understanding Poetry* (196), though whether this suggests an affiliation or an ironic rebuff is a matter of interpretation.

sought amusement in speculating upon the relative velocities of their several descents toward the foam below" (239). He notices, however, that certain objects resist the vortex. He tries to explain to his brother, who is panicked with fear, but his brother does not understand. He lashes himself to a cask and jumps from the boat. The currents of the whirlpool buoy him, without drawing him any deeper. He survives, while his brother, incapable of this sort of detached observation, clings to the boat and is carried to destruction.

For McLuhan, "A Descent into the Maelstrom" offers a parable of how to survive the vortex-like condition of modernity. "A whirling phantasmagoria can be grasped only when arrested for contemplation. And this very arrest is also a release from the usual participation." Such amused observation might easily seem irresponsible. "Many who are accustomed to the note of moral indignation will mistake this amusement for mere indifference. But the time for anger and protest is in the early stages of a new process." Once a process has established itself, anger and protest will do nothing—one must learn to surf the vortex's waves. In *The Mechanical Bride* "media" is not yet the key term of McLuhan's thinking, but the conviction that some force is shaping our lives in deeper ways than we understand, and that it can only be understood through a sort of nonjudgmental, even amused, contemplation, would remain central. Poe's story offers an allegory for how we exist in media—trapped in an overwhelming maelstrom. McLuhan's later persona, and insistence that "the medium is the message," would provoke and confound his audiences who were looking for some clear moral statement about the situation, about, for instance, whether television was good or bad. But McLuhan's sense of media as environmental, as even a catastrophe akin to Poe's maelstrom, remained throughout McLuhan's later work and accounts for his, at times frustrating, insistence that media were not something to be judged, so much as understood. While McLuhan's critics would see in him a determinist (and his writing is full of moments that seem to describe media as single-handedly *causing* certain social and historical effects), McLuhan positions himself as the sailor, bemusedly contemplating the action of the media maelstrom. Agency is possible only through understanding the environment. Judging the whirlpool is futile. In Poe's story, the storyteller's brother is swallowed by a process that he cannot bear to understand.

What McLuhan offers is an alternative. "There is absolutely no inevitability as long as there is a willingness to contemplate what is happening" (25), declares a page in *The Medium is the Massage* (1967). It's McLuhan's idealistic hope that understanding can mitigate the powers of the media.

The transition from *The Mechanical Bride*'s pedagogic modernism, with its goal of liberating its readers from the culture of advertising through education, to the better-known McLuhan of the 1960s involved a number of changes and began by wedding his symbolist-inspired historicization of culture to a longer history of media.

A History of the History of Media

Every theory of media, and indeed every theory of modernism, presupposes some *history*. The history that shaped McLuhan's thinking is inextricable from his time at the University of Toronto, where he met both Harold Innis (who died shortly after McLuhan's arrival) and Eric Havelock. Innis, like McLuhan, had been deeply influenced by the modernist writer, and fellow-Canadian, Wyndham Lewis, though McLuhan insisted that Innis had "misread Wyndham Lewis radically" (to be fair, an easy enough error to fall into) (Gordon 149). Havelock and Innis were already in conversation with each other, and each would have a profound influence on McLuhan by helping him situate his own argument within a much longer history.[6] Together, Innis, Havelock, and McLuhan would form the core of what has been called "the Toronto School" of media studies.[7] David Olson explains that "the Toronto School denied that new media simply spread the same information as

---

[6] It is possible that McLuhan encountered parts of Havelock's argument while a student at Cambridge. I. A. Richards, in a 1947 radio address, printed in *The Listener* the same year, references the argument Havelock would publish in *Preface to Plato* (1963): "Eric Havelock has suggested that we may see in Plato's rejections of Homer the revolt of the writing mind's mode of apprehension against the pre-literate mind's other, less abstract and intellectual, way of ordering itself" (204).

[7] Derrick De Kerckhove credits Jack Goody with introducing the term "in a mildy unflattering footnote" (73).

earlier media, insisting rather that the media themselves put an indelible stamp on the structure of knowledge and on the 'mentality' of their users" (355). The Toronto School is defined by "the notion of communications as a distinct phenomenon, an idea that they abstracted out of the broader disciplinary concerns within which it had been embedded" (Blondheim and Watson 7). This focus resulted in a broad rereading of history from the perspective of communications media. While never a student or professor at the University of Toronto, Walter Ong, whose focus on the psychological and social consequences of literacy is summarized in *Orality and Literacy* (1982), belongs in this group as well. The Toronto School relies on a broad concept of media, which includes writing as perhaps the earliest and most crucial media technology. Their history of media is as long as available history, stretching from antiquity to the present, and divided into periods based on the dominant media technology—most broadly into periods of orality, literacy, print, and post-print media technologies. The scope of this history is one of the things that separate McLuhan, and the Toronto School more broadly, from other approaches discussed in this book. And within such a history, modernism often appears not simply as radically new but as a return to a preprint condition, or even a condition of orality.

The origins of this long history of media, however, predate Havelock and Innis. Indeed, this history of media has itself a history, which extends to what scholars of classical literature call the "Homeric Question." This is, in fact, a series of questions about Homer and his work: How and when were the epic poems the *Iliad* and the *Odyssey* composed? Do they share a single author? To what extent do they describe a historical reality? Was there, for instance, a real Trojan War? These questions, which may initially seem antiquarian and narrowly philological, stand behind much of the Toronto's school's media ecological thinking.

In 1935, after conducting research in Yugoslavia, Milman Parry began work on what was to be a new theory of the composition of Homer's poems. A classics scholar, Parry's dissertation examined the use of epithets and formulas in the *Iliad* and the *Odyssey*. Why, in those poems, are characters so often described by repetitive short descriptions? Surely the reader understands that Achilles can run fast without him constantly being described as "swift-footed"? Likewise, the numerous patronymics (Achilles as "Peleus's son";

Agamemnon as "son of Atreus"; even "Zeus the son of Cronos") seem to insist on parentage at moments where such information is of dubious relevance. The explanation of such epithets, Parry had argued, lay in their meter. These short, metrically regular phrases helped the poet to meet the demand of dactylic hexameter. If the epithets seem repetitive or unnecessary (as, to a contemporary reader, they often do), it is because their function is metrical rather than descriptive or narrative.

Parry's early work on Homeric epithets opens on to the larger question of the structure and authorship of Homeric epic poetry—the "Homeric Question" proper. Parry was not the first to observe the formal peculiarities, as well as inconsistencies and "inconcinnities" (as they are often called by scholars) in the Homeric epic poems. Since the later eighteenth century, approaches to the Homeric Question fell into two broad traditions: "Analysts" and "Unitarians." The Analysts sought to break down the Homeric texts (to *analyze* in its etymological sense) in order to separate an "authentic" text from what were posited as later interpolations and corruptions, chiefly on the grounds of inconsistencies within the poem. The Unitarians, by contrast, insisted on the unity of the poems. The poems, they argue, were too clearly coherent and unified to be broken apart, and so represented the work of a single poet, and a single act of poetic creation. "The whole nature of the debate changed, however," writes Robert Fowler, "with Milman Parry's discovery that the poems' many formulas combine in extensive and economical systems, in origin explicable only as aids to oral composition-in-performance; moreover, they had to be the creation of tradition, not of any one bard" (221). The metrical motivation of the epithets, that is, is best understood as a consequence of the poem's medium—the needs and exigencies of "composition-in-performance." The oral medium, here, operates as a sort of unacknowledged agent, or shaper, of the text.

In order to study such oral composition, Parry traveled to investigate a still living tradition of Serbo-Croatian bards, or *guslars*, who sang epic narratives similar to the Homeric works. His purpose was to study oral poetry not on the page, but as a living tradition. In the first half of the 1930s, Parry recorded more than 1,000 epic songs, as well as thousands of other items (including more than 11,000 "women's songs"). Parry's own ability to formulate and investigate this question is itself a product of the media environment of the 1930s. Guslar performances were recorded on aluminum phonographic discs, using a phonographic recorder that Parry customized for the purpose.[8] The aluminum discs could record only three and a half minutes at a time. Interrupting the performance would, however, contaminate the very object of Parry's analysis (the guslar poet *in* performance), so Parry's device allowed him to toggle between two recorders, adding new discs without interrupting the performance.

His research convinced him that the *Iliad* and the *Odyssey* were originally oral works, and that their oral medium is reflected in the form of the poems (this is sometimes called the "oral formulaic theory"). Walter Ong summarizes the importance of Parry's work this way: "virtually every distinctive feature of Homeric poetry is due to the economy enforced on it by oral methods of composition" (21). The oral-formulaic understanding, as propounded by Parry and his student and collaborator, Albert Lord, suggests that the Homeric epics, as we understand them, are transcribed versions of poems that would have been experienced, and indeed composed, in performance. The poets would draw on memorized formulaic units to improvise the poem–units that include not only epithets, but also broader, structural and thematic structures and conventions. While the performers with whom Parry spoke, for instance, would insist that they had performed the "same" poem on different occasions, Parry's recordings revealed differences between performances. The quest for the "correct" text of the Homeric poems is impossible and motivated by a misunderstanding of the poem's medium. The search for a correct or uncorrupt text was a consequence of assuming that all texts are *written*. The Homeric poems were not written; nor were they even "memorized" in the conventional sense. They instead reflected an entirely oral form of organization. The recognition of the oral character of Homeric epic changes how we understand it radically. Previous readers had been misled by a bias inherited by treating these oral works as though they were written. Ong writes, "deep inhibitions have interfered with our seeing the Homeric poems for what they in fact are" (18).

---

[8]The recordings and transcriptions are today part of the extensive Milman Parry Collection, held by Harvard University. For a description of Parry's recording methods, see David Elmer's "The Milman Parry Collection of Oral Literature."

In embryonic form, this investigation of ancient Greek epic poetry contains an entire program of media studies. Parry's study of Homer reveals how a medium can exert a hidden, shaping force on a text. For McLuhan and Ong, and many others, Parry's realization opened far beyond the Homeric Question. Orality defined not simply a mode of composition or textual circulation; it was a mode of social organization. McLuhan writes in *The Medium is the Massage*,

> Homer's 'Iliad' was the cultural encyclopedia of pre-literate Greece, the didactic vehicle that provided men with guidance for the management of their spiritual, ethical, and social lives. All the persuasive skills of the poetic and the dramatic idiom were marshaled to insure the faithful transmission of the tradition generation to generation.
>
> (113)

McLuhan here proposes the epic poem as oral encyclopedia. D. H. Green elaborates,

> Any society with a sense of self-awareness has to store essential information about its past, and in an oral society this has to be done by memory rather than by writing, by professional remembrancers rather than by trained scribes. In the light of this need the poet in an oral society must be seen, not primarily as an entertainer or as a creative artist, but rather as one who possesses the skill of making language memorable and can thus fulfill the task of mnemonic preservation of what his society needs to retain of its past.
>
> (272)[9]

Yet, even this suggestion may not sufficiently recognize how profoundly we are separated from an oral culture. After all, the *encyclopedia* that McLuhan invokes is itself an invention of print. Havelock, in *A Preface to Plato* (1963), writes that,

---

[9] The idea of orality's tendency toward "memorable" language is explored at length by Ong. It is evident, Ong suggests, in the typology of characters one finds in epic— larger than life, generic heroes, rather than the more "round" characters of the novel, for instance (69–70).

> The metaphor which describes Homer as a tribal encyclopedia is in fact loose if we use the term encyclopedia in that bookish sense which is proper to it. For Homer continually restates and rehandles the *nomos* [law] and *ethos* [beliefs] of his society as though from a modern standpoint he were not quite sure of the correct version. What he in fact is quite sure of is the overall code of behaviour, portions of which he keeps bringing up in a hundred contexts and with a hundred verbal variants.
>
> (92)

The repetitions are part not simply of an oral poetics, but of an entire organization of social life. Without writing to codify, organize, and store ideas about behavior, the law (*nomos*) and ethics (*ethos*) only exist through such oral enactments, where redundancy is not superfluous but essential. The epithets and repetitions that seemed to mar the greatness of Homeric epic are revealed to be part of an alien mode of social organization.

Parry's philological investigation of the "Homeric Question" opens onto a vertiginous prospect, whose precise depths were described by Havelock, Ong, and McLuhan, and others. The recognition of orality as a mode of textual circulation raises questions about memory that were of a concern to Plato himself. Ong writes, "Homeric Greeks valued clichés because not only poets but the entire oral noetic world or thought world relied upon the formulaic constitution of thought" (23). Cliché is how social memory exists in a world without writing. The recognition of orality as an alternate mode of understanding has consequences at both the individual and collective level; its implications are both cognitive and social.

The importance of Parry's research, as summarized by Albert Lord, to McLuhan's understanding of media is evident in the opening *The Gutenberg Galaxy* (1962). "The present volume," McLuhan writes, "is in many respects complementary to *The Singer of Tales* by Albert B. Lord" (1). Later in *The Gutenberg Galaxy* McLuhan points to a second key influence. "The present volume to this point might be regarded as a gloss on a single text of Harold Innis: 'The effect of the discovery of printing was evident in the savage religious wars of the sixteenth and seventeenth centuries. Application of power to communication industries hastened the consolidation of vernaculars, the rise of nationalism, revolution, and new outbreaks of savagery in the twentieth century'" (245, quoting Innis, *Bias* 29).[10] McLuhan's work builds on key ideas from these two thinkers to develop its own peculiar account of the problem of modern media. Parry's approach to the Homeric Question helps us recognize the mediacy of not only print and writing, but orality itself. The voice, in this description, is a medium as much as any other, with powers and affordances and limitations. Innis's work attempts to offer a wider, political history of that distinction.

Like McLuhan himself, Harold Innis was a Canadian. The two met at the University of Toronto, and Innis, though less widely known than McLuhan, is central to Toronto School media studies.[11] By training he was an economist and his early work focused on the way that regions of the Canadian economy and social organization were dictated by the staple commodities they produced. His attention and sensitivity to such staples are reflected in his later work on communications media,[12] where Innis treats these media as staples, contrasting the particular materialities of clay, papyrus, parchment, and paper. Like Ong, Innis charts a long history of media from antiquity to the present. But while Ong elaborated the "oral noetic world" implicit in the medium of orality, discovered by Milman Parry, Innis's focus was more decidedly political and historical. To the broad distinction between orality and literacy that is central to Milman and Parry, and, later, Ong, Innis adds finer distinctions within the history of literacy, often based on the specific writing technology. He contended, for example, that the cultural effects of

---

[10] Elsewhere in *The Gutenberg Galaxy*, McLuhan describes the work as "a footnote of explanation to his work" (56).

[11] Innis is so central that the editors of *The Letters of Marshall McLuhan* trace McLuhan's most famous slogan, "the medium is the message," to Innis's statement "The significance of a basic medium to its civilization is difficult to appraise since the means of appraisal are influenced by the media, and indeed the fact of appraisal appears to be peculiar to certain types of media. A change in the type of medium implies a change in the type of appraisal and hence makes it difficult for one civilization to understand another" (Innis qtd. in McLuhan et al. 219–20). Here we see the degree to which McLuhan's penchant for the quotable made him the Toronto School's ad-man.

[12] The shape of Innis's career is itself a subject of debate, summarized by Blondheim (70n22). Paul Heyer notes, for instance, the way that Innis's description of the manufacture of papyrus recalls his descriptions, in the first part of his career, of beaver and codfish (47).

cuneiform and clay writing technologies are not the same as papyrus or parchment, to speak nothing of the effects of the printing press.

And while Innis is sometimes described, like McLuhan, as a "technological determinist," at many points he seems to recognize that the relationship between media and history is mutually constitutive. In *The Bias of Communication* (1951), Innis suggests that cuneiform evolves beyond pictographic writing because of the "difficulties of writing on moist clay" (36). Here, geography (and geology) determines the medium as much as the medium determines culture. The media logic of papyrus, similarly, is a function not only of its materiality (its lightness, but relative lack of durability), but the geographic conditions of its production as well. "Papyrus was produced in a restricted area and met the demands of a centralized administration whereas parchment as the product of an agricultural economy was suited to decentralized system" (*Bias* 48). These details of production, as much as the media themselves, are crucial here. Papyrus, a thick paper-like material, is made from the papyrus plant which grows in wet, swamp-like conditions along the Nile river valley. Its production is therefore centralized around these areas. Parchment, which is made from animal skins, by contrast, is less bound by space, and can be produced elsewhere. Centralized and less durable papyrus was biased in the favor of space and administration; more durable and decentralized parchment biases a culture in the direction of time. What Innis shares with McLuhan is a penchant for drawing large-scale conclusions. From this division between time-biasing media and space-biasing media, in turn, Innis draws still further consequences. Parchment's bias toward temporal duration and time, Innis suggests, disposes a society toward religion, the centralization of papyrus toward political hierarchy and empire.

In this way, tablets, scrolls, and codices all reflect differing modes of cultural organization. Innis shares with cultural historians of media like Jonathan Sterne and Lisa Gitelman a strong, narrative attention to history. Yet while the histories offered by Sterne and Gitelman tend be deep, Innis's are broad, bridging multiple centuries in as many paragraphs. His writing feels at times like paratactical lists of assertions, re-summarizing history with particular attention to media (and, in particular, to the history of writing technologies). Menahem Blondheim describes Innis's style in his late works this way: "Facts of history are marched chronologically, one by one, and Innis, the philosopher in the grandstand, gains insight and contributes comments on them, as they relate to his philosophical focus: the determining influence of communication on society and culture" (69).

While Innis valorizes societies that achieve a socially coherent balance of time- and space-based media, Innis generally seems concerned to preserve orality over against the incursions of space-based media. He finds a sort of idealized balance between orality and writing in ancient Greece, where the "strength of the oral tradition bend[s] the alphabet to suit its needs" (*Bias* 41). Here too it is possible to note the ways that Innis's account of media history is not strictly deterministic. The *cultural* strength specific to Greek oral tradition, of which Homer is exemplary, rather than *orality itself*, was able to control the space-bias that Innis generally detects in the alphabet as a technology, and which in Rome led to empire-building. In space-biased media, Innis regularly detects a tendency toward imperialism and militarism. His essay "A Plea for Time" worries that a space-bias connected to print threatens Western civilization.

> Lack of interest in the problems of duration in Western civilization suggests that the bias of paper and printing has persisted in a concern with space. The state has been interested in the enlargement of territories and the imposition of cultural uniformity on its peoples, and, losing touch with the problems of time, has been willing to engage in wars to carry out immediate objectives.
>
> (*Bias* 76)

Innis was often more pessimistic than his peers. Ong saw in late-twentieth-century media technology (including computers) a return to some of the properties of orality paired with some of benefits of literacy—a condition he called *secondary orality*, and generally celebrated this return. McLuhan, in his descriptions of "the electric age" and "global village" (the sense that electronic media could overcome or even abolish geographic distance), could sound downright giddy. Innis was less optimistic.

Indeed Innis directly picks up the modernist tradition of offering a critique of modernity. Innis is explicit in linking his concern about the spatial bias of print, and post-print media to Wyndham Lewis's diagnosis of the time-centric condition of modernity in *Time and Western Man* (1927). While the terminology between the two may at first seem inconsistent, when Lewis says time he means something like the ephemerality of the moment, as evident in such modernist phenomena as the vitalist philosophy of Henri Bergson or the stream-of-consciousness narration of James Joyce. Or, as Innis puts it, citing Lewis, "In art classical man was in love with plastic whereas Faustian man is in love with music. Sculpture has been sacrificed to music" (*Bias* 90).[13] His description of "Faustian man" here draws not simply the story of Faustus, but on the deeply pessimistic conservatism of Oswald Spengler explicated in *The Decline of the West* (1923). Innis's media theory connects Lewis's suggestion that the permanence of the plastic arts, and of sculpture in particular, has given way to a celebration of music as the central art, with a much wider, and darker, political vision. While Innis's politics are not typically explicit, a conservatism underlies them. The space-biases of the newspaper, the radio, and film, in Innis's account, are eroding "culture." In a moment that recalls Greenberg's description of the origin of kitsch in mass literacy, Innis suggests that with the dominance of newspaper, radio, and film, "Superficiality became essential to meet the various demands of larger numbers of people and was developed as an art by those compelled to the meet the demands" (*Bias* 82). More dramatically, Innis contrasts the ear and eye, in ways that anticipate McLuhan, "Communication based on the eye in terms of printing and photography had developed a monopoly which threatened to destroy Western Civilization first in war and then in peace" ("A Plea for Time" 80). The conservative critique of modernity that runs through the modernism of writers like Wyndham Lewis and T. S. Eliot is replayed by Innis in media theoretical terms.

McLuhan approached Innis from the perspective of a literary critic. His distinction between time and space, chiefly a contrast between duration and extension, is aestheticized and individualized

---

[13]Innis here cites Lewis, *Time and Western Man*, pgs. 295 and 299.

in McLuhan's work. Of course, the distinction itself was already potentially aesthetic. Lessing's *Laocoon*, that was so crucial to Clement Greenberg's account of modernism, relies on precisely such a distinction between the arts of space and those of time. It was left to McLuhan, however, to explain those resonances.

McLuhan, Prosthesis, Humanism

Central to McLuhan's theorization of media is a definition of media as extensions of the human body in which the senses provide a counterforce to the materiality of the media themselves. The transition from orality to literacy, for instance, is, in McLuhan's phrase, the trading of an ear for eye. All media, for McLuhan, extend a particular sense. We might call the contention that all media extend, alter, or augment human senses the *prosthetic thesis*. Defined as "extensions of man," as the subtitle of *Understanding Media* puts it, almost all technology or tools can be understood as "media," not only communication technologies: the wheel is an extension of the foot and clothing is an extension of the skin. Such a thesis is not without complications. It takes quite an imaginative leap to see the book as an extension of the eye, rather than say, a container of thought or a script for a performance of speech. Television, peculiarly in McLuhan's reading, extends not the sense of vision (or even *presence*), but of *touch*. And if McLuhan's particular equations of technology with the body seem confounding, the prosthetic thesis itself is certainly debatable. As Kenneth Burke notes, "many human inventions conceivable might *not* be 'extensions' of the human body," but in McLuhan's account "the whole subject is sufficiently vague to allow for McLuhan's mediumistic geneaology" (167).

The prosthetic thesis not only extends McLuhan's thinking to objects we might not conventionally consider *media*, it also grounds the way that media affect individuals in an understanding of a unified perceiving subject. As prostheses, the power and agency of media are grounded, and limited, by the human body and sensorium. The complex question of the materiality and agency of technology is simplified by grounding it in the human subject. While McLuhan is more famous for insisting that media massage us, or "work us over completely" (McLuhan, *Medium* 26), the prosthetic thesis limits that power in certain ways. The power of media, which otherwise in McLuhan's work can seem virtually omnipotent, is limited by the scale and abilities of the human. This limiting is clearest in McLuhan's description of "sense ratios." He describes an economy among the senses, such that the augmentation of one sense necessarily affects the others. "As an intensification and extension of the visual function, the phonetic alphabet diminishes the role of the other senses of sound and touch and taste in any literate culture" (*Understanding Media* 84). The balance, between space and time-based biases in the work of Innis, becomes a balance among the sense ratios in McLuhan. Thus, the extension of the eye through first writing and then print creates rationalism by deadening the involvement and emotion that McLuhan associates with the ear. In Ong's terms, "writing restructures consciousness."

In this model of media, the artist is an individual with heightened senses. "The serious artist is the only person able to encounter technology with impunity, just because he is an expert aware of the changes in sense perception" (McLuhan, *Understanding* 18). McLuhan here echoes Pound's dictum, "Artists are the antennae of the race" (80). The antennae-like sensitivity of art is why McLuhan grants it pride of place in his attempt to come to terms with media change. If media form environments which, like the water in which fish swim, are invisible to those who inhabit them,[14] the artist is uncannily able to see the present. While most, in another McLuhanism, experience the world through a rear-view mirror, the artist lives fully in the present. McLuhan was originally trained as a scholar of Elizabethan literature; his dissertation was on the playwright Thomas Nashe (1567–1601). But just as that period was shaped by the displacement of manuscript culture by the printing press, McLuhan saw modernism as reflecting the displacement of book culture by newer media technologies, and it was modernist artists and writers who best understood this shift.

In an early essay, "Joyce and Mallarmé and the Press" (1954) McLuhan describes Joyce and the French poet Stéphane Mallarmé as recognizing the power of the newspaper. The "popular press as an

---

[14]"Fish know nothing of water," reads an aphorism in McLuhan's *Culture is our Business* (70). Kenner echoes this remark in "McLuhan Redux" (227-8).

art form has often attracted the enthusiastic attention of poets and aesthetes while rousing the gloomiest apprehensions in the academic mind" (McLuhan, "Joyce" 5). In Mallarmé's challenging poem *Un Coup de Dés* (1897), with its typographic experimentation with the page and its obscure lack of a clear narrator, McLuhan discovers the newspaper: "it was Mallarmé who formulated the lessons of the press as a guide for the new impersonal poetry of suggestion and implication. He saw that the scale of modern reportage and of the mechanical multiplication of messages made personal rhetoric impossible" (McLuhan, "Joyce" 11). *Ulysses*, in its one-day structure, reproduces the newspaper. "With its date-line June 16, 1904, *Ulysses* is, newspaperwise, an abridgement of all space in a brief segment of time." And Joyce's novel *Finnegans Wake* (1939) condenses all time into a short space, using the aural qualities of radio and broadcast technology ("Joyce, Mallarmé, and the Press" 50–1). Joyce is readable in McLuhan's narrative as standing on the cusp of a transition to a new electric age of communications, the return of orality now mediated through electric technologies. *Ulysses* faces backward toward print, while the puns of *Finnegans Wake* face toward the electric media.

Even as McLuhan was centrally involved with key modernist figures and achieved an unsurpassed level of celebrity for an English professor, an avowedly McLuhanite school of art or literary criticism never emerged. Yet, one nevertheless can detect a McLuhanite spirit in more recent scholarship on modernism, even if McLuhan himself is not present. In arguing broadly for a continuity, rather than a disjunction, between modernism and its technological environment, McLuhan anticipates Tim Armstrong's *Modernism, Technology, and the Body* (1998) and Sara Danius's *The Senses of Modernism: Technology, Perception, and Aesthetics* (2002). Both offer accounts of modernism that reject what Danius calls the "the antitechnological bias of high-modernist art" (40). Against the understanding of modernism as being itself deeply antimodern—evident in complaints about cinema and mass culture, a return to myth—Armstrong and Danius both seek to reveal the continuities between technology and modernist literature. And the McLuhanite prosthetic thesis is central to both of these accounts. Armstrong does not discuss McLuhan, but his account of the period's fascination with the image of technological augmentation, and the ambivalent character of that fascination, which contains "both utopian possibilities and a wounding and fragmentation of the self," is akin to McLuhan's rhetoric of prosthesis and amputation (*Fiction* 101). Danius's *Senses of Modernism* offers a rich account of intersections between modernism and its media as manifested through the senses. She thus rereads *Ulysses*, Joyce's "epic of the human body," "as a record of the modernist reinvention of the human body" (152). The novel features extensive meditation on the senses, whether through Stephen's experience on the beach in "Proteus" or Bloom's considerations of blindness. At the level of the sentence, Danius suggests, Joyce's prose represents the visual by adapting methods of cinematic framing (164), while sound is recorded, phonographically, without distinctions between human and inhuman (157). In the novel "each sensory organ now appears to operate independently and for its own sake" (151). And yet the novel as whole masters these rogue senses and, true to McLuhan's prosthetic thesis, manages to hold them together. Yet rather than the eclipse of the book that McLuhan (and later, Friedrich Kittler, discussed in Chapter 5) describes, Danius describes *Ulysses* as illustrating the triumph of the book for its ability to hold these errant senses together. "In bringing various artforms into contiguity with one another, *Ulysses* attempts to transcend the increasing differentiation of modes of cultural production in the age of mechanical reproducibility, notably their increasingly specialized ways of addressing the senses" (185).

The Typewriter

To better understand McLuhan's approach to media, let us look at a particular media technology—the typewriter. It is a counterintuitive selection to exemplify McLuhan's thinking. It was post-print "electric" technologies, and television in particular, with which he was most often associated, and it is has been the rise of the internet that seemed to confirm his claims about a "global village." Compared to television or the internet, the typewriter seems a clumsily mechanical vestige of a previous era. Yet it offers a clear case study of how a technology can reshape aesthetic expression, and how McLuhan's perspective might inform our understanding of modernism. To understand the typewriter, we must understand it "environmentally," that is, as intelligible only with reference to a wider ecology of media technologies. Its commercial success, for instance, is inextricable, in McLuhan's description, from that of the telephone. "It was the telephone, paradoxically, that sped the commercial adoption of the typewriter" (*Understanding Media* 262). A new technology of connection (the telephone) required new technology of recording (the typewriter). It will also offer an intriguing paradox, for while many media-oriented critics will see in the typewriter (and similar technologies) a becoming *visual* of poetry, McLuhan himself will find just the opposite. And this paradox illustrates something crucial about McLuhan's conceptualization of media.

McLuhan's comments on the typewriter are typical of his approach to media. While his language is deterministic, he is often sensitive to the full range of effects a technology can have. When he asserts, for instance, that "when the first wave of female typists hit the business office in the 1890s, the cuspidor manufacturers read the sign of doom" he condenses a media history *and* a history of gender into a formulation that links diverse areas of culture: "the uniform ranks of fashionable lady typists made possible a revolution in the garment industry. What she wore, every farmer's daughter wanted to wear, for the typist was a popular figure of enterprise and skill" (*Understanding Media* 259). Call it a probe. It lacks sufficient explanation or grounding in evidence. (Is it true that spittoon, or cuspidor, manufacturers realized the changing dynamics of the late nineteenth-century workforce ahead of anyone else?) But, it also reflects the mode of response McLuhan imagined appropriate to his own electric age—reaching across diverse areas of culture to link together surprising effects.

The role of the typewriter is particularly clear in poetry. One does not need to be a media determinist to acknowledge that Apollinaire's calligrammes, for instance, exploit the visual dimension of the page to be meaningful (see Figure 3.1). Such meanings are unavailable to poetry that takes as its medium the lyric orality descending from Homer and inhering in rhyme or meter, organizing sound through time rather than position in space. Ong attributes the sort of visual space that Apollinaire exploits not directly to the typewriter, but to the meaningfulness of typographic space inaugurated by print (what Ong will call a "hypervisualized noetic world," 125). While

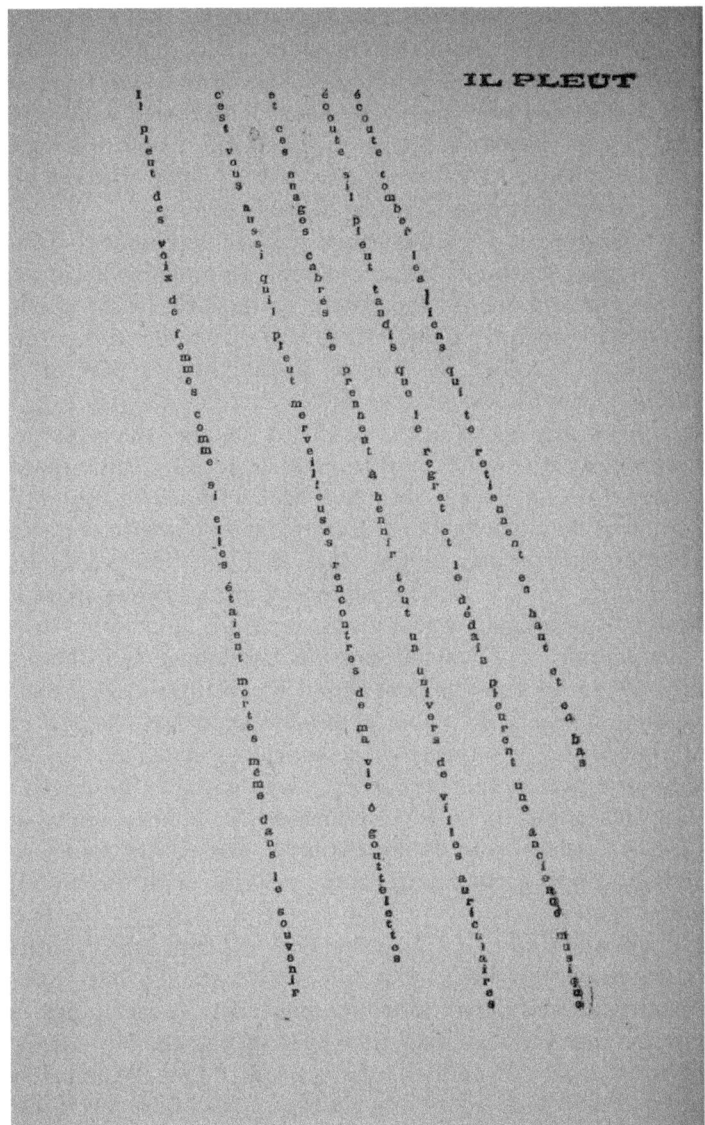

FIGURE 3.1 *Guillaume Apollinaire, "Il Pleut" from* Calligrammes: poèmes de la paix et da la guerre, 1913–1916, *Courtesy of The Internet Archive.*

any sort of writing organizes language spatially, that organization is not meaningful without the regularity and reproducibility of print. This is evident well before the modernism of the typewriter, in seventeenth-century poems like George Herbert's 1633 poems "Easter Wings" (which looks, on the page, like a pair of wings) or "The Altar" (which looks on the page like an altar) or in the blank page in Laurence Sterne's *Tristram Shandy* (1767).

The tradition of McLuhanesque reading represented by Ong locates a modernism of the typewriter as an intensification of the typographic focus on the visual, particularly in the tradition of "concrete poetry." Concrete poems, like the calligrammes of Apollinaire, exploit their visual appearance as part of their meaning. The tradition of concrete poetry is accelerated by the typewriter, which places in the hands of the poet the tools of the typesetter. The typewriter enables readier access to this space as an element of typographic meaning. Mallarmé's *Un Coup de Des* and some of the poems of E. E. Cummings are further evidence of this modernist tradition. As Ong says, in a poem like Cummings's untitled poem no. 276 (the grasshopper poem), "White space is so integral to Cummings's poem that it is utterly impossible to read the poem aloud" (127). Modernism is here allied with the visual against the aural/oral. The poet Dick Higgins invokes McLuhan in explaining the visual character of modernist poetry: "As McLuhan says, you can't make the new medium do the old job .... What interests me now is that new poetry isn't going to be poetry for reading. It's going to be for looking at ..... I mean book, print culture, is finished" (qtd. in Emerson 98, first ellipsis mine). Such a reading of McLuhan equates the typewriter with the becoming visual of poetry.

McLuhan's student, Hugh Kenner, expands this tradition, equating the typewriter not simply with visuality, but with the modern break away from conventional form. Kenner points to a machinic logic broader than the typewriter itself, but expressed through it, that is evident in the poetry of Ezra Pound. Pound emphasized the work of art as a concentration of energy; it was to be judged according to machinic principles of efficiency (e.g., "use no superfluous word," in his essay "A Retrospect"). Kenner extends the term *machine* as widely as McLuhan does *media* to include a broad range of phenomenon. A machine, Kenner insists, "need not connote iron nor hardware" but "applies to any economical self-activating system for organizing resources" (Kenner 54). The *Oxford English Dictionary*, in its marshaling of the history of the English language, is a machine; the critical editions of ancient poems that Pound drew on extensively for translations like "The Seafarer" (1911) or "Homage to Sextus Propertius" (1919) are likewise machinic in their organization. And, the modernist poem as a form, by compressing emotion and lived experience into the most effective and efficient language, what Pound calls "an intellectual and emotional complex in an instant of time" is a machine of experience ("Retrospect" 113). The poem "economized and concentrated human perception, human expression" (Kenner 52). The modernist poem privileges efficiency over the orality of form. This stress on "the clean efficiency" of form accounts for a mode of lineation that is itself indebted to the typewriter. Kenner points to Pound's "The Return" (1912), as a poem with a machinic efficiency. Its irregular lines create a visual, rather than oral, rhythm. Transforming spacing into a meaningful element of the poem, however, requires "a way of creating the poem in one's workroom in a form close to the form in which it will be printed. So *The Return* is an early example of what has become a twentieth-century genre, a poem that could only have been composed on the typewriter" (47–8). Less obviously than concrete poetry, "The Return" nevertheless testifies to a visual logic that poets access through the typewriter.

More recently, Lori Emerson has taken up this line of analysis in *Reading Writing Interfaces* (2014), tracing the role of McLuhan in a tradition of concrete poetry that extends into "dirty" concrete poetry contemporary with McLuhan's own popularity in the 1960s and 1970s. Dirty concrete poetry radicalizes concrete poetry's use of the typewriter. These poems "deliberately courted a visual and linguistic nonlinearity and illegibility by putting the typewriter to the test. As these poets created smeared letters with inked ribbons or different carbons while turning and twisting the page, the result was often the imprint of letters that appeared literally dirty or rough around their edges" (100). Creating poetry using mimeograph or xerox machines in addition to typewriters compounds the immersion of such works in their media. While concrete poems like Apollinaire's "Il Pleut" use their visual element to reduce the distance between form and content (the poem looks like what is describes), dirty concrete poetry, Emerson suggests, replaces the message with the medium. The refusal of orality evident in Cummings's grasshopper poem brings form and content into closer unity. The movement of the letters of the poem on the page might be read as more accurately representing, or even as *enacting*, the movement of the grasshopper. Dirty concrete poetry, however, does not better align form and content, but exposes something about form directly—the medium by which the poem is materially created. Such poems often lose all semantic intelligibility and become instead a purely visual testimony to the fact of mediation itself, works "whose content is the noise of media transmitting this same content" (Emerson 111). Here, in dissolving conventional semantics and meaning, the medium radically becomes the message of the poem.

Perhaps the most radical typewriter poem in this tradition is bpNichol's simple "The Complete Works" (1968). This poem reproduces the letters of the alphabet (capital and lowercase), as well as numbers and punctuation marks, grouped and ordered as they might appear on a typewriter keyboard. It participates in, but radicalizes, the combinatory logic of a work like Raymond Queneau's *Cent mille milliards de poèmes* (1961). Queneau's book presents the reader with ten sonnets, each with the same rhyme scheme, and each printed with its lines on separable pieces of card, so that a line from one poem could be recombined with any lines from the other ten poems. The result is a combinatory work through which the reader can, theoretically, generate literally millions of individual sonnets. Nichol's "Complete Works" offers a similar gesture, inviting the reader to create "any possible permutation of all the listed elements." Similar to the "infinite monkeys" who, through chance, can produce any work of literature (often Shakespeare),[15] Nichol's poem contains all possible poems. It illustrates the power of the alphabet as a technology of reduction, discussed at length by Ong and others. Yet, Nichol's "Complete Works" is not simply a poem about the power of alphabetization. It points to a medium that is more concrete and particular than the alphabet—the typewriter. The poem presents not simply "the alphabet," but the range of letters and characters of a keyboard (digits, punctuation, accented characters). Arranged in four horizontal groups, each of which

---

[15]Darren Wershler-Henry offers the best discussion of the typewriter and monkeys in *The Iron Whim*, Chapter 22 (185–99).

contains two lines, it reproduces the standard QWERTY keyboard layout. As a tool, the typewriter reduces the infinite potential of language to mechanism. Emerson sees this logic, evident in dirty concrete poems, as continuing a longer modernist tradition. "Dirty concrete poems are not an aberration in the history of twentieth-century poetry but rather representative of one of the mainstays of innovative writing: an active engagement in hacking both writing and writing media that treats both as process and product, the two unavoidably intertwined" (126).

Ong, Kenner, and Emerson all see the effect of the typewriter as an increase in the visual dimension of poetry, with concrete poetry being the vanguard mark of the typewriter. McLuhan himself, however, views the typewriter in almost diametrically opposed terms. Even as the typewriter extends the regularization of the printing press ("Typewriters caused an enormous expansion in the sale of dictionaries," *Understanding Media* 262), its chief effect, McLuhan contends, is essentially oral. Orality, in this broader sense, is not simply a matter of speech, but suggests live performance, akin to a rhapsode performing a Greek epic or, perhaps, the improvization of the jazz performer. "Seated at the typewriter," McLuhan writes, "the poet, much in the manner of the jazz musician, has the experience of performance as composition. In the nonliterate world, this had been the situation of the bard or minstrel" (*Understanding Media* 260). With Eliot and Pound, "the typewriter was an oral and mimetic instrument" (*Understanding Media* 262).

Like Ong, McLuhan points to Cummings as exemplary of this tradition. But it is the Cummings of "In Just-" (1920) rather than the Cummings of the untitled grasshopper poem. If the grasshopper poem approaches illegibility in its oral inarticulability, or, more precisely, if it reveals the gap between *reading* and *reading aloud*, "In Just-" is eminently amenable reading and performance. It is the sense of spontaneity and improvisation that bear the mark of the typewriter. McLuhan invokes Charles Olson, who in his essay "Projective Verse" (1950) equates the typewriter with orality and the poetry of *breath*. For Olson, poetry in the age of print has lost touch with its oral/aural qualities. "Projective Verse" calls for a return to orality and the voice in poetry, and a renewed focus on "breath." The typewriter frees the poet from the burden of rhyme and meter by enabling a musical score-like representation of orality.

> It is the advantage of the typewriter that, due to its rigidity and its space precisions, it can, for a poet, indicate exactly the breath, the pauses, the suspensions, even of syllables, the juxtapositions even of parts of phrases, which he intends. For the first time the poet has the stave and the bar a musician has had. For the first time he can, without the convention of rime and meter, record the listening he has done to his own speech and by that one act indicate how he would want any reader, silently or otherwise, to voice his work.
>
> (1058)

Olson too points to Homer as central in this progression, and like McLuhan, Havelock, and Ong, suggests a fundamental connection between poetry and orality that print has distorted. For Olson as for McLuhan, the typewriter paradoxically does not heighten the visual dimension of poetry but restores its orality. It extends the logic of type, but in so doing reverses it. In *Understanding Media* McLuhan offers a principle: "during the stages of their development all things appear under forms opposite to those that they finally present" (*Understanding Media* 34). The typewriter by intensifying typography also reverses it; the visual becomes the oral (what McLuhan will later call "the reversal of the overheated medium").[16]

The typewriter and its relationship to modernism provide an illustration of both the subtleties and the frustrations of McLuhan's approach to media. The nuance of McLuhan's description of the typewriter's orality may refute accusations of simplistic media determinism; in equating orality and the typewriter, however, McLuhan might just as easily be accused of a sort of capricious inconsistency. If his description of the orality of the typewriter nicely explains some things (Henry James's late prose as a product of dictation, the poetics of Charles Olson) it does not explain others (the grasshopper poem, concrete poetry).

---

[16] Late in his career, McLuhan attempted to further formalize this by articulating four so-called "Laws of Media" ("McLuhan's Laws of the Media"). Any technology *amplifies* some sense, *obsoletes* some existing technology, *retrieves* some older technology, and *reverses* into its opposite. In 1988, after McLuhan's death, a book of this title was published under the editorship of his son, Eric.

Humanism and Its Discontents

The paradox of McLuhan's characterization of the typewriter as an oral medium is instructive in a deeper way as well. It shows the degree to which McLuhan's prosthetic theory of media is fundamentally humanist in orientation. The media archaeological tradition Emerson invokes, and which is at the center of Chapter 5, is often described as posthumanist or even anti-humanist in orientation. Dirty concrete poetry, "whose content is the noise of media transmitting this same content" (Emerson 111), seems to aptly illustrate McLuhan's claim that "medium is the message." Yet his understanding of media as prostheses imposes a human scale and economy on media. It is this economy that reverses the visual output of a typewriter into an oral medium. Defining media as "extensions of man" invests them with distinctly human meanings. A medium can never produce mere *noise*. And McLuhan's humanist theorization of media shares the discontents of such humanisms in general. It presumes a normative model of *the human*. The weaknesses of this model are evident in three areas: (1) the prosthetic model of media draws on without sufficiently theorizing disability; (2) its stress on *orality* fails to engage relevant ideas about race; (3) the history on which it is based develops an ethnocentric notion of the *West*.

The metaphor of the prosthesis silently adapts ideas about disability without attention to the complexity of disability as a category. While naturalizing prosthesis and defining, as Ong does, alterity as essential to humanity, the Toronto School in some ways troubles any straightforwardly normative understanding of the body. Yet ideas about disability are given a central place in McLuhan's account of media, without sufficient attention and analysis. Disability is at once central and unexamined. Debates about orality and Homer, who is traditionally figured as blind,[17] already place the nature of disability at the center of the Toronto School lineage. The language of disability recurs throughout McLuhan's descriptions of the experience of media change. McLuhan cites Arnold Toynbee's *Study of History*, observing

---

[17] Alexander Beecroft reads Homer's blindness in classical biographies of Homer as a proxy for the biographies' authors' attitudes toward literacy.

"Toynbee's explanation of how *the lame and the crippled* respond to their handicaps in a society of active warriors. They become specialists like Vulcan, the smith and armorer" (*Understanding Media* 68–9, my emphasis). Media change as an experience of amputation or disabling is the other half of imagining media as prosthesis. In *Understanding Media*, for example, he writes, "The electric technology is within the gates, and *we are numb, deaf, blind, and mute* about its encounter with the Gutenberg technology, on and through which the American way of life was formed" (*Understanding Media* 17–18, my emphasis). McLuhan's language here is at times callous. But more importantly, disability is central to his analysis, and yet is never explicitly theorized. It may be possible to rewrite the history of media that is so central to McLuhan as a history of disability.

A similar question attends the way that orality operates in the Toronto School, which is at times inattentive to the way race has shaped understandings of literacy and its others. The trope of the talking book, for instance, as discussed by Henry Louis Gates in *The Signifying Monkey* (1988), figures the relationship between orality and literacy with specific attention to the role of literacy in the history of American slavery, and the subsequent intertextual revisions of this trope within black literature. Understanding orality and literacy may be impossible without attention to race. Michael North's discussion of the poetry of Claude McKay in *The Dialect of Modernism* (1994), for instance, reveals that whether he was writing in vernacular Jamaican English, or in standard English, McKay's reception was shaped by race. This focus on sound and race is evident more recently in Alexander Weheliye's *Phonographies: Grooves in Sonic Afro-Modernity* (2005). Weheliye brings attention to the ways that sound, orality, and technology are shaped by race. He seeks to disrupt and displace "the grand narratives of reason and technological progress by incorporating those who fall outside of these categories into the mix, which disruption, in turn, revamps the meanings of modernity as it resists separating these two spheres (modernity and minority cultures) into neatly distinct categories, asking us to rethink the very source of this putatively universal and homogenous sphere" (23). The humanism of the Toronto School is one of those grand narratives that may need disruption before it can usefully help us understand modernism and its media. The most direct critique of the concept of orality in the Toronto School comes in Jonathan Sterne's essay "Theology of Sound" (2011). Sterne traces Ong's understanding of orality to an essentially theological distinction between the spirit and the letter—a distinction Ong himself would sometimes invoke (73). Sterne offers a history of the Toronto School approach to media in an attempt to separate its productive strands (including Innis's media history) from its less productive strands (including the concept of *orality*).

The problem of ethnocentrism indeed runs beyond orality alone in Toronto School thinking. Humanism, in general, offers a sort of false universalism, making declarations about what is true of "humanity" or "man" (e.g., the subtitle of *Understanding Media*, "the extensions of *man*"), when what is really meant is something more narrow. Ong is sensitive about this sort of simplistic chauvinism. He prefers, for instance, the term *oral* cultures to *preliterate* cultures because preliterate "presents orality—the 'primary modeling system'—as an anachronistic deviant from the 'secondary modeling system' that followed it" (13). However, the broad references to "the West" that remain a central part of McLuhan and Ong's thinking, as well as the centrality of strong claims for an essential distinction between alphabetic and other writing systems, evidence residual Orientalism.[18] One point of origin for such claims is Ezra Pound's own reification of the Chinese character as a medium for poetry, which McLuhan references approvingly at points including in letters to Pound (*Letters* 218). Christopher Bush's excellent and thorough *Ideographic Modernism* (2010) traces the way the ideograph moves through modernist thinking as a response to wider shifts in media. One could certainly extend Bush's argument to elements of McLuhan and the Toronto School's thinking about media.

---

[18]Thomas J. Farrell embraces this aspect of Ong's writing, arguing in the vein of Samuel Huntington, explicitly that "certain features of Western culture have made it distinctive historically and have set it apart from the rest of the cultures of the world." Ongian literacy stands behind modernity, including "print culture, modern science, modern capitalism, modern democracy, the Industrial Revolution, and the Romantic Movement" (Farrell 271). Ongian literacy comes to name a crucial part of the "inner-directed" way of life that is, unlike "tradition-directed" cultures, "highly compatible with modern capitalism" (Farrell 279). Farrell's short essay, in my estimation, exemplifies precisely these ethnocentric dangers.

Thomas Mullaney's recent *The Chinese Typewriter: A History* (2017), similarly, reveals the ways that even in seeking to avoid essentialist claims about race or difference, theorizations of media technology reinscribe those differences. The role of the alphabet in Toronto School thinking, for instance, often repeats what Mullaney calls a nineteenth-century "fetishization of the alphabet." A long history of evolutionist arguments about writing, extending at least back to Hegel, argued that Chinese writing was intrinsically inferior to the alphabet. Pound's celebration of Chinese reverses this judgment, and sees in "ideographic" writing a superior, more immediate mode of inscription. As Bush shows, this celebration of Chinese is often simply a mirror image of these arguments—celebrating the attributes that had falsely been attributed to Chinese writing in order to derogate it.

As Mullaney compellingly argues, while these sorts of arguments have been discredited as claims about language, they continue to influence understandings of technology. In granting so much agency to media and writing systems, the Toronto School threatens to reproduce at the level of technology a racist argument about language and writing systems. The broad contrast between the alphabet and other writing systems often resituates cultural difference as technological, preserving the racism implicit in arguments from figures like Hegel. Mullaney nicely summarizes how this old, Hegelian argument resurfaces:

> Perhaps Chinese speakers are able to express themselves as completely as those of Western languages in a cognitive sense, and so Hegel was wrong. Yet *technologically*, speakers and writes of Chinese were demonstrably hindered by their onerous script, one that obstructed literacy and the adoption of modern information technologies such as telegraphy, typewriting, stenography, punched-card computing, and more—and so Hegel was *right*.
>
> (72)

Mullaney's history of the Chinese type provides a useful corrective. Even as typewriter manufacturers declared their typewriters "universal," "not one of these companies ever succeeded in breaking into the Chinese-language market" (10). The "Chinese typewriter" offers a key image of the sort of false universalism that inheres in many humanist approaches to media, and at least to some extent in the Toronto School as well. What looks, from one perspective, to be the inadequacy of Chinese writing to modern technology, Mullaney reveals, is a product of a particular history. Understanding the history of media, or of the typewriter, thus requires looking outside the history of media as prostheses alone, to a broader history that shapes and informs the history of media.

4

The Work of Modernism in the Age of Mass Media: The Frankfurt School

While we have occasionally caught glimpses of the public or the mass audience (in "Avant-Garde and Kitsch," or in Innis's treatment of politics), the idea of media for both the Toronto School and the Greenbergian tradition is clearest at the level of individual media. And, in different ways, they both stress medium specificity. The history to which we now turn is less interested in the specific character of particular media than in their social consequences. Media technologies in the modernist period reorganized the relationship between the producers and consumers of media. Earlier technologies—the printed book and the newspaper—had created mass publics. However, radio, film, and television, intensified the sense of a *mass* audience, of a large group of people all hearing, viewing, or reading the same thing. Print itself underwent a similar "massification" in the period, both with increasing rates of literacy and new printing technologies (including halftone technology, which simplified printing of images and text together). And no theorization of modernism and its media focuses more intensely on the specifically *mass* character of modern media than that of the Frankfurt School.

While "media" is a key category for the art historical tradition descending from Clement Greenberg explored in Chapter 2, and is *the* key term for the Toronto School discussed in the previous chapter, "media" is not itself as central a term for the thinkers associated with the Frankfurt School discussed in this chapter. They are more likely to think in terms like "mechanical reproduction" or "the culture industry," which highlight the social relations enabled and produced by modern media, rather than their materiality. Founded in 1923 at the Institute for Social Research in Frankfurt, Germany, the Frankfurt School was (and remains) a Marxist research institute which, in the course of its history and in the writing of its most widely recognized figures, developed a novel way of thinking about history and culture. Like other modes of Marxist cultural history, the Frankfurt school offers a materialist history, where *materialist* largely means economic. Unlike other modes of Marxist criticism, the Frankfurt School grants more agency and autonomy to culture. The *dialectical* account of history developed in the thinking of Theodor Adorno and Max Horkheimer offers a sharp contrast with any account of culture which reduces it some other social force—whether the economic (as in some early Marxist accounts of culture) or media.[1] Media in the Frankfurt School's thinking are not a secret cause of culture or social change (as they are for the Toronto School), but are enmeshed within, and expressive of, larger social forces. Media (like literature and culture in general) thus offer a terrain where social life is constructed and upon which larger forces struggle.

Yet this is not the same thing as discounting or ignoring media technologies entirely. The Frankfurt School differs sharply from the other traditions we've considered: it offers neither a quest to purify (Greenberg's term) or reinvent (Cavell's and Krauss's) media in service of art; nor does it seek to reveal media as a primary force in the history (the Toronto School). Instead, it asserts that the most important fact about media is how it restructures social and political relations. If media are important in the modernist period, it is because they are *mass* media. Modernist technological change reorganized and massified social life. The Frankfurt School approach to media, even as it has shaped both media studies and modernist studies, can easily feel somewhat outdated and certainly at odds with many of the dominant trends of the New Modernist Studies. This chapter will both explain why the Frankfurt School often seems outdated, while highlighting its continued relevance.

---

[1] Thomas Misa, for instance, contrasts the media-determinist thinking of Lewis Mumford with that of Marx (Misa 308).

At the center of this chapter are two figures (indeed, friends) who have defined a tension in modernist studies: Theodor Adorno and Walter Benjamin, who offer opposing tendencies within the Frankfurt School. In caricature, Adorno is an elitist snob, interested in difficult art and classical music, while Benjamin is a superfan of Chaplin and Mickey Mouse. Adorno recoils from popular culture in horror, while Benjamin embraces it; Adorno is a dour pessimist, retreating to an ivory tower (what Georg Lukács called the "Grand Hotel Abyss"), while Benjamin is the poptimist celebrant of movies and Parisian arcades. Adorno, with his Hegelian vocabulary, classical piano training, and uncompromising antipathy to jazz, seems diametrically opposed to Benjamin, who found great meaning in the detritus of modern life, and saw revolutionary potential in film. These are oversimplifications, but they capture a real dichotomy. Yet, as with all dichotomies in Frankfurt School thinking, it is a dialectical one—rather than a simple pair of opposites, each thinker contains elements of the other in his thinking.

To the question of how modernism relates to its media, the Frankfurt School answers with history. It is an answer completely different from both Greenbergian formalism and McLuhanite determinism. Yet this refusal of media determinism is made not out of some faith in the power of the individual nor of liberal progressivism. What it offers instead is a thoroughgoing historicism that sees media as inextricable from the social world of which they are part.[2] Such a history is less empirical, less grounded in specific dates and the particular microevolutions of individual media, than the media history of scholars like Jonathan Sterne and Lisa Gitelman, who take their bearings from a cultural studies tradition. It is a Marxist sense of history (history as class struggle) but it is also a sense of history indebted to thinkers like the sociologist Max Weber (1864–1920). For Weber modernity is defined as a process of disenchantment. In *The Protestant Ethic and the Spirit*

---

[2]While broadly "historical" or "sociological," Adorno and Horkheimer's dialectical history is at odds with many definitions of *historicism*. Marjorie Levinson nicely contrasts "the difference between historicism and dialectics," as "a distinction between conserving and redeeming the past" (113). This sense of *redemption* finds its grounding in the Marxist orientation of the Frankfurt School, and is especially evident in Walter Benjamin's notion of history, as articulated in his "Theses on the Philosophy of History," and captured in his description of the "Angel of History."

of Capitalism (1903), Weber describes modernity as demanding the obligations of Puritan asceticism without its justifications.

> One of the fundamental elements of the spirit of modern capitalism, and not only of that but of all modern culture: rational conduct on the basis of the idea of the calling, was born ... from the spirit of Christian asceticism ... The Puritan wanted to work in a calling; we are forced to do so. For when asceticism was carried out of monastic cells into everyday life, and began to dominate worldly morality, it did its part in building the tremendous cosmos of the modern economic order. This order is now bound to the technical and economic conditions of machine production which to-day determine the lives of all individuals who are born into this mechanism.
> (180–1)

Weber famously describes this modern condition as an "iron cage."

Whether it is a modernity defined by the experience of shock and the fragmentation of experience, as it is for Benjamin, or Adorno and Horkheimer's account of an ever-encroaching instrumental reason, history has a sort of meaning and direction that media express. In viewing media as inextricable from larger historical forces, Adorno, Horkheimer, and Benjamin (whom for convenience I will, with some inaccuracy, generalize under the name Frankfurt School)[3] provide this book's clearest and most sophisticated rejection of media determinism. Mechanical reproduction changes culture not through some medium-specific property (the indexicality of film; the stasis of the photograph; the uniform character of print), but by reorienting how it creates publics by bringing together the producers and consumers of culture. Even that language—producers and consumers, rather than artists and audiences, or authors and publics—suggests a radical shift. The perspective offered by the Frankfurt School on modernism and its media grows out of a

---

[3] The description of the Frankfurt School offered here ignores figures like Leo Löwenthal, Ernst Bloch, and others, even as it affords pride of place to Benjamin, who, strictly speaking, was not a "member" of the Frankfurt School, in the sense of holding a formal position in the Institute for Social Research. If such a portrait seems partial and out of step with the Frankfurt School as it actually existed, it is nevertheless the one most frequently encountered in American literary studies.

recognition that technology restructures the relationship between the consumers and producers of media.

Massification and Commodification

Communication technologies were enabled and shaped by two related developments in the modernist period: the emergence of an industrialized urban mass population and the increased commodification of the media. Raymond Williams, in *Keywords* (1976), notes the emergence of the term *the masses* to describe urbanizing populations starting in the first half of the nineteenth century (192–97). Industrialized, machine technology drew people together to labor. Peter Gaskell describes how "the steam engine has drawn together the population into dense masses" (qtd. in Williams, *Keywords* 194). These new, urban crowds had cultural and aesthetic consequences. For the French poet Charles Baudelaire (1821–1867), they were a force of uniquely modern, erotic excitement. The crowd offered an environment in which the *flaneur*, or urban stroller, could get lost. Of the flaneur, Baudelaire writes, "The crowd is his element, as the air is that of birds and water of fishes. His passion and his profession are to become one flesh with the crowd." In the same passage, Baudelaire describes experience of the crowd as itself a media experience, "we might liken [the flaneur] to a mirror as vast as the crowd itself; or to a kaleidoscope gifted with consciousness, responding to each one of its movements and reproducing the multiplicity of life and the flickering grace of all the elements of life" (9). By the twentieth century, the term *mass* was being used to describe uniquely modern phenomenon: mass movements, mass markets, and mass production. These masses are, however, an ambivalent thing. One may celebrate the masses as a source of democratic power or the embodiment of the people (as in mass movements), but also describe them as mere herds, passive objects of manipulation (by mass media, for instance). This new thing, *the masses*, was the explicit focus of Gustave Le Bon's 1895 study *The Crowd* and earned the attention of Sigmund Freud in *Group Psychology and the Analysis of the Ego* (1921) and *Civilization and Its Discontents* (1930). Films like Eisenstein's *Battleship*

Potemkin (1926) dramatized crowd scenes, elevating the crowd or mass into the role of central character.

The emergence of some concept of "the masses" around the start of the twentieth century is the obverse side of modernism's exclusivity and elitism. John Carey, in *The Intellectuals and the Masses: Pride and Prejudice among the Literary Intelligentsia, 1880–1939* (1992), detects in modernism a Nietzschean hostility to this newly emergent culture of the masses, akin to Greenberg's hostility to kitsch. A similar hostility to the masses is present, he argues, in the work of many modernists and theorists of modernism, including T. S. Eliot and José Ortega y Gasset. The literary critic F. R. Leavis's first pamphlet, *Mass Civilization and Minority Culture* (1930), makes this relationship explicit. The pamphlet anticipates some of the themes that would motivate the journal *Scrutiny*, which Leavis co-founded in 1932. The mass media, in Leavis's view, is a corrosive force, against which a "minority" modernist culture is defined. As he later writes in *Culture and Environment* (1937), "Films, newspapers, publicity in all forms, commercially-catered fiction—all offer satisfaction at the lowest level" (3). Mass production in culture, in the press and in film, is a "levelling-down, so that 'Civilization' and 'culture' are coming to be antithetical terms" (*Mass* 17).

The same mass character that horrifies Leavis, however, might be seen in less panicked terms. The German sociologist and critic Siegfried Kracauer (1889–1966), who would provide a key inspiration for the Frankfurt School, similarly focuses on the mass character of modern culture, but where Leavis sees only degradation, Kracauer sees an expression of national consciousness. Rather than in its politics or its works of high art, the meaning of a culture is most legible in those superficial and disposable things that Leavis was eager to discard. David Frisby's *Fragments of Modernity* (1998) offers a valuable overview of Kracauer and other key influences on the Frankfurt School. Frisby quotes Karsten Witte's observation that Kracauer trained his analysis on "the marginal zones of high culture and came to rest on the media of popular culture: the cinema, streets, sport, operetta, revues, advertisements and the circus ... deciphering social tendencies immediately out of ephemeral cultural phenomena" (qtd. in Frisby 110). The Tiller Girls offer an excellent example of one such cultural phenomenon. Like the Rockettes (their closest contemporary analogue), the Tiller

Girls were a large precision dance group. Popular at the start of the twentieth century, they offered a spectacle of regularized motion. In Kracauer's reading, the regimented spectacle of the Tiller Girls' performances removes all individuality from the dancers. In his essay "The Mass Ornament" (1923), Kracauer writes, "Only as parts of a mass, not as individuals who believe themselves to be formed from within, do people become fractions of a figure" ("Mass Ornament" 76). Within this spectacle an individual dancer's body loses its own coherence and becomes a mere collection of parts that is reunified and made intelligible only as part of a mass. The individual melts into an arrangement, legs and arms disappear into spirals and designs. Such spectacles, Kracauer suggests, are not erotic, nor do they work like military drills to create camaraderie or express fellow feeling. Instead, they reflect the conditions of capitalist mass production itself.

> The structure of the mass ornament reflects that of the contemporary situation. Since the principle of the *capitalist production process* does not stem purely from nature, it must destroy the natural organisms which it regards either as a means or as a force of resistance ... Like the mass ornament, the capitalist production process is an end in itself. The commodities that it spews forth are not actually produced to be possessed; rather, they are made for the sake of a profit that knows no limit.
> (78)

In the precision movements of the Tiller girls Kracauer sees a sort of aestheticism (form for form's sake) that ultimately reflects the conditions of modern capitalism—mass production for mass production's sake.

That the mass media are not simply debased culture, but expressive of the logic of modern, capitalist culture, is especially clear in the case of film. Film is a collective medium in both its production and its consumption. It is experienced collectively, by viewers gathered together in theaters, and is produced through the collaborative labor of actors, screenwriters, set designers, and cinematographers. Unlike a poem or novel, film is never simply the expression of a single artist. Rather than the straightforward manipulation of mass psychology and leveling down described by Leavis, Kracauer sees film, and mass culture more broadly, as a rich text demanding interpretation to be understood—even if what it reveals is ultimately the degrading effects of capitalism or fascism. In his influential *From Caligari to Hitler: A Psychological History of the German Film* (1947), Kracauer argues that German film of the post–First World War period expresses something like national consciousness or psychology. He traces, for instance, how the original screenplay (written by Hans Janowitz and Carl Mayer) for Robert Wiene's 1920 film *The Cabinet of Dr. Caligari* offered a clear antiauthoritarian allegory that Wiene's film utterly distorted. The film tells the story of Cesare, who, under the hypnotizing power of Dr. Caligari, commits murders. In Mayer and Janowitz's screenplay, Caligari is a psychiatrist who manipulates Cesare into these crimes. "According to the pacifist-minded Janowitz," Kracauer writes, "they had created Cesare with the dim design of portraying the common man who, under the pressure of compulsory military service, is drilled to kill and to be killed." The screenplay critiques war and nationalist violence, by representing Cesare as a victim of the manipulations of Caligari. Yet, Wiene's film alters this story by adding a frame story which reveals that the film's narrative is offered by a character who is an inmate of an insane asylum. The pernicious Caligari of the central narrative is the asylum's director. In this twist, the story of Caligari's manipulation is revealed as an irrational fantasy. Kracauer explains, while "the original story exposes the madness inherent in authority, Wiene's *Caligari* glorified authority and convicted its antagonist of madness. A revolutionary film was thus turned into a conformist one" (*From Caligari* 67).

In so twisting Mayer and Janowitz's postwar critique of authority, Kracauer suggests, the 1920 film reveals the longing for authoritarianism in German culture that would engulf the nation in the following decade with the rise of fascism. The character of Caligari offers a "premonition of Hitler ... in the sense that he uses hypnotic power to force his will upon his tool—a technique foreshadowing, in content and purpose, that manipulation of the soul which Hitler was the first to practice on a gigantic scale" (*From Caligari* 72–3). The film captures the lost potential of post–First World War Germany, which would ultimately culminate in the absolute submission to authority evident in the rise of Hitler. Such a vision of film puts Kracauer at odds not only with Leavis (for whom films "involve surrender, under conditions of hypnotic receptivity, to the cheapest emotional appeals," *Mass Civilization*

14), but with those who see in film a mode of artistic expression as individual as any other medium. As Vicky Lebeau notes, Kracauer's vision of film, as a mass medium, sees it as reflecting the collective psyche of the German people. It provides a "royal road" to the national unconscious, akin to the royal road to the unconscious Freud believed he had discovered in dreams (Lebeau 6). Mass media, for Kracauer, offer a modern mythology, a window on to the psychology the newly emergent masses.

Kracauer's mode of analysis provided a key influence on the Frankfurt School. His fascination with the detritus of modernity would be taken up by Benjamin, and his sense of mass culture as a modern mythos would be formalized in Adorno and Horkheimer's dialectic of enlightenment. Yet for Adorno and Horkheimer, terms like popular, vernacular, or even *mass* culture ignored the fact that this culture had been brought under a rationalized, instrumentalist logic. To focus on its mass character alone ignores the ways in which it is shaped by the demands of commodification. This culture was in no way "popular"; it was a product of what Adorno and Horkheimer term "the culture industry." This phrase itself now lacks the condemnatory force that Adorno and Horkheimer imagined it to have. The *Kulture* (culture) of "culture industry" (*Kulturindustrie* in the original German) suggests a realm of higher values. The very notion of treating such values as an "industry" suggests degradation. The idea of the "culture industry" describes the same massification that fascinated Kracauer, but sees this process as not simply a matter of massification, but of commodification or "reification."

In the most general sense, reification (from the Latin *res,* or "thing") describes the process of treating something that is not a thing as if it were. The term is elaborated within Marxist cultural theory by the Hungarian philosopher Georg Lukács, in his 1923 essay, "Reification and the Consciousness of the Proletariat." This account of reification is a sort of generalization of the account of commodity fetishism first offered by Marx. In early societies, commodity exchange represented only a part of society. Ethics, law, art, or religion all remained independent of the production, distribution, sale, and consumption of commodities. Reification names the process under capitalism whereby commodity exchange reshapes all of human experience. In Lukács's description, the commodity relation not only transforms the whole world into saleable objects, "It stamps its imprint upon the whole consciousness of man; his qualities and abilities are no longer an organic part of his personality, they are things which he can 'own' or 'dispose of' like the various objects of the external world" (100). This process of reification is evident in art and literature as well. Modernist and naturalist fiction, for Lukács, offers only atomized description rather than the fully coherent narration achieved by the high realist fiction of writers like Balzac. As Tyrus Miller explains in *Modernism and the Frankfurt School* (2014),

> Reification leads to literary manifestations of an atomized positivism, which cleaves to surface details of social life, registering disconnected and meaning-deprived facts, while failing to penetrate to the underlying relations, dynamics, and structural principles. He found these effects of reification to be exemplified in the naturalist novels of Emile Zola and Upton Sinclair, as well as in the modernist montage-novels of James Joyce, John Dos Passos, and Alfred Döblin.
> (15)

While reification names the negative consequences of mass culture, it is not impossible to imagine mass culture as positive force. The fact of mechanical reproduction—the ability to easily reproduce works of art and make them widely available—holds out the promise of making art more accessible. For most of history, art forms like orchestral performance or canvas painting were utterly beyond the reach of the majority of people. Seeing a painting or orchestral performance was necessarily limited and so governed by a logic of scarcity, resulting in the snobbery and elitism long associated with art. Technologies of mechanical reproduction seem to alleviate this scarcity. Through reproductions the paintings of Vermeer can be more broadly accessed, the symphonies of Beethoven experienced by all on phonograph record or radio broadcast. One might quibble that the means of reproduction are still too crude—that reproductions fail to do justice to the colors of a Matisse or the textured impasto of a Van Gogh; that the scratchy sound of a record lacks the fullness of performance, or that the limited recording length of a record means that a symphony must be enjoyed in parts. Yet, such objections are not really objections to the democratizing power of technology in art, but complaints about its imperfections—problems for which one could imagine technological solutions (higher resolution! better fidelity!).[4] This vision of technology as a means to spread culture informed the first director of the BBC, John Reith, who imagined a mission for radio derived from Matthew Arnold—to share "the best that has been thought and said." Such an understanding of mechanical reproduction's consequences is essentially liberal. It imagines a modest improvement in culture by better sharing an already-established set of values, rather than challenging them in any way.

This liberal image of media technology enabling broader access to culture provides a useful point of reference, because both Benjamin and Adorno and Horkheimer, though in dialectically opposite ways, sharply reject it. For Benjamin, such a position is mere empty bourgeois ideology, artificially preserving a realm of "art" independent from life. What Benjamin describes mechanical reproduction doing, in his famous essay "Work of Art in the Age of Its Mechanical Reproducibility" (1935) (discussed at greater length below), is far more radical than increasing the accessibility of an existing canon. Mechanical reproduction overturns our most basic ideas about art. It does not simply make great works of art more widely available, but reconfigures the very definition of art. In removing the scarcity that shapes the experience of art, mechanical reproduction reveals the extent to which key ideas from art—genius, originality, creativity—are not necessarily properties of art itself, but reflect the bourgeois class structure in which art under capitalism is produced. By undermining this scarcity and its attendant ideologies, mechanical reproduction for Benjamin has an essentially revolutionary potential.

For Adorno, by contrast, this apparent democratization is just the final triumph of reification. Art is indeed made more accessible, but only by becoming an empty commodity. In his essay "A Social Critique of Music" (1945), Adorno asks of radio, "Are the masses really participating in music culture or are they merely forced consumers of musical commodities?" (232–3). The real problem

---

[4]In his essay "The Radio Symphony: An Experiment in Theory" (collected in *Current of Music*), Adorno argues that the conditions of reproduction of radio are so fundamentally different that indeed the experience of the symphony on the radio is simply not the same experience.

with art was never access to the objects and media of art, but the unjust distribution of leisure and education imposed by the class system. "The abolition of educational privilege by disposing of culture at bargain prices does not admit the masses to the preserves from which they were formerly excluded," Adorno and Horkheimer write in *Dialectic of Enlightenment* (1944), "but, under the existing social conditions, contributes to the decay of education and the progress of barbaric incoherence" (130). For Adorno, Horkheimer, and Benjamin, the Reithian desire to treat technology as a mere means to better spread an Arnoldian vision of culture ignores the way that culture is organized by the class structure of a society. In the Frankfurt School tradition, the mechanical reproduction enabled by modern media technology can only be understood in relation to the mass culture that it both expresses and enables.

"Work itself is given a voice"

For Benjamin, the greatest promise of the new media technologies of the turn of the twentieth century lay in their restructuring of the relationship between cultural producers and consumers. One thing media do, as the Toronto School insisted, is shape the experience of time and space. Yet they also imply a social relationship. The telephone bridges distances in space like broadcast media, but it allows a conversation rather than a broadcast. It enables a mutuality, rather than a hierarchy. McLuhan's description of print focuses chiefly on effects like the rationality, linearity, and objectivity that he associates with print's intensification of vision and sight at the cost of hearing and orality. Yet one of the most important consequences of print is the asymmetrical relationship between reader and writer that it introduces. The printed page is (or, over its history, becomes) qualitatively different from the written page. Mass reproduction of printed texts creates a clear separation of roles between authors and readers. Indeed, as many have argued (including McLuhan), modern ideas of authorship, and attendant ideas including copyright, only emerge with print, which heightens the asymmetry between reader and author.

The potential reorganization of this relationship is one of Benjamin's central themes. His essay "Author as Producer," written in 1934, traces the consequences of the relationship between cultural producers and consumers for the politics to art. The question of art's relationship to politics is often posed as one of propaganda. Should an artist advocate political positions in their work? Does political advocacy compromise aesthetic value? Is all political art simply propaganda? Is propaganda necessarily bad art? These questions are common enough (and still asked). But for Benjamin they represent a dead end. To resolve this question, he offers instead a "dialectical approach," which focuses not on "such rigid, isolated things as work, novel, book. It has to insert them into the living social contexts" ("Author as Producer" 80). Any discussion of art's politics is meaningless if it does not consider the work within the relationship of producers and consumers. "Author as Producer" insists authors must recognize themselves as members of the working and producing class (rather than an aloof intelligentsia). Only then can they understand themselves not in terms of creativity or genius, but as playing a role within the "relations of production," or more simply, as a part of the economy. Only by understanding it at the level of the relations of production does the question of art's politics become meaningful. The author's individual attitudes about these conditions are irrelevant: "a political tendency, however revolutionary it may seem, has a counter-revolutionary function so long as the writer feels his solidarity with the proletariat only in his attitudes, not as a producer" ("Author as Producer" 84). This shift of perspective also makes media uniquely relevant. "Rather than asking 'What is the attitude of a work *to* the relations of production of its time?' I would like to ask, 'What is its position *in* them?'" ("Author as Producer" 81). Understanding a work's position within these relations, that is how art exists within the economy, requires attention to how works are made, reproduced, and circulated. It requires, in short, attention to media. Changes in media are important because they can reshape this relationship and the author's place within it.

Politics here occurs at the level of the medium rather than the message. Writing politically progressive novels or poems will do little, or nothing, if the relations of production remain unchanged. But what are the "relations of production" when it comes to culture? Insisting that the author is a *producer*, and so involved in class struggle, is part of understanding the intersection of culture and relations of production in a more conventionally Marxist sense. In this most stridently political of Benjamin's essays, the writer must betray the bourgeois culture that is the source of their education, their audience, and which has provided the traditional image of what a writer is. Instead, the writer must "transform[] himself from a supplier of the productive apparatus into an engineer who sees it as his task to adapt this apparatus to the purposes of the proletarian revolution" ("Author as Producer" 93). To become genuinely political, a writer cannot simply write pamphlets advocating a political position. Becoming a producer requires the author to transform themself from a bourgeois *writer* to a proletarian *engineer*. Treating the author as producer removes the halo of creative genius which has attended that figure at least since romanticism. In his most famous essay, "The Work of Art in the Age of Its Mechanical Reproducibility," Benjamin offers a similar contrast between the painter and the cinematographer by comparing them to a magician and a surgeon, respectively: "The attitude of the magician, who heals a sick person by a laying-on of hands, differs from that of the surgeon, who makes an intervention in the patient" (35). Such a contrast makes explicit a fundamental hostility to the romantic ideology of creativity that traditionally justifies art—the ideology of aesthetic autonomy present in Clement Greenberg, and the almost religious reverence for modernist evident in Michael Fried (both discussed in Chapter 2). Rather than treating *culture* as an elevated sphere of creativity, Benjamin compels a recognition of it as a sphere of production, and one where media play a crucial (perhaps even determining role).

What would it actually look like for the author to assume this role as producer? We can catch a glimpse in one of the degraded cultural forms that Benjamin celebrated—the newspaper. By contrast, for Lukács, the newspaper exemplifies reification. He writes, "The journalist's 'lack of conviction,' the prostitution of his experiences and beliefs is comprehensible only as the apogee of capitalist reification" ("Reification" 100). Yet Benjamin celebrates precisely this same element of journalism for dethroning the artificial distinction between art and life. The newspaper is a medium that indiscriminately absorbs all aspects of contemporary life. It is a "literarization of the conditions of living." Because the newspaper is organized simply by the events of everyday life, which it digests and redistributes, it reflects a closer relationship to the life of the masses than a form like the novel. This "literarization" creates a possibility of bringing life more directly itself into writing and undermining the separation between the writer, as intellectual, and the masses. As Benjamin puts it, with the religious overtones typical of his writing, "it is at the scene of the limitless debasement of the word—the newspaper, in short—that its salvation is being prepared" ("Newspaper" 360). Where Lukács had seen only debasement, Benjamin sees a preparation for (political) redemption.

Still newer technologies of mechanical reproduction, such as photography and especially film, offer an even more radical promise of restructuring the relationship between culture and production, and further empowering the masses. When newspapers publish letters to the editor, they reveal that nearly anyone could write for that medium. But film extends this power even broader. "*Any person*," Benjamin writes, "*can lay claim to being filmed*" ("Work of Art" 33, original emphasis). In contrast to the division of writers from readers and, more profoundly, of literacy from non-literacy, the camera (in this, admittedly somewhat counter-intuitive formulation) is open to anyone. "The Work of Art" essay echoes "Author as Producer" and extends its argument into the medium of film, asserting that with film, "Work itself is given a voice" ("Work of Art" 34).[5] The contrast with thinkers like Ong and McLuhan could not be clearer. For them literacy represents a key step along a humanist discourse of improvement. For Benjamin, it is a matter of class politics.

Aura

Benjamin's most famous and sophisticated account of politics, art, and their relationship to the masses comes in his discussion of *aura*. Aura is Benjamin's name for the quality that traditionally attaches to original works of art. It is the reason why we assume that, even if you know what the *Mona Lisa* looks like, you need to travel to a museum in Paris to *really* see it. Even in the most perfect reproduction, Benjamin explains, "*one* thing is lacking: the here and now of the work of art—its unique existence in a particular place" ("Work of Art" 21). However perfect the reproduction of a

---

[5] Benjamin repeats this theme in his essay "Newspaper" (359–60) and offers similar terms—"Work itself has its turn to speak"—in "Author as Producer" (83).

famous painting, we treat it as somehow lacking. Aura is Benjamin's name for what is lacking. The original artwork has *aura*, while the reproduction lacks it.[6] It is the mark of the artwork's complete and utter uniqueness.

Such a notion of aura is almost religious. In Tyrus Miller's description, it is "a sort of halo around the work that evokes a spiritual realm foreign to that of work and everyday life" (42). Aura carves the work of art out from the rest of everyday life, and grants it a special existence. Benjamin traces the origin of this almost magical power to art's origins in ritual and religion:

> the earliest artworks originated in the service of rituals—first magical, then religious. And it is highly significant that the artwork's auratic mode of existence is never entirely severed from its ritual function. In other words: *the unique value of the "authentic" work of art always has its basis in ritual.*
> ("Work of Art" 24)

Art's auratic power, however, persists even after art is no longer associated with ritual or religion. Art becomes a sort of secularized religion in the modern period. Exemplified by museums, theater going, and novel reading, the modern secular religion of art maintains aura by treating art as separate or autonomous from the rest of life.[7] E. M. Forster's description of the Schlegel family in the novel *Howards End* (1910) captures well this secularized religion of art. The Schlegels attend concerts, read and argue about literature, as a key element of a modern, liberal way of life.

Benjamin comes, however, not to praise aura but to bury it. Viewing art in relation to aura allows Benjamin to narrate its history, from its origin in ritual to the present, along broadly Marxian lines. In this history the autonomous, bourgeois work of art is essentially aligned with capitalism, while the destruction of aura would help lend work a voice, and bolster an emergent socialism. Aura separates art from the rest of life. By destroying aura the last lingering connection between art and cultic value,

---

[6] For a rich analysis of this question, see Latour and Lowe, "The Migration of the Aura, or How to Explore the Original through Its Facsimiles."
[7] Terry Eagleton discusses literature as a replacement for waning religious faith in modernity (*Literary Theory* 22–4).

evident in bourgeois aesthetic autonomy, is finally complete, and art is subsumed fully into the culture out of which it emerges: *"as soon as the criterion of authenticity ceases to be applied to artistic production, the whole social function of art is revolutionized. Instead of being founded on ritual, it is based on a different practice: politics"* ("Work of Art" 25). Aura, by separating the artwork from the rest of social life, depoliticizes art. It grants a false autonomy and preserves a bourgeois, individualist mode of consumption. It disempowers the masses and thwarts any revolutionary mode of perception. Many of the key terms that Benjamin celebrates—automaticity, habit, the elimination of individuality—might strike us as antithetical to the very idea of art. But that is Benjamin's point; categories like uniqueness, genius, and individuality are all indebted to an outmoded, and indeed politically regressive, idea of aura.

The destruction of aura, rather than an increase in accessibility, is the power Benjamin ascribes to technologies of reproduction. As Reith imagined, reproductions indeed allow artworks to circulate more widely. Benjamin admits, reproductions now "meet the recipient halfway, whether in the form of a photography or in that of a gramophone record. The cathedral leaves its site to be received in the studio of an art lover; the choral work performed in an auditorium or in the open air is enjoyed in a private room" ("Work of Art" 22). But mechanical reproduction has more radical consequences by removing the uniqueness of the work of art, and thereby destroying its aura. It does not simply make art more available through copies, it changes how we understand what art is.

Of course, the fact of a copy of the Mona Lisa does nothing to destroy the Mona Lisa itself, or even reduce its aura. Thousands continue to throng to the Louvre to see Da Vinci's painting, despite the ready availability of copies. Benjamin's argument, however, is that technologies like film and photography eliminate any meaningful notion of an *original*. Because a photograph only exists as a copy, photography makes aura impossible. The singular photographic negative is part of the artwork's production, but any single print made from that negative is as "original" as any other. No print can claim to be the *real* work, certainly not in the way that a particular piece of canvas on a wall in Paris can claim to be *the Mona Lisa*. In photographs and films, there is only a proliferation of copies. The most important consequence of mechanical reproduction is not improved access to "great works of art"—a position which would only further solidify the authority of the past—but this destruction of aura which completely redefines art by reconfiguring the relationship between art and the masses, and opening up the possibility of a revolutionary future.

While some have seen the power Benjamin confers on technology as bordering on deterministic,[8] he did not believe that the sheer technological fact of film or photography guaranteed any particular politics or outcome. The destruction of aura is not a technological event alone, but has its "social basis" in "the increasing emergence of the masses and the growing intensity of their movements" ("Work of Art" 23). The erosion of aura frees up art for political purposes—but there is no necessary politics to the erosion of aura itself. For Benjamin, while the technological fact of film enables the eradication of aura, it does not automatically produce it. When Benjamin wrote "The Work Art" essay, film as a narrative form was still emerging. The conventions of continuity editing and the Hollywood star system were, for Benjamin, attempts to squash the medium's radical potential and reestablish aura within film. His essay is as much a plea to seize the radical potential of film's nascent state as it is a description of its anti-auratic properties. "It should not be forgotten, of course, that there can be no political advantage derived from this control until film has liberated itself from the fetters of capitalist exploitation. Film capital uses the revolutionary opportunities implied by this control for counterrevolutionary purposes" ("Work of Art" 33). Hollywood movie studios replace the cultic value of art with the cult of the film star. For Benjamin, therefore, "the expropriation of film capital is an urgent demand of the proletariat" ("Work of Art" 34). Even, therefore, as Benjamin ascribes power to film as a medium, it is a power that is politically realized only when seized by social forces—of capital or of revolution.

Written during the rise of European fascism, the "Work of Art" essay, in its closing section, spells out the relationship between the modern masses and industrialized technology in the starkest political terms. Technology and the emergence of modern masses demand, in Benjamin's view, a reorganization of class society. New technologies empower humanity, but what will be done with this power? Capitalist property relations, like aura, represent an outmoded and obsolete

---

[8]Terry Eagleton has described a "technologism" as a part of the idealism that exists in tension with the materialism of Benjamin's Marxism (175–7).

way of understanding and organizing the world. Maintaining an old social system under new technological conditions, Benjamin suggests, is only possible through violence. Fascism, he writes, "attempts to organize the newly proletarianized masses while leaving intact the property relations" ("Work of Art" 40). It does so by transforming politics into aesthetics. The aestheticization of politics is central to the mass spectacles of Nazi Germany, captured in Leni Riefenstahl's 1935 film *The Triumph of the Will*. Incredible violence combines with gratuitous aestheticization, and the power of technology—to end hunger or to equitably share wealth—is diverted away from the creation of a more just society.

Benjamin sees a similar aestheticization of politics in the Futurist celebration of war as "beautiful." When Filippo Marinetti, in "The Founding and Manifesto of Futurism" (1909), writes that "We will glorify war" (42) and offers lavish praise for violence and machinery, Benjamin detects the necessary outcome of technological improvement in the absence of social justice. Art's autonomy here transforms into a sort of nightmare. The separation of art from life, under such technological conditions, leads to a world in which even human destruction becomes a spectacle to behold aesthetically. Just as reification leads the individual to treat her own existence at a remove, as an object, so the destruction of war becomes a mere object of contemplation. Benjamin argues that humankind "which once, in Homer, was an object of contemplation for the Olympian gods, has now become one for itself. Its self-alienation has reached the point where it can experience its own annihilation as a supreme aesthetic pleasure. *Such is the aestheticizing of politics, as a practiced by fascism. Communism replies by politicizing art*" ("Work of Art" 42). In fascism reification reaches a crisis point. Either the masses are empowered by technology, and politics supplants aesthetics by claiming art for itself (a process that Benjamin, in the closing sentence, associates with communism), or the reactionary reappropriation of technological power aestheticizes life in fascism.

It is a stark contrast, made only starker by Benjamin's own tragic death, fleeing the Nazis. Yet, Benjamin's celebration of the destruction of aura, and its hostility to traditional bourgeois art might not strike all readers as cause for celebration. Benjamin eagerly welcomes the waning of individuality and uniqueness, to be replaced by more political, more revolutionary, values. Yet some may see in such a process something to fear, even if they otherwise share Benjamin's political commitments. Such was Benjamin's friend and correspondent, Theodor Adorno.

Adorno

In a 1936 letter to Benjamin, his friend Theodor Adorno responded to "The Work of Art" essay with some ambivalence. Adorno was as dismayed by the rise of fascism as Benjamin, yet where Benjamin celebrates film and the potential disappearance of aura, Adorno wishes to preserve aura as a force that resists capitalist culture. In a crucial, and often quoted passage, Adorno writes of the relationship between art and popular culture such as film, between what he calls the "dialectic of the highest" and the "dialectic of the lowest":

> '*Les extrêmes me touchent*' [Gide], just as they touch you—but only if the dialectic of the lowest has the same value as the dialectic of the highest, rather than the latter simply decaying. Both bear the stigmata of capitalism, both contain elements of change (but never, of course, the middle-term between Schönberg and the American film). Both are torn halves of an integral freedom, to which however they do not add up. It would be romantic to sacrifice one to the other, either as the bourgeois romanticism of the conservation of personality and all that stuff, or as the anarchistic romanticism of the blind confidence in the spontaneous power of the proletariat in the historical process—a proletariat which is itself a product of bourgeois society.
> (*Aesthetics and Politics* 123)[9]

For Adorno, Benjamin's celebration of the destruction of aura falls into this second romanticism. It enthuses over the anti-auratic potential of film itself without paying enough attention to the social forces in which this technological fact is embedded. Benjamin's hope relies on the "spontaneous power of the proletariat in the historical

---

[9] Exactly what the highest and lowest mean here is not entirely clear. As Deborah Cook notes, while Fredric Jameson has suggested that the "torn halves" represent not *art* and the *culture industry*, but serious art and light art, Adorno's comments, responding to Benjamin, seem to clearly anticipate his later development of the idea of the "culture industry" (Cook 105–6; cf. Jameson, *Late* 133).

process," without sufficiently acknowledging the degree to which this same proletariat is produced by bourgeois society. These forces—the forces of capitalism—appear, in Adorno's estimation, almost inescapable.

This sense of capitalism's crushing, pervasive, inescapability is one of the hallmarks of Adorno's writing. Even as he shares Benjamin's socialist vision of a post-capitalist society, Adorno is far less quick to detect its potential in elements of popular culture like film. In the dedication to his aphoristic 1951 text *Minima Moralia* (the title cynically echoes Aristotle's treatise on ethics, the *Magna Moralia*), Adorno describes the degraded condition of contemporary life as one impoverished by the forces of modernization, or, more precisely, reification. "What the philosophers once knew as life has become the sphere of private existence and now of mere consumption, dragged along as an appendage of the process of material production, without autonomy or substance of its own ... Our perspective of life has passed into an ideology which conceals the fact that there is life no longer" (*Minima Moralia* 15). Here is a fine instance of Adorno's nearly unremitting pessimism. Forces of rationalization and administration have so thoroughly infiltrated all aspects of the world, that "there is life no longer." Life in a rich, full, proper sense—life beyond mere biological existence—has been crushed by capitalism. Instead of life, we have what amounts to shopping ("mere consumption, dragged along as an appendage of the process of material production"). Under such conditions the very idea of *ethics* or *morality* seems laughable. Or, as Adorno famously puts it, "Wrong life cannot be lived rightly" (*Minima Moralia* 39). Art, however, offers some resistance to this process.

While Adorno's diagnosis of mass culture shares many elements with Benjamin, their assessment of popular art and the value of aura differ sharply.[10] Benjamin imagines that the elimination of aura makes the work of art available for politics, but for Adorno

---

[10] In a letter to Benjamin, Adorno proposed publishing his essay "On Jazz" alongside Benjamin's "Work of Art" essay. Jamie Daniel calls "On Jazz" "a long variation on the theme of Benjamin's comment in [the 'Work of Art' essay] that human subjectivity was now alienated from itself and its own best interests to such a degree that 'it can experience its own destruction as an aesthetic pleasure of the first order'" (42). Yet what Benjamin describes as occurring at the social level, in fascism, Adorno detects in the individual's enjoyment of jazz music. Adorno describes jazz as "easily adapted for use by fascism'" ("On Jazz" 61).

the destruction of aura simply moves art from the frying pan of reification into the fire of the commodity form. Completely freed from its cult value, the work of art has only pure exhibition value. But this exhibition value, Adorno writes, in his posthumously published *Aesthetic Theory* (1970), "is an *imago* of the exchange process" (45). It offers not a moment of revolutionary potential, but the triumph of reification over the last forces which resist or escape it. To eliminate aura entirely, under capitalism, is to reduce art to a commodity. The complete desacralization of art that Benjamin celebrates in mechanical reproduction is, Adorno argues, undialectical. "Aura is not only—as Benjamin claimed—the here and now of the artwork, it is whatever goes beyond its factual givenness, its content; one cannot abolish it and still want art" (*Aesthetic Theory* 45). Art is only truly art when it has some existence beyond its commodity status. There must always be *some* aura, some irreducible distance, between the work and the world in order for art to truly exist in Adorno's estimation.

Adorno's dialectical treatment of aura in response to Benjamin's essay anticipates the similar treatment of myth in *Dialectic of Enlightenment* (1944). In this defining work of Frankfurt School Critical Theory, Adorno and Max Horkheimer offer a history of civilization as a process of "enlightenment." The book describes enlightenment not as a single event in history, but as the dialectical process by which reason seeks to master and overcome the irrationality of myth. The eighteenth century is often described as an age of reason, or more simply as "the Enlightenment," exemplified by philosophers (John Locke, Jean Jacques Rousseau) and economists (Adam Smith). It represents the overcoming of superstition (often including religion), the emergence of modern science, and might even be considered as the beginning of the modernity we continue to inhabit. Enlightenment, as the philosopher Immanuel Kant put it in "What is Enlightenment?" (1784), "is the human being's emergence from his self-incurred minority [*Unmündigkeit*; also translatable as immaturity]" ("An Answer" 17). Enlightenment (or a fully developed sense of reason) frees people to no longer simply accept authority (as a child must). *Dialectic of Enlightenment* questions Kant's confidence that enlightenment is over or complete. It treats enlightenment as a continuing process, and one that is more ambivalent than Kant's description allows. Enlightenment's opposite, in Adorno and Horkheimer's description, is *myth*. In a 1982 lecture, Jürgen Habermas, a second-generation member of the

Frankfurt School, explains that enlightened thinking both differs from, and combats, myth. It differs from myth because it refuses the authority of tradition and elevates "the non-coercive coercion of the better argument." It opposes myth by offering an alternative—the exercise of individual reason as a way to break the "collective spell of mythical powers" (14). The promise of enlightenment was a better world, based on rational, non-coercive ideals. Perhaps most simply, enlightenment means *improvement*.

Yet, for Adorno and Horkheimer, writing during the Second World War and the Holocaust, the promise of enlightenment described by Kant is self-evidently empty. At its most rudimentary level, enlightenment promises improvement, and there is little evidence of *improvement* in a world marked by war and genocide. "Enlightenment, understood in the widest sense as the advance of thought," Adorno and Horkheimer write, "has always aimed at liberating human beings from fear and installing them as masters. Yet the wholly enlightened earth is radiant with triumphant calamity" (*Dialectic* 2). In the face of industrialized war, of the rationalized murder of millions, and, later, nuclear proliferation and environmental degradation (which is ongoing even as I write these words), how should we understand this failure of reason? To be sure, the enlightenment continues to have its defenders and even partisans,[11] but Adorno and Horkheimer refuse to consider enlightenment as simply a force for good. They see in reason not the achieved maturity of mankind, that Kant describes, but mastery run amok. The failure of enlightenment stems from a fundamental misunderstanding about its nature. Where partisans of the enlightenment from Kant forward see the distinction between superstition (or myth) and enlightenment as absolute, Adorno and Horkheimer find them woven together throughout history. As their title suggests, myth and enlightenment form a dialectic—an ongoing, historical process, in which each term produces the other.

The concept of *dialectic* is central to Adorno's work, and so crucial to his understanding of media and modernism. Drawing on both Marx and Hegel, Adorno's reworking of the dialectic late in

---

[11]Steven Pinker, for instance, insists that when seen in the proper context, despite the apparent catastrophes of the twentieth century, Enlightenment continues apace, and improvement continues—things are getting better. Far more moderately, Adorno's own student, Habermas, speaks of *modernity* as an "unfinished project."

his career (as "negative dialectics") is one of the most challenging aspects of an already formidable thinker's career.[12] The basic idea of dialectic, however, begins with conversation—etymologically, dialectic is related to the art of rhetoric and debate. It includes the interrogatory method of Plato's dialogues, by which truth is reached not through simple deduction but a process of discourse and disagreement. As Williams notes, nineteenth-century German philosophy (chiefly Hegel) "extended the notion of contradiction in the course of discussion or dispute to a notion of contradictions in reality," becoming in Marxism "a progressive unification through the contradiction of opposites" (*Keywords* 92). Adorno and Horkheimer's "dialectic of enlightenment" stages just such a process between the apparent opposites of *enlightenment* and *myth*. In each term, they detect an element of its apparent opposite. Myth, they insist, is already a form of enlightenment. It abstracts the world and tries to account for it, to explain it. Think, for instance, of origin myths. Such stories "sought to report, to name, to tell of origins—but therefore also to narrate, record, explain" (*Dialectic* 5). Such beliefs do not meet science's criteria for explanation, yet they nevertheless represent an attempt, perhaps the first attempts in human history, to render the world comprehensible and, crucially, to bring it under the sway of human control. Ceremony, ritual, and magic are already a step toward engineering the world through scientific mastery.

Just as myth is already a sort of enlightenment, so too is enlightenment itself always, at least potentially, mythic. Despite its pretensions to rationality, it harbors myth within itself and can easily collapse into a fetishistic worship of impersonal forces, akin to the fetishism of commodities described by Marx. The "free market," for instance, is mythologized as an agent, as perhaps, even, a god who can only be propitiated through rituals of quantitative easing, interest rate adjustment, and fiscal stimulus.[13] The judgments

---

[12] Adorno's *Negative Dialectics* offers a radical revision of the concept of dialectic which seeks to preserve the sense of process and development without collapsing into the identity or synthesis which is typically imagined as emerging from a dialectical process, and which sometimes introduces the (to Adorno, false) idea that the dialectic moves toward a goal or *telos*.

[13] For a brisk and excellent account of our contemporary economic moment, and how it reproduces some of this faith in markets, see Stephen Metcalf's "Neoliberalism: The Idea That Swallowed the World."

of science can take on a mythic quality—not because they are "untrue" in the narrow sense, but because they are incomplete, and so end up soliciting the kind of worshipful reverence once reserved for myth. The world, to science, appears only as something to be measured, counted, and empirically analyzed. "The world as a gigantic analytical judgment, the only surviving dream of science, is of the same kind as the cosmic myth which linked the alternation of spring and autumn to the abduction of Persephone" (*Dialectic* 20). Or, more tersely (and more damningly), "Animism had endowed things with souls; industrialism makes souls into things" (*Dialectic* 21). Such is the central thesis of *Dialectic of Enlightenment*. Adorno and Horkheimer offer a quasi-history of human existence that extends from prehistory to the present, modifying similar accounts offered by Hegel and Marx. While a Marxian sense of the mode of production informs this history, Adorno and Horkheimer's focus is not the mode of production per se, but the historical development of reason, and its fate under the conditions of industrialized capitalism.

The Culture Industry

But what does this have to do with media? Adorno and Horkheimer trace enlightenment's inability to deliver on its promise of an improved world to the deceptions and failures of mass culture under capitalism. They conclude the first chapter of *Dialectic of Enlightenment* writing that the advance of knowledge has finally made possible the English philosopher Francis Bacon's (1561–1626) dream of humanity using "its knowledge for the betterment of its condition" (*Dialectic* 1). Since Bacon, knowledge has sufficiently developed to make that possibility real. "But in the face of this possibility enlightenment, in the service of the present, is turning itself into an outright deception of the masses" (34). This "deception of the masses" thwarts and impedes the dialectic from overcoming its present condition, becoming what Adorno and Horkheimer call *the culture industry*, and what others have called "mass culture"—that mode of cultural production that emerged in the second half of the nineteenth century and is, for a whole host of figures, modernism's peculiar shadow twin.

Art of an earlier period, prior to the emergence of the culture industry, offered an image that prefigured the utopian freedom which enlightenment promises. The pleasure and beauties of art reconciled the individual and the collective. In art, freedom and necessity are not in opposition. Kant's idea of beauty as expressing "purposiveness without purpose" (*Critique* 73)—a sense of meaningfulness which is nevertheless unconstrained by any particular meaning—is a similar formulation. Adorno follows the nineteenth-century French writer Stendhal (whom he is fond of referencing) in imagining that art offers a promise of happiness—a promise, not the thing itself. This image of freedom and happiness contained in art was necessarily imperfect, because it was only ever an unrealized image. Art, in this view, reaches its apex around the turn of the nineteenth century. As Martin Jay elaborates, "if Adorno ever had a positive vision of the reconciled work of art as a prefiguration of a rationally totalized, yet non-dominating social whole, it was in the music of Beethoven's middle period" (143). While Adorno's writing can feel relentlessly pessimistic, his descriptions of Beethoven offer respite, granting a rare glimpse of what freedom might actually look like. "Beethoven represented the highest moment of bourgeois humanism, the clearest embodiment of practical reason in sensuous terms, the greatest realization of active subjectivity in objective musical patterns" (Jay 141). Beethoven specifically, but bourgeois art more broadly (roughly, the art of the late eighteenth and early nineteenth centuries), offered something that was neither pure speculation nor practical action, but a realm of individual, subjective freedom. This is the freedom to which Adorno's halves no longer "add up." The freedom expressed in bourgeois art was limited in fundamental ways: only a small, cultural elite could appreciate works of bourgeois culture (like Beethoven's music), and, more fundamentally, it was limited by being a purely *aesthetic* experience—it was a promise of happiness, not happiness itself. Yet even in this limited state, the vision of enlightened freedom offered by art was a genuine glimpse of a reconciled social world, free from exploitation and instrumentality. It offered an image worthy of utopian ambition. With the progress of enlightenment however, that only-ever partial refuge has been torn asunder and replaced by, on the one hand, a culture industry that offers a degraded vision of happiness as mere pleasure or entertainment, and modernist art, which keeps art's "promise of happiness" alive only negatively, by more thoroughly denying it and testifying to its absence.

To the culture industry, this realm of art, like nature itself, loses any positive identity of its own and becomes the raw material for the manufacture of commodities. It is taken over and colonized by the same enlightenment reason that dethroned superstition and mastered nature. Jameson calls the idea of the culture industry "Adorno's single most influential—and also provocative, and even notorious—concept" (*Late* 139). The culture industry describes "the implacable expansion and penetration of 'enlightenment' (or of 'positivism', if you prefer another version) into the mind itself, into subjectivity, in modern times" (*Late* 107). When instrumental reason invades culture, it produces a quantifiable, standardized product. Differences within the products of the culture industry, of genre or quality, are merely superficial. What the culture industry produces is uniformity and sameness. You're free to like jazz or country music, to prefer Cary Grant to Grant Cooper, comedies to melodramas, *Star Trek* to *Star Wars*, Coke to Pepsi, Brittany to Beyoncé. But such preferences are empty and meaningless. As Adorno and Horkheimer put it, "Something is provided for everyone so that no one can escape" (*Dialectic* 97).

The culture industry then operates as away of managing the masses. The films, music, and entertainment of the culture industry are offered to "those who want to escape the mechanized labor process" (*Dialectic* 109). But in reality it offers no escape at all. While Benjamin suggests that film provides a sort of training for modernity and celebrates distraction as a modern mode of aesthetic appreciation ("Work of Art" 37–9), Adorno and Horkheimer see it as an empty distraction from suffering. Popular culture merely placates people to keep them working. Hollywood films and popular music offer only a parade of uniformity. Movie plots are repetitive and simplified; characters are flattened. Popular music offers an endless parade of purportedly novel songs, all of which are fundamentally similar, exemplifying "the most deep-seated contradiction of capitalism" in the realm of culture: a simultaneous desire for novelty and sameness, for something "original" that is "just like" what has already been successful ("On Jazz" 54). As a result, all the culture industry really provides are "after-images of the work process," entertainment that delivers only another version of the same oppression that it promises escape from. Even in cartoons, Adorno and Horkheimer detect the exploitation of the larger social system. "Donald Duck in the cartoons and the unfortunate victim in real life receive their beatings so that spectators can accommodate themselves to theirs" (*Dialectic* 110). And so "Entertainment is the prolongation of work under late capitalism" (*Dialectic* 109). In granting such a key role to entertainment, *Dialectic of Enlightenment* departs from traditional Marxist understandings of culture as merely epiphenomenal, as a *superstructure* that expresses some more fundamental logic of the mode of production. In this older model, social change and evolution must occur at the level of the *base*—of the economy or the mode of production. Adorno and Horkheimer, however, grant power to culture in its ability to manipulate reason and to deceive the masses. If enlightenment is the force that gradually subsumes all nature and human life, the culture industry represents its extension into the realm of art and human subjectivity. This at once makes the realm of culture more important and, as the culture industry, more insidious. Rather than a mere epiphenomenon, culture comes to play a key role in the maintenance of capitalist domination.

The culture industry, blob-like, absorbs the incidental differences between media. While Adorno and Horkheimer are not inattentive to differences between media technologies (indeed some of Adorno's most fascinating writing on media comes in his essays on the gramophone, on radio, or his later essays on film), the particular properties of individual media are all subsumed by the power of the culture industry. The specific technological characteristics of individual media do not have the importance that they did for McLuhan (or will, later, for Friedrich Kittler). "Interested parties," they write, "like to explain the culture industry in technological terms." However, the uniformity and standardization that Adorno and Horkheimer detect in the culture industry "should not be attributed to the internal laws of technology itself but to its function within the economy today" (*Dialectic* 95). The archival orientation of contemporary media studies is often at odds with such generic conclusions. The undifferentiated sameness of the commodity form that Adorno and Horkheimer find lurking beneath every object of popular culture belies any insistence on medium specificity. Adorno and Horkheimer's understanding of media nevertheless provides a key model for understanding media as inextricably enmeshed in, and an expressive of, social forces and histories outside technology itself. As Jonathan Sterne, one of the preeminent contemporary scholars of media studies, notes

> Adorno and Horkheimer's analysis of mass culture has been much maligned in the past few years as elitist, but a serious reading of their work shows their attention to many of the issues now dominating the analysis of mass culture—the increasing concentration of media ownership and the commodity status of entertainment—as well as their attention to the aesthetic dimensions of mass-cultural experience.
>
> (*Audible* 157)

The Frankfurt School focuses on those larger forces that operate through media rather than the media themselves. The idea of the "culture industry" works against the medium specificity that motivates much of more recent media studies. N. Katherine Hayles's insistence on "the importance of media-specific analysis," for example, is decidedly at odds with Adorno and Horkheimer's understanding of a single "culture industry." For Hayles, understanding *radio* or *film* necessarily requires a fine-grained attention to medium. (We might even begin to think that perhaps *the medium is the message*.)[14] To use a more recent term, we might say the culture industry exists *transmedially*.[15] Adorno and Horkheimer describe a system where "a branch of art follows the same recipe as one far removed from it in terms of its medium and subject matter," where a film is cobbled together from the plot

---

[14] As Hayles notes, "medium specific analysis" is "[i]n many ways this is a return to the agenda set by Marshall McLuhan" ("Print" 68fn1).

[15] The idea of *transmedia* was popularized by Henry Jenkins to describe the way that popular culture (especially franchises like Star Wars, the Marvel Universe, and others) operates across media. To use it to describe "the culture industry" may seem surprising (given Jenkins's largely positive, and celebratory assessment of transmedia, and popular culture more broadly). But Adorno and Horkheimer already note the way that culture industry products operate across media in *Dialectic of Enlightenment*. In comparing the culture industry to the logic of advertising, they note how the uniformity and regularity of the culture create a "factory-like" situation where every film exists chiefly as a preview for the others ("anyone arriving late cannot tell whether he is watching the trailer or the real thing"), and which is "factory-like not only in the film studio but also, virtually, in the compilation of the cheap biographies, journalistic novels, and hit songs" (132). Indeed, when Jenkins describes "transmedia storytelling" in an age of "convergence culture," it can easily feel like the chief thing that separates his analysis from Adorno and Horkheimer's account of the culture industry under late capitalism is that Jenkins celebrates those very forces that Adorno and Horkheimer condemn.

of a novel and a piece of a Beethoven symphony (*Dialectic* 96). Under such conditions, attention to the particular materialities and affordances of a medium is not useful. Such a perspective may even be debilitating, missing the forest of cultural production under capitalism for the medium-specific trees.

Radio provides an interesting opportunity both to examine Adorno's approach to a particular medium and how medium specificity ultimately pales in importance to the facts of reification and the commodity form. In a number of essays, some only published recently,[16] Adorno offers more medium-specific and textured analysis of radio.[17] These works show an attention to medium that is absent in Adorno's better-known writing (to English speakers) on the culture industry and media (including *Dialectic of Enlightenment* and "On the Fetish Character of Music"), though this work remains consistent with the notion of the culture industry. David Jenemann's *Adorno in America* (2007) shows how important Adorno's experience working in America, studying the culture industry directly, was to Adorno's understanding of media. After fleeing Nazi Germany, Adorno (after a stay in Oxford) arrived in the United States in 1938 and worked as part of Paul Lazarfeld's Princeton Radio Research Project. Lazarfeld's work used surveys and empirical social science to study radio reception and its effects on listeners. Jenemann shows how the position articulated in *Dialectic of Enlightenment* is not simply an aloof dismissal of the culture industry, but reflects the perspective of a critic and scholar who had seen directly the ways that listeners were quantified and dissected for advertisers.

So, how did Adorno understand the specificity of radio as a medium? As a sound medium, radio radically separates the hearer of a sound from its producer. In theory, this makes it a potentially rich channel for modernist experiments sound, like those described of Pierre Schaeffer or the BBC's radiophonic workshop. Schaeffer, the founder of *musique concrète*, used recorded sounds and sound manipulation in the service of music composition. Schaeffer sought an autonomy for sound similar to the purification that Greenberg

---

[16]Much of Adorno's work on radio stems from his time working with the Princeton Radio Research Project. Much of this work is collected in *Current of Music*, published in English in 2009.

[17]Adorno also addresses specific media in his essays on the phonograph, "The Curves of the Needle," and his essay on film, "Transparencies on Film."

describes in modernist painting. In his *Treatise on Musical Objects* (1966), Schaeffer describes *acousmatic sound*, sound without reference to its origin or source (in an instrument, say), as enabling a "pure listening" (97). Such sound technologies were at the center of the experiments of the BBC's radiophonic workshop, starting in the late 1950s, as described in Louis Niebur's *Special Sound: The Creation and Legacy of the BBC Radiophonic Workshop* (2010). Radio could enable modernist works like the radiophonic poem, "Private Dreams and Public Nighmares" (1962), written by Frederick Bradnum with music composed by Daphne Oram. Rather than being chiefly a way to disseminate music, radio might itself become an instrument. Adorno could certainly imagine this possibility. "The idea," Adorno wrote at one point, "is that we should no longer broadcast over the radio but play on the radio in the same sense that one plays on a violin" (qtd. in Hullot-Kentor 115). In a brief comment, Adorno even considers the theremin, a musical instrument that is played by moving one's hands between two antennae to alter the pitch and volume of a tone, as one potential avenue for exploiting the radio as a medium of artistic creation *rather than* a technology of reproduction (Hullot-Kentor 115). Perhaps surprisingly, for a figure often caricatured as old-fashioned, Adorno seemed similarly open to the potential of electronic music at the end of his career.

Yet such possibilities of radio as a *modernist* medium are downplayed in Adorno's analysis of radio. This reflects the historical fact that these possibilities remained dormant and largely unrealized within radio as a medium, as the culture industry instrumentalized the medium toward other ends. Indeed, the experiments of the BBC's radiophonic workshop were most successful when they ended up as part of the culture industry—as in the theme for the television show *Dr. Who* that the radiophonic workshop developed. The culture industry treats radio, like all mass communication technologies, solely as a means, and so fails to fully explore the inherent properties of the medium itself. The culture industry employs radio as a *reproducer* of other sounds, and so effaces its own mediating power. Radio ends up being, in Robert Hullot-Kentor's words, "a mode of production that characteristically imitates nature rather than fulfills its own productive potential" (112). Adorno focuses not on radio as it could be, but on actually existing radio, as it was used by the culture industry. He treats radio, in Jenemann's words, "as a symptom of an entire network of social processes" (54). Stemming from his work with the Princeton Research Project, the bulk of Adorno's writing on the radio examines its potential as a way to broadcast (rather than make) music, and his assessment is unsurprisingly negative. Adorno's account of radio focuses on (1) the radio as commodity; (2) a phenomenological consideration of the experience of radio listening, with a particular focus on the *voice*; and (3) a focus on the *broadcast* character of radio. At each of these levels, like the culture industry more broadly, what radio presents deceives the listener. It promises one thing, while being in reality another. Consider even the last recourse of the listener who is utterly frustrated by what she hears on the radio—simply turning the device off. Adorno describes observing "people switch off their radios with a sort of wild joy, just as if they were shouting, 'I shut his mouth for him!'" Such a gesture, Adorno writes, "is the most fruitless of all. It creates the illusion of might and power, but it really means only that the rebel is withdrawing from contact with the very public events he believes he is altering" (*Current* 113). What looks like social action (a response to the radio, shutting it off) is, in reality, a sort of retreat from action.

A similar sense of deception is reflected in radio's relationship to the commodity character of modern society. While one must purchase a radio, listening to the radio seems to be free. Tuning in to a broadcast and listening feels wholly different from *buying* something. Radio's ambient availability makes it feel as free as the very air through which its waves travel. But in fact, for Adorno and Horkheimer, this indicates that the reified commodity form has only been more totally absorbed by the medium. Rather than escaping reification, radio emblematizes the wider condition of art in which "the commodity character of art disintegrates just as it is fully realized" (*Dialectic* 128). And so while one freely tunes in, behind the scenes radio's financial existence is supported by corporate advertisers who offer broadcasts of symphony performances for the public benefit. "The deception takes place indirectly *via* the profit of all the united automobile and soap manufacturers, on whose payments the stations survive" (*Dialectic* 128). In obscuring the commodity capitalism on which it nevertheless depends, radio is guiltier than other media of the *deception* which Adorno and Horkheimer identify as the chief work of the culture industry. "[Radio] thereby takes on the deceptive form of a disinterested, impartial authority, which fits fascism like a glove" (*Dialectic* 129).

This *fascistic* dimension of radio, however, is even more evident in the experience of listening to radio. While the radio itself does not speak, it nevertheless, Adorno suggests, has a voice of its own. The radio voice, as Adorno calls it, is the force that permeates every content the radio might broadcast. Adorno's "radio voice," as Brian Kane notes in a 2016 essay, "is the sound *of* the radio, not any particular voices or any particular content heard over the airwaves. It is the name Adorno gives to radio's how elements, taken in toto" ("Phenomenology" 98). As used in actual broadcast, it is the *medium* rather than simply its particular messages or content that is fascistic. A key element of the radio voice is a sense of closeness and proximity to the listener.[18] The effect of such closeness is to elide the mediating role of the radio itself. While it is clear to all listeners that the radio *itself* is not speaking, nevertheless, the radio voice "can dispense with the intermediary, objectivating stage of printing which helps to clarify the difference between fiction and reality" (*Current* 47). A medium like print has the advantage of being self-evidently *not* the thing it mediates, its mediation is explicit and clear. But radio, like film in Adorno's analysis elsewhere, is slavishly dedicated to the task of reproduction. Hullot-Kentor writes, "Radio broadcast ... transforms music into a relation between original and reproduction. The original necessarily becomes a fetish that the reproduction seeks to achieve" (114). Technological reproduction here does not eliminate aura, as Benjamin hoped, but parasitically feeds off it. In moments of privacy, the radio voice seems to uniquely address the listener, rather than foregrounding its reproducible anonymity. Rather than undoing aura, radio dissembles the mechanical reproduction that enables it and strives to establish a false intimacy with the listener, with, for Adorno, predictably dire effects. The Nazi use of radio is a key example for

---

[18] We might trace some of this deceptive closeness to another technology, the microphone. While early phonograph recording required artists to sing, speak, or even *yell* into a horn, the development of electrical microphones allowed a voice to be recorded that would have been far too quiet to be recorded by earlier means. The *crooning* of crooners, like Bing Crosby, was enabled by this technology which creates a sense of proximity between the recorded voice and the listener that can be closer than anything one could experience at a concert (Chanan 68–9).

Adorno's thinking, and he traces much of German fascism's power to radio as a technology. What looks like the "*Führer*'s metaphysical charisma" is in fact simply the ubiquity of radio, "the omnipresence of his radio address" (*Dialectic* 129).

Adorno's Modernism

Adorno's brief interest in radio experiments reflects the way that his understanding of media is always in connection to the larger forces that make those media meaningful. In modernity, no art or medium has its meaning outside relation to the culture industry. Modernism too is submitted to this requirement. If the culture industry is one product of instrumental reason's expansion into culture, modernism is another. The dialectical process that tore apart the limited experience of freedom accessible in Beethoven and the high bourgeois culture of the nineteenth century produced the two broken halves that Adorno described in his 1936 letter to Benjamin. Genuine art in the period of the culture industry, for Adorno, was necessarily difficult and challenging; it was modernist art, exemplified by figures like Samuel Beckett (to whom Adorno had planned to dedicate his posthumously published *Aesthetic Theory*) in literature and, in music, Adorno's own former teacher Arnold Schoenberg. Not all the art that conventional histories describe as "modernist," however, met Adorno's, at times idiosyncratic, criteria. Stravinsky, famously, earned Adorno's disdain, as did the later work of Schoenberg (which moved from so-called "free atonality" to a more rigid embrace of a twelve-tone system of composition). Unlike Benjamin, Adorno was no fan of Dadaism or the other European avant-gardes (in Peter Bürger's sense), who, in their zeal to reunite everyday life and art, Adorno thought, artificially healed the wound of modernity that true modernism must seek to express.

Whatever one makes of Adorno's judgments about individual artists, Adorno's understanding of genuine modernist art was dialectically united to his vision of the culture industry. As Tyrus Miller puts it, the culture industry is "modernism's dialectical complement and secret sharer" (81). If instrumental reason has corrupted the domain of art and created the culture industry, genuine art can survive only by acknowledging this state—not by pretending it didn't happen and continuing to create art as it had previously done. To continue to write novels as Charles Dickens and George Eliot did, or to compose symphonies in the style of Beethoven, would be as hollow and empty as Adorno and Horkheimer find the culture industry itself. Modernist art absorbs the reified state of the world in order to reflect it back as an inoculation against ultimate destruction. "The history of modern art," Adorno writes, "is largely that of the ineluctable loss of metaphysical meaning" ("Art and the Arts" 383). This disappearance of "metaphysical meaning" in modern art is evident in the loss of many traditional aesthetic categories across the arts: harmony in classical music, representation in the visual arts, or plot, character, and even *meaning* in literature. Adorno offers an essentially social and historical explanation for why these fundamental categories disappear in modernist art. Art is swept up in a gradual "erosion" of meaning. Yet, "[t]he nonmeaningful realities that find their way into the domain of art in the course of erosion are potentially salvaged as meaningful by art, at the same moment as they fly in the face of the traditional meaning of art" ("Art and the Arts" 385). Art may look as though it is falling apart, because it "fl[ies] in the face of the traditional meaning of art," but it is instead engaged in a salvage operation, recovering some vestige of genuine meaning from a world where such meaning is being eroded away by the totalizing force of capitalism.

It is in this sense that we should understand Adorno's most widely quoted maxim: that there can be no poetry after Auschwitz. It means almost the opposite of what it is typically taken to mean: not the weakness of art in the present situation, but its profound strength. As Jameson notes, "If everything in Adorno leads into the aesthetic, everything in Adorno's aesthetics leads out again in the direction of history" (*Late* 239). Even as modernist art forsakes the conventional structures and pleasures of art, it nevertheless has an almost world-historical importance. "Art presents humanity with the dream of its doom so that humanity may awaken, remain in control of itself, and survive" ("Art and the Arts" 385). The dissolution of bourgeois culture was necessary because it was not true to the concept of culture, which requires *freedom for all*. Post-bourgeois art, i.e. modernist art, keeps that hope alive, even in a damaged and unrealized form. As Adorno elaborates,

> While the present situation no longer has room for art—that was the meaning of the statement about the impossibility of poems after Auschwitz—it nevertheless has need of it. For reality without images is the counterpart of another condition without images: the condition in which art disappears because the utopia encoded in every work of art has been fulfilled. In itself art is not capable of such a demise.
>
> ("Art and the Arts" 387)

While the tone of *Dialectic of Enlightenment* is relentlessly pessimistic, in the most surprising dialectical turn of all, Adorno is a fundamentally optimistic figure, detecting in modernist art a utopian grasping toward a way of living that has finally realized the promise of enlightenment, and achieved a world without exploitation.

Adorno's binary definition of modernism and the culture industry as mutually exclusive recalls Clement Greenberg's earlier contrast between avant-garde and kitsch. Adorno and Greenberg both, as Richard Leppert notes in his commentary on Adorno's essay on "Music and Mass Culture" (2002), "understood kitsch as commercial, mass-produced, formulaic, standardized, and aesthetically and politically rear-guard ersatz culture, which feeds off genuine culture but only for the purpose of enjoying the profits that might accrue from the recognition and/or patina of prestige and comfort that such culture might provide" (Leppert in Adorno, *Essays* 363). Both Greenberg and Adorno describe kitsch as *predigested* art. Kitsch, Greenberg writes, "*predigests art* for the spectator and spares him the effort, provides him with a short cut to the pleasure of art" ("Avant-Garde and Kitsch" 13, my emphasis). Adorno echoes Greenberg, in describing the "*pre-digested quality*" of mass cultural objects, which are preformed by the culture industry for the ready consumption of a universal consumer. Such culture is, Adorno writes, "baby-food ... based upon the infantile compulsion towards the repetition of needs which it creates in the first place" ("Schema of Mass Culture" 67). Yet, these remarkably similar descriptions belie very different understandings of modernism. Greenberg's account of the relationship between avant-garde and kitsch is as binaristic as Adorno's description of modernism and the culture industry, and is, at least in his early essays, equally grounded in a socioeconomic context. Yet, Adorno's binarism is always a dialectical one, in which the "torn halves" remain indissolubly related to one another. The art that Greenberg celebrates as a value in itself is, for Adorno, intelligible only in relation to the degraded state of the world. Its power is that it preserves negatively a vision of an unrealized and utopian possibility. Where Greenberg sees a quest for purity, Adorno sees a strategic retreat, or an embattled way station in a still incomplete history. Despite their apparent similarities, then, Adorno rejects the value of purity in Greenberg's sense. For Adorno, the autonomy of modernist art was never absolute. Instead, "autonomy was a relational phenomenon, not a mechanism to justify formalist amnesia" (Huyssen 57). The "great divide" between modernism and mass culture is not an absolute separation, but what Andreas Huyssen calls, drawing on Freudian psychoanalysis, a "reaction formation" (57). If Greenberg describes modernist art as fragmenting into its constituent arts, each on a quest to purify itself in relation to its medium, Adorno suggests, instead, that each art dialectically struggles against its own medium, or what Adorno calls "the chance nature of its quasi-natural aspects." What unites the disparate arts as *art* is not some shared quest for medial purity, but simply *negation* itself ("Art and the Arts" 383).

Such negation is not simply destructive, but is the Hegelian force that propels the dialectic, that maintains the utopian promise of enlightenment by rejecting its incomplete realization in the present. J. M. Bernstein notes that, unlike Greenberg, "Adorno was not trying to prescribe the future course of art; rather he was intent on revealing the truth content of high modernism, a truth content he knew to be fast disappearing" (20).[19] Modernism is therefore not a *purely* aesthetic experience; it has "truth content." Aesthetic autonomy in Adorno's sense means not utter separation from the social world, but being sufficiently distant to allow art to reflect and critique the social world from which it emerges. It injects works of a high modernist tradition (or at least Adorno's version of that tradition), with an ability to enact social critique. Even works like the plays of Samuel Beckett or the fiction of Franz Kafka, which seem to lack any political content, become political in this wider sense. To those who do not accept, or are uninterested in the larger

---

[19]This is perhaps unfair to Greenberg, who was often explicit that he was not *prescribing* what art should do.

dialectical history which Adorno's perspective on modernism reflects, this is a distinction without a difference—it is a lot of hemming and hawing to ultimately insist on a position that might still look like the elitism of Greenberg. But within the dialectical history Adorno and Horkheimer offer, modernism emerges not as a retreat from the world, but as the fiercest critique of it.

This understanding of modernism, however, exists in tension with the understanding of modernism elaborated by the New Modernist Studies over the past two decades. Where the latter is expansive, Adorno is exclusive; where it undoes barriers, Adorno's modernism, just as much as Greenberg's, is defined by what it excludes. While many of the Frankfurt School's preoccupations—with politics, with understanding media in relation to larger social forces and histories—persist in the New Modernist Studies, Adorno's modernism bears a defining, essential relationship to negativity that is absent from most of the New Modernist Studies.

The example of radio provides a useful opportunity to chart these similarities and differences. Modernist radio, from the perspective of the more recent scholarship, is a more complex, and less singularly determined phenomenon than Adorno's account allows. Where he sees a medium whose potential has been reduced and shaped by the singular, fascistic imposition of the commodity form, more recent scholarship explores radio as inflected by categories like nation, gender, race, and class in ways not captured by a focus on the culture industry alone. Beginning with the essays of *Broadcasting Modernism* (2009), edited by Debra Rae Cohen, Michael Coyle, and Jane Lewty, this scholarship broadens an understanding of radio in the modernist period beyond the mainstream commercial radio broadcasts that Adorno takes as typical and opposes to a proper high modernism. The New Modernist Studies does so in two directions: first, by examining the challenging uses of radio as an aesthetic medium by Samuel Beckett and Dylan Thomas, among others, as well as the broadcasts of radio by writers like T. S. Eliot, Ezra Pound, Louis MacNeice. Melissa Dinsman's *Modernism at the Microphone: Radio, Propaganda, and Literary Aesthetics During World War II* (2015) continues this excavation, examining the radio work of Ezra Pound, Dorothy Sayers, and writers at the BBC, to explore the connections between war and radio. But it also turns its attention to neglected uses of radio—uses that are neither high canonical nor mainstream and commercial, but attempts to take advantage of the medium's possibilities for other ends. Indeed, the sharpest distinction between the Frankfurt School's account of modernism and its media and the New Modernist Studies' is the latter's utter lack of interest in preserving the sharp binary between modernism and mass culture. The Frankfurt School views culture as absolutely split (those torn halves again), where the New Modernist Studies tends to see, and celebrate, a different model of culture, as either an undifferentiated plane on which cultural items and figures interact or a network of individual nodes, connecting and relating in sometimes surprising and unanticipated ways. Dinsman, for instance, reads Adorno's work on radio alongside the panic surrounding Orson Welles's 1938 *The War of the Worlds* broadcast (32–54).

In the "radio voice" in particular, the New Modernist Studies discovers a phenomenon less univocal than Adorno describes. Rather than the singular radio voice that Adorno discusses, Pamela Caughie suggests that the disembodied voice (evident as well in the telephone and the phonograph) "serves to destabilise class, racial and gender identities" and so "gives rise to a new kind of subjectivity in the modernist era" (94). The alienation from the self created by technologies of mass reproduction is a more uneven and ambivalent phenomenon than the Frankfurt School account of it allows. A disembodied voice alienates the individual from herself, but it also reveals the ways that categories like gender and race shape our understanding of voice. Indeed, as much recent modernist scholarship has insisted, the idea of a radio voice looks very different once race and gender are considered. Such alienation not only enables mankind to contemplate its own destruction with aesthetic pleasure (as Benjamin describes) or masochistically revel in its own debasement (as in Adorno's account of jazz) but creates an ambiguous space for identity. "Sound technology raises the possibility of a discrepancy, not a correspondence, between the individual and its vocal embodiment" (Caughie 107). The place of accents, to signify class or race, plays a key role in the history of the phonograph, for instance (as discussed by Lisa Gitelman, *Scripts* 119–47). The disembodied voice in the New Modernist Studies is a more variously inflected phenomenon than Adorno's account allows.

The New Modernist Studies shares with Adorno an understanding of media as intrinsically political, though with an expanded understanding of what politics is. The political focus of recent scholarship on modernist radio typically highlights categories more granular than the Frankfurt School's concentration on fascism and capitalism alone. Rather than the history of art and mechanical reproduction, or the development of enlightenment, the New Modernist Studies inserts radio into histories that are more textured and local. Viewing radio in relation to nation, empire, and war has proved to be a particularly fruitful avenue. In addressing Irish radio, Emily Bloom's *The Wireless Past: Anglo-Irish Writers and the BBC, 1931–1968* (2016) and Damien Keane's *Ireland and the Problem of Information: Irish Writing, Radio, Late Modernist Communication* (2014) complicate our sense of radio's relationship to nation. Bloom notes that in the Irish context, radio (because an acoustic, and largely linguistic medium) seemed well-suited to the nationalist cause—as a venue for Irish-language broadcasts and a platform for nationalist education. Indeed, the first Irish radio broadcast (in Morse code, using a radio unit seized from a ship) was during the 1916 Nationalist Uprising (as McLuhan notes, *Understanding* 304). Yet radio waves do not respect national borders, and radio's promiscuity as a broadcast medium meant that it "was quickly reinterpreted by its listeners as an instrument for transnational communication" (Bloom 12). Bloom continues, "While radio often originates out of national institutions and while broadcasting structures tend to stem from a nationalist ethos, in practice they have the potential to mediate across national borders, revealing the fluidity if not the arbitrariness of those borders, and to create transnational imagined publics" (15). Here, as in much post-Frankfurt School media studies, reception is reimagined, not as a passive acceptance, but as a process of negotiation between a broadcast and its listeners. Keane's account reads radio alongside other forms to explore the complexity of Ireland's interwar position (Ireland remained neutral during the Second World War).

Where Adorno and Horkheimer seek to articulate how radio expresses the dominant forces of capitalist instrumental reason, the New Modernist Studies often seems to be excavating those moments that resist or escape this logic. In *Writing the Radio War: Literature, Politics, and the BBC, 1939–1945* (2018), Ian Whittington notes that "these complex and multiple listening publics were not passive vessels for the reception of a version of national or imperial identity dictated from on high, but were instead critical and reflexive communities whose engagement with radio spilled over into adjacent media" (12). In a discussion of the Jamaican poet Una Marson and her radio work, Whittington describes "the ambivalent power wartime broadcasting offered to British colonial subjects" (157). Even as writers like Marson wished to join anti-fascist wartime broadcasts, they had to negotiate the complexities of the BBC in a colonial context. "Many late-colonial writers were reluctant to broadcast on behalf of the BBC because of the complicated signals such cooperation sent to listeners overseas" (157). The politics of radio here is ambiguous. Even as the radio voice of the BBC was foremost the voice of empire, it also allowed the creation of communities of resistance that otherwise might not exist. Indeed, Tom McEnaney captures a similar ambivalence in a very different context in *Acoustic Properties: Radio, Narrative, and the New Neighborhood of the Americas* (2017), suggesting that far from being uniformly subsumed by fascist uses in the way Adorno describes, "radio broadcasting technology became the chosen medium for writers and political activists to theorize, represent, and construct a political voice through which the people can speak" (141).

There are also important methodological differences between Adorno's treatment of radio and the recent burst of interest in modernist radio. Much of this recent scholarship is grounded in archival research. It often stresses details that the Frankfurt School approach ignores, but also reveals the role that various institutions played in shaping the production and radio—including governmental and state institutions like the BBC and Radio Free Europe. The BBC emerges as a crucial institution connecting modernist and postcolonial writers in Peter Kalliney's *Commonwealth of Letters: British Literary Culture and the Emergence of Postcolonial Aesthetics* (2013). This research also tends to highlight "intermediality," exploring radio through its relationship to other media (especially print) rather than either the Toronto School's medium-specific mode of analysis, or the Frankfurt School's tendency to see in all media a single culture industry. Debra Rae Cohen's "Intermediality and the Problem of the *Listener*" (2012) illustrates this well by focusing the BBC magazine *The Listener*, published by the BBC as a sort of adjunct to its broadcasts, complicating the separate categories through which we typically understand the media of the first half of the twentieth century.

While the sense of history and the mode of politics that the New Modernist Studies finds in media, including radio, is more ambiguous and textured than the story of reification charted by Adorno, contemporary studies of modernist radio follow the Frankfurt School in seeing radio not simply as a technology, but as expressing, and shaped by, larger social forces. The New Modernist Studies rejects the flat uniformity of the radio voice as described by Adorno, and his characterization of the medium's politics as more or less fascist. Yet, rather than a simple rejection, we might equally understand contemporary approaches to modernist radio as enriching and complicating the Frankfurt School's tradition of understanding technology in relation to processes of mass culture, reification, and commodification. It shows these processes to be more complex, shot through with markers of race and class that were themselves able to be made into commodities, and it explores the more ambivalent and variegated elements of the medium's politics.

5

Friedrich Kittler and Media Archaeology: The End of the Book and the Birth of the Modernist Discourse Network

The tendency of individual media technologies to be dissolved into "the culture industry," discussed in the previous chapter, finds its sharpest contrast in the work of Friedrich Kittler. Where the Frankfurt School's dialectical history understands media as expressions of capitalism, Kittler's focus is resolutely on the media technologies themselves. Like McLuhan, he grants technology priority; unlike McLuhan, it is the materiality of the media themselves to which Kittler grants power, not their function as prostheses. The theories of previous chapters have imagined media as the bearers of other forces—of art, of the human senses, of history. Kittler is fascinated by the mechanism itself.

Kittler's media theory is an exorcism. It is an act of disenchantment, which seeks to purge all metaphysics from our understanding of meaning. Where German idealist thought had imagined a Geist, or Spirit, informing history—a vision still detectable (albeit in altered ways) in the Frankfurt School—Kittler sees a brute materialism. While meaning had seemed to be the expression of some ineffable substance, understood as soul, spirit, or even simply "the human,"

Kittler contends it is nothing more or less than the machinations and interactions of inscriptive technologies. In rejecting the unifying and meaning-granting figure of the human subject, Kittler departs from McLuhan and the Toronto School, with whom he might otherwise easily be aligned. His penchant for sloganeering ("media determine our situation"; "The entertainment industry is ... an abuse of army equipment"), is decidedly McLuhanesque, but the humanism that underwrites those slogans (media as prostheses, his faith that media studies could empower individuals) is not simply absent. It is forcefully rejected. Such a perspective opens Kittler to the charge of media determinism, and he has little interest in rebutting it.

At the broadest level, we might say that Kittler's contention is that the development of technological media—the media, that is, of modernism—undid conventional understandings of meaning itself, and revealed meaning as an effect, rather than a cause. While other ways of understanding meaning (Kittler is thinking especially of nineteenth-century hermeneutics) sought to uncover and reconstruct the human meanings embedded within texts, Kittler argues that this model is so much humanist claptrap. Technological media reveal such attempts to recapture meaning as a mere effect of the book as a media technology. In place of meanings, Kittler focuses on "discourse networks" and their materialities. A discourse network is "the network of technologies and institutions that allow a given culture to select, store, and process relevant data. Technologies like that of book printing and the institutions coupled to it, such as literature and the university, thus constituted a historically very powerful formation, which in the Europe of the age of Goethe became the condition of possibility for literary criticism" (Kittler, *Discourse* 369). Literary criticism, and indeed literature itself, are consequences of the book as a technology. This definition, as often in his work, redescribes the past in terms more appropriate to Kittler's present. He not only calls book printing a technology but redescribes the operations of culture as a largely technological matter of selecting, storing, and processing data. Modernism is thus not a set of aesthetic practices but is defined instead by the discourse network enabled by the technological media (the gramophone, film, and typewriter, in Kittler's typology) that displace the book.

Media Archaeology

Every theorization of modernism and its media implies a history of media, and these histories have shapes: the splintering shape Greenberg describes as "Art" fragments and each individual art form develops autonomously; the figure of deviation from, and return to, orality that is central to the Toronto School's media history; the oscillating shape of the Frankfurt School's dialectical history of myth and enlightenment emerging into the mass deception of the culture industry. Such media histories not only offer a set of dates and events, but chart continuities and breaks. When did things begin, when did they change? When did they continue as they had been before? And why? Histories are, in short, stories. The media archaeological account at the center of this chapter offers a history that refuses any sense of direction or teleology. In part because it refuses to identify any master term (whether that be reason, aesthetic autonomy, or simply the human as a category), it can easily (as in the case of Friedrich Kittler) fall into a sort of media determinism. It is perhaps best understood, however, as refusing to understand the history of technology as a linear, teleological development. In this regard, Kittler's work can be usefully considered alongside a larger constellation of theory and artistic practice, sometimes called "media archaeology." While only loosely defined, *media archaeology* brings together a range of approaches to media.[1] It combines, at the level of theory, elements of post-structuralism (including a Foucauldian attention to history and a Derridean interest in processes of signification), while in practice it explores alternative and lost media.

Media archaeology's relationship to "archaeology" is best understood as metaphorical. It recovers or "excavates" overlooked

---

[1] This approach to history extends beyond scholarship. Jussi Parikka suggests that Steampunk—the nineteenth-century-inspired genre of science fiction and its associated culture—captures the spirit of media archaeology (*What* 1). Its combination of Victorian and computational cultures, and its counter-narratives of do-it-yourself tinkering and hacking all capture something of the interest in history conjoined with technological play present in media archaeology. Perhaps interestingly, though, steampunk leaps over the period conventionally called modernism in jumping from Victoriana to digital culture in a single leap.

remnants of past media. This attention to the forgotten, the failed, and the unrealized, Wolfgang Ernst elaborates, separates media archaeology from media history. "Archaeology, as opposed to history, refers to what is actually there: what has remained from the past in the present like archaeological layers, operatively embedded in technologies" (241). Such a description recalls Walter Benjamin's account of the past as "an image which flashes up at the instant when it can be recognized and is never seen again" (*Illuminations* 255). The person who imagines the past this way, Benjamin explains, stops treating history linearly "telling the sequence of events like the beads of a rosary. Instead, he grasps the constellation which his own era has formed with a definite earlier one" (*Illuminations* 263). While Benjamin was concerned with a history broader than media history, his method is echoed in the work of media archaeologists. The past, in this vision, is not comprehensible in its own terms, but only from the perspective of the present. Abandoned, unsuccessful, or merely antiquated technologies illuminate, and are illuminated by, the present. It is for this reason that media archaeology has developed alongside the study of "new media," as an attempt to understand digital, computational media. Lori Emerson's media archaeology lab, for instance, collects obsolete media from the late-nineteenth century to the present in order to defamiliarize them. Older computers and their interfaces reveal the ways that our encounters with technology, and what seems "natural" or "intuitive," are shaped by a history that quickly disappears beneath the surface of the new.[2] Such technologies develop so quickly that they seem to obsolesce before our very eyes. Paying attention to obsolescent technologies and missed opportunities complicates and upends a narrative of technology that is driven chiefly by progress.[3]

---

[2]See *https://mediaarchaeologylab.com/about/* as well as the MAL's website more broadly for a sense of the materials they collect and share.
[3]Jonathan Sterne's analysis of the mp3 file format, for instance, offers a media archaeology of a file format. Sterne's account works against a narrative of music technology which stresses increasing *fidelity* as the sole measure of a representation of sound. The mp3, as a technology, does not represent an improvement over earlier digital representations of sound in terms of fidelity or accuracy; but, because it compresses audio files into smaller sizes, it is more portable. Sterne reveals a media technology—here, the mp3—as a negotiation between competing forces, rather than a simple improvement over previous technologies.

In rejecting teleology, media archaeology departs from both the dialectical history of the Frankfurt School and the developmental histories of the Toronto School and Clement Greenberg. While media archaeology shares Benjamin's fascination with the detritus of the past, Benjamin preserves some sense of *meaning* in history, if only in negative form. In his "Theses on the Philosophy of History," Benjamin describes the "angel of history" (from Paul Klee's drawing *Angelus Novus*) as "turned toward the past. Where we perceive a chain of events, he sees a single catastrophe which keep piling wreckage upon wreckage." The angel longs to fix this catastrophe, but a storm carries them into the future. "This storm is what we call progress" (257–8). Even as this famously elliptical passage rejects conventional ideas of historical progress, it nevertheless preserves a meaning or telos in history through its sense of catastrophe (which awaits, in Benjamin's writing, messianic redemption). Media archaeology rejects all such meanings. Gods and *zeitgeist* alike are exorcised from its history of media, the angel of history just as surely as the god Progress.

Banishing teleology requires understanding media history on new scales. Gone is the long triumphal march of orality, writing, print, culminating in the ascension of a secondary orality inaugurated by electronic media (in the McLuhan/Ong narrative). In its place is a more uneven, detailed, and textured history of media, where failure, obsolescence, and forgotten experiments can be as interesting and important as major innovations. (Kittler himself, though, remains deeply fascinated by inventor-hero figures like Thomas Edison and Alan Turing.) Not just photography, but the zoetrope; not just film but the mutoscope and tachistoscope; not just the computer, but predigital schemes and technologies of (to use Siegfried Zielinski's term) *combining*.[4] This alternative history, or archaeology of media, works, above all, to free media history from narratives of progress. In the work of cultural historians like Lisa Gitelman's *Scripts, Grooves, and Writing Machines* (2006), who in most regards departs sharply from Kittler, the result is finely detailed, archivally grounded histories of specific technologies, which recover the complexity of technologies' first emergence. Charles Musser's history of "screen practice," in *The Emergence*

---

[4]E.g., Kittler on the phonautograph (*Gramophone*, 73–4); Crary on the zootope (*Techniques* 100); Gitelman on souvenir foils ("Souvenir Foils").

of Cinema (1990), similarly works to dislocate the history of film from the film camera alone, and insert it within a longer history of projected images. In Siegfried Zielinski's *Deep Time of the Media* (2006), this same refusal of linear, progressive narratives means unusual juxtapositions between historical moments, comparisons across centuries, freed from context. Such juxtapositions reveal common concerns or motifs in history, what Erkki Huhtamo calls *topoi* ("From Kaledoscopic" 222).

If modernism is yoked to notions of the novel and the new, media archaeology refuses the clear sense of linearity that newness assumes. Rather than a series of absolutely new irruptions, media archaeology sees longer continuities between the present and the past. Zielinski recovers forgotten elements of media history to construct a history of the new in the old. The presentist, teleological tendency of media history, Zielinski contends, sees "[p]ast centuries were there only to polish and perfect the great archaic ideas" (3). Media archaeology, by contrast, offers an opportunity to resist this presentist distortion. It "finds from the rich history of seeing, hearing, and combining using technical means: things in which something sparks or glitters ... and also points beyond the meaning or function of their immediate context of origin" (34). One sees such a project in Shane Butler's provocative *The Ancient Phonograph* (2015). Butler argues for an understanding of ancient literature as a sort of *phonograph*; such a deliberately anachronistic suggestion is meant to complicate our concepts of voice and reveal how entwined they are with media. Butler suggests that writing in ancient Greece was understood phonographically, that is, as a recording of *voice*. If such an understanding of writing seems peculiar today, it is because, as Kittler would insist, our understanding of what it means to record a voice has been (re)shaped by the phonograph and other media technologies.

At one extreme, a media archaeological orientation might motivate the recreation of old (or even imaginary) technologies. This is the approach Jentery Sayers calls "prototyping the past" in a 2015 essay of that title. It is a process of using contemporary fabrication technologies associated with "maker" culture (3D printing, computer-controlled routers, and similar tools), to build/recreate items from the past. He describes, for instance, recreating a nineteenth-century, electric stickpin, designed by Gustave Trouvé and manufactured by Auguste-German Cadet-Picard. This decorative pin features a small skull, a "death's head," which was designed to move its eyes and its jaw.[5] Recreating obsolete (or even unrealized) items, Sayers, suggests, "understands technologies as entanglements of culture, materials, and design, and it explains how and why technologies matter by approaching them as representations *and* agents of history" (158). In its recombination of the new and the old (using new fabrication technologies to recreate Victorian jewelry) and its refusal of teleology (capturing a sort of dead end, or unrealized possibility), the project described by Sayers exemplifies a media archaeological practice oriented toward the late-nineteenth, and early-twentieth centuries. Such projects may seem at odds with, or simply irrelevant to, the conventional study of literature, culture, and "the humanities." But the contours of the humanities, and indeed of the *human*, are what are at stake in the media archaeological project, and in the work of Friedrich Kittler in particular.[6]

Discourse Networks

Of all the thinkers explored in this book, Kittler is the least interested in aesthetic modernism in the narrow sense. His discussion of the modernist media ecology—or what he calls "discourse network 1900"—certainly includes the experiments in literary form we associate with figures like Gertrude Stein, Djuna Barnes, or James Joyce, but Kittler seems uninterested in modernism per se. Even as he often uses literature as a key element in his arguments, it is not separated from the wider media environment of which it is a part. Modernist artists lose their status as exceptional figures—they are no longer prophets of the new media, nor explorers of

---

[5]Sayers and the University of Victoria Maker Lab have also built a working replica of the earliest magnetic sound recording device (*http://maker.uvic.ca/jacob2/*). Their "Kits for Culture" provide details on how to reproduce such projects and include a number of others. See *http://maker.uvic.ca/container/*.
[6]While I am suggesting media archaeological practice is offered as an alternative to (or, in Kittler's case, a rejection of) traditional humanistic interpretation, Sayers suggests that "prototyping the past is deeply intertwined with hermeneutics and close reading" (159).

the medium's inherent properties, nor autonomous preservers of a realm outside instrumental reason. Instead, they are just one more actor in a discourse network. Modernism is neither an achievement to be defended (as it is for Greenberg), a herald of the new age (as it is for McLuhan), nor a refuge in a damaged world (as it is for Adorno). It is instead an epiphenomenal expression of some more fundamental process. If modernism means anything to Kittler, it is as a periodizing term, denoting a particular historical moment, defined by its "discourse network."

Modernism, in this narrative, is the period between the decline of the book and the rise of digital media. It is an odd moment where media materialities proliferate in between periods dominated by single, dominant media forms. The modernist discourse network emerges with the technological media that dethrone the book: specifically the gramophone, film (projected moving images, not photography, in Kittler's narrative), and the typewriter. The book was once the central mode of representing and storing information. What Kittler calls "discourse network 1800"—what cultural or literary historians might call nineteenth-century Romanticism—is defined by the book's centrality as a media technology. The period, in Kittler's account, was able to so completely naturalize literacy that reading became a hallucinatory experience, and the book as a medium was capable of representing the full range of sense experience. But with the emergence of technological media the book loses this monopoly. By the end of the nineteenth century, the book's monopoly has been broken, and new cultural storage technologies emerge to compete with the book as stores of "serial data." These technologies capture different types of sense experience in different technological channels: film and photography are able to capture the visual, while the audible finds itself trapped in wax, vinyl, and, later, magnetic tape. Modernism is a Cambrian explosion of media materialities. However, that explosion—from the unity of the book to the diversity of modernist media materialities—is short-lived. Like an exploding star, it soon collapses back in on itself. After the Second World War, with the rise of computers, information technology reunifies the representation of culture within a single medium as the digital comes to play the role the book once did: the chief medium of all sense experience. Modernism is thus a period of media fragmentation between two monopolies, that of the book and that of the digital.

This historicization of modernism is indebted to the intellectual climate of the 1960s. Kittler writes in the aftermath of the post-structuralist turn in critical theory and literary criticism and mixes a range of theorists, including Jacques Derrida and Jacques Lacan, with a McLuhanite emphasis on media. In shifting the focus to the *materiality* of media, rather than its operation as a system of signification, Kittler is a hinge between post-structuralism and whatever we might call what happens *after* post-structuralism (call it new materialism, posthumanism, or similar). Of the post-structuralist thinkers Kittler draws on, it is Michel Foucault who offers the most important precedent for Kittler's theorization of media. The *discourse network* can thus be understood as a revision of Foucault's own notion of *discourse*. Discourse, in Foucault's specific sense, is "a systematic organization that cannot be reduced to the demands of logic or linguistics" (199). To understand a historical period's discourse is to reveal (in a Kantian phrase) the conditions of possibility for claims about truth and experience. Discourse makes truth—or what counts as truth within a historical period—possible. Studying discourse reveals the historical conditions that allow things to appear as true.

Foucault's notion of discourse is interested in truth and meaning, not paper or files. Kittler sees Foucault's historicism as flawed by this inattention to media technology. Discourse only exists when it is materialized, and it is media, for Kittler, that provide the conditions of possibility for experience, rather than discourse in some abstract sense. It is no accident, for Kittler, that Foucault's account of discourse ends just as discourse network 1900 is emerging. By attending to media, Kittler out-Foucaults Foucault. Just as Foucault relativizes the idea of truth historically, Kittler relativizes Foucault's historicism through attention to media materiality. Markus Krajewski's *Paper Machines: About Cards and Catalogs, 1548–1929* (2011) takes this inspiration directly. A media archaeology of paper information management systems, it traces the way card management systems reshaped knowledge. The seemingly banal card catalog freed knowledge from the book as a medium by allowing facts to circulate and be organized outside its unity. Library card catalogs enabled a range of systems of organization to exist simultaneously, rather than a single hierarchy of information. Structures of knowledge are enabled by a series of materialities, including such easily ignorable facts as a standardization of paper card sizes. The technology of such systems spread from library to business and accounting. Beneath knowledge and business both, Krawjewski unearths the machinations of the card catalog.

Recent work in modernist studies has similarly sought to uncover the media underpinnings of knowledge, law, and literature. James Purdon's *Modernist Informatics: Literature, Information, and the State* (2016) tracks a tension between modernist literature and an emergent culture of information. Purdom finds in the work of Joseph Conrad, Ford Madox Ford, Graham Greene, Elizabeth Bowen, and others "a new understanding of the relationship between the technologies of information management and the conditions of everyday life and thought in modern societies" (7). In Purdon's account, literature exists in tension with this new mode of information. Many writers seem to see information as the cold merely factual quality against which the literary was defined. And so "a concern with information surfaces where the survival of literariness is itself in question. It is information against which the idea of the literary must be defined" (16). Cornelia Vismann, in *Files: Law and Media Technology* (2008; German edition, 2000), similarly identifies a tension between modernist fiction and information technology.

> Narratives by Kafka and Melville do not merely illustrate the machine and apparatuses of the law, or the logic of bureaucracy driven to its extreme. As narrative residues discarded by the grand tales of the origin and evolution of the law, they stand at the end of a process of differentiation that also entailed a removal of literature from the law.
>
> (xiii)

Literature is that which is expunged from the bureaucratized realms of information and law. Yet for Purdon, "information and literary narrative have a history of entanglement as well as antagonism, and that this relationship—the productive challenge posed to literature by the genres of information—was a significant factor in the cultural shaping of modernist narrative" (4).

Such works trace a medium-specific, material grounding for Foucault's account of discourse. Vismann and Purdon do not simply offer histories of the office, bureaucracy, and law. They show the way that such institutions and discourses express an underlying media system. As Michael Wutz puts it, Kittler and media archaeology "played Marx to Foucault's Hegel: they pulled discourse analysis off its textual and discursive head and set it on its media-technological feet" (xxii). Media also provide the absent motor to Foucault's history. Frederic Jameson once noted that Foucault's history offers a series of stages without offering any explanation for how or why one stage shifts into another (*Prison* 193–4). Foucault's historicism, because it lacks a concept like the *mode of production* or a sense of *class struggle* (or even Adorno and Horkheimer's dialectic of enlightenment), reduces history to a series of unmotivated events—an empty sequence. Kittler provides an answer to this objection (though not a Marxist one) by locating the primary mover of history in technological change. Foucault's failure to recognize the media technological underpinnings of his history limited his analysis to the age of the book. Kittler explains, "discourse-analytic studies had trouble only with periods whose data-processing methods destroyed the alphabetic storage and transmission monopoly, that old-European basis of power. Foucault's historical research did not progress much beyond 1850" (*Discourse* 369). Foucault's history necessarily misses what is unique and peculiar to the modernist period—the radically altered discourse network created by industrialized media technology.

Focusing on a discourse network (rather than on simply discourse and their histories) widens the scope for understanding the discursive conditions of possibility beyond the library. "All libraries are discourse networks, but all discourse networks are not books" (Kittler, *Discourse* 369). A period's discourse network includes not only the technologies, but the institutions that develop from, and sustained, those technological materialities. "Discourse network 1800" is centered around the book as a technology, but also includes the institutions, concepts, and ideas that helped maintain that discourse work. Crucially important for the discourse network that preceded modernism is the gendered establishment and naturalization of literacy through an ideology that links literacy to pedagogy and imagination. Kittler explains,

> In 1800 the system of equivalents Woman = Nature = Mother allowed acculturation to begin from an absolute origin. A culture established on this basis speaks differently about language, writes differently about writing. Briefly put, it has Poetry. For only

when phonetics and the alphabet shortcircuit the official route from a natural source to those on the receiving end can a kind of speech arise that can be thought of as an ideal of Nature. This placing of mothers at the origin of discourse was the condition of production for Classical poetry, and the Mother was the first Other to be understood by poetical hermeneutics.

(*Discourse* 28)

At the center of discourse network 1800 was a naturalization of the alphabet, evident in phenomenon as diverse as alphabet books and in cookies, baked in the shape of letters (29). Reading became second nature by naturalizing the alphabet, and through pedagogical practices focused on the mother and the mother's body (the Lacanian psychoanalytic dimension of Kittler's thinking is particularly evident in some of his discussions of the mother). Discourse network 1800 knots together a particular set of media technologies (the alphabet, the book), social practices (of pedagogy and instruction), libidinal investments and fantasies (in the mother), and the state (who is chief beneficiary of this naturalization of literacy—in the form of clerks and bureaucrats who can staff modern nation-states). The romantic idea of "Literature" (or what Kittler calls "Poetry") emerges enmeshed within a single network that includes these institutions and technologies. As Terry Eagleton notes, it is "only with what we now call the 'Romantic period' that our own definitions of literature began to develop" (18). Kittler traces the emergence of the idea Literature as a unique mode of imaginative writing that expresses human interiority to discourse network 1800. And all of this comes falling apart when that discourse network is undone by the new technologies of inscription of discourse network 1900.

The fraying of discourse network 1800 with modernist technologies is evident in a number of ways. For instance, the typewriter undoes the gendered logic of writing that prevailed in discourse network 1800. In that earlier period, men were writers, and women readers (and, crucially, *teachers*). He describes metaphors that gendered writing similar to "the metaphor of literary paternity" Sandra Gilbert and Susan Gubar describe in their ground-breaking 1979 work of feminist criticism, *The Madwoman in the Attic* (6). Kittler similarly notes "an omnipresent metaphor equated women with the white sheet of nature or virginity onto which a very male stylus could then inscribe the glory of its authorship" (*Gramophone* 186), or what Gilbert and Gubar trace as the equation of the pen and the penis. The typewriter undoes this heterosexualized division of literary labor. It not only changes how people wrote, but undoes this gendered division of labor. As Kittler notes, the typewriter was both a machine and a gendered occupation—the word "typewriter" could refer not only to the device but the (typically female) person operating it. Women entered offices as secretarial workers at the end of the nineteenth century and, alongside this new writing technology, displaced the largely male clerical workers that preceded them. "Typescript amounts to the desexualization of writing, sacrificing its metaphysics and turning it into word processing" (*Gramophone* 187). Yet, as Jennifer Fleissner notes in a 2000 essay on *Dracula*, Kittler overstates how absolute the break introduced by female secretarial labor and the typewriter really was. "Kittler's epistemic version of history disallows the possibility of continuity alongside disruption" (Fleissner 425). Indeed, his treatment of gender and the typewriter nicely illustrates the media deterministic tendency of his thinking. Fleissner shows that, rather than simply undoing metaphors of gender, those same metaphors persisted, shaping women's entrance into office work. The office was imagined as a domestic space, tended by women; the mechanical work of typewriting was analogized to piano playing, which was imagined as particularly well-suited to the female body; secretarial labor required women both to work but appear as if they were not working, and so "retain symbolically the 'apartness' that gives bourgeois domesticity its uncorrupted charm" (Fleissner 447). Kittler's materialist Foucauldian model of historical ruptures introduced by technological changes ignores these continuities.

Kittler's Inhumanism: The Body as Site of Inscription

Foucault's relevance to the New Modernist Studies is inextricable from its relation to post-structuralism more broadly. And post-structuralism's place is decidedly vexed. At once an inspiration for undoing the conventional, restricted narratives of modernism, and foundationalist transhistorical narratives about "Literature," poststructuralism's descriptions of breaks and ruptures can be equally sweeping and unnuanced. For the archivally motivated and the historically specific, such broad gestures can impose a theoretical framework on a historical reality that is messier. For instance, Foucault's account of discourse, like structuralist and post-structuralist thinking more broadly, represents a "decentering of the subject." The human individual is not an agent who controls discourse. Discourse instead is an inhuman force that produces the subject. Foucault, near the close of *The Order Things* (1966; English 1970) famously writes, of "man" as a relatively recent invention, and one which may one day disappear, "like a face drawn in sand at the edge of the sea" (*Order* 387). Kittler shares with Foucault this vision of the humanist subject as produced by, rather than producing, discourse. Yet in Kittler's thinking what decenters the subject is not simply discourse but media.

Rather than the Romantic author, confidently expressing themself through language, it is the medium which is expressed in the work. Where the artist had a unique power over the medium in McLuhan's history, Kittler replays a poststructuralist theme with a media materialist emphasis. Roland Barthes's famous essay "The Death of the Author" (1967) imagines the *author* as disappearing in a manner similar to Foucault's, effaced, in Barthes's description, by the operation of writing itself. For Kittler, however, it is not writing in the abstract—the *écriture* of post-structuralism—that eclipses the human agent, but media technology. The death of the author, Barthes famously declares, is the "the birth of the reader" (148). Kittler's vision of the decentered subject, by contrast, is less liberatory. It is not the reader, but media itself that replaces the author: "Record grooves dig the grave of the author" (*Gramophone* 83). This same decentering of the human, David Welberry notes in his introduction to Kittler's *Discourse Networks*, is evident in Kittler's shift away from hermeneutics (concerned with recapturing *meaning*, as produced by human subject) to a focus on the "psychophysics" of media (xxix). A similar shift is evident in Jonathan Crary's media archaeological account of the change, starting in the second half of the nineteenth century, in how vision was understood. As discussed in Chapter 1, Crary describes a shift away from models of the camera obscura as the chief metaphor for perception, to the physiological models of the later nineteenth century grounded in the organs of perception themselves. The human is not a subject, but a body, a physiological structure that interacts and with the matter of technology. This is a "materialism" of sorts, but it is a very different kind of materialism than the essentially economic one which one motivates Marxist accounts of culture, including Adorno and Horkheimer's. Kittler is, Geoffery Winthrop-Young suggests, not simply *posthuman*, in the sense described by Katherine Hayles in *How We Became Posthuman* (1999), but posthuman*ist* ("Silicon Sociology" 393). That is, Kittler doesn't imagine technology as allowing humans to transcend their circumstances, but as simply leaving humans behind.

This media materialist revision of the post-structuralist decentering of the human subject also marks Kittler's difference from McLuhan and the Toronto School. The body is as central to Kittler's thinking of media as it is to McLuhan's, but while McLuhan imagines media as a prosthetic augmentation, Kittler treats the body as a surface on which media, like the nightmarish machine described in Kafka's "In the Penal Colony" (1919), inscribe. *Inscription* rather than *augmentation* provides the central metaphor for Kittler's account of media and the body. The direction of the agency is reversed; for McLuhan, humans act through media, even if those media deform, translate, and change the human sensorium in ways that cannot be controlled or anticipated. By contrast, Kittler explains in a 1996 interview that media influence the body, but are essentially independent of and prior to it.

> I don't believe in the old thesis that thus the media are prostheses of the body, which amounts to saying, in the beginning was the body, then came the glasses, then suddenly television, and from the television, the computer. The mythology is that everything frees itself from the body, dissolves and submerges in it again.
> (Kittler, Griffin, and Herrmann 738)

Such a model informs Thomas Elsaesser's description, in "Media Archaeology as Symptom" (2016), of how recent films—he mentions *Gravity* (2013), *Interstellar* (2014), and even *Avatar* (2009)—take advantage of new digital film-making technologies to dislocate the human scale. In such films, Elsaesser writes, "the whole body becomes a perceptual surface" (205). Such a vision of the human as a surface inscribed upon by media departs from the essentially humanist perspective of McLuhan.

War and Media

If there is an agential force in Kittler's history of media it is neither a human subject, nor a historical subject like Enlightenment, but war. *Gramophone, Film, Typewriter* (1999, German Edition 1986), Winthrop-Young suggests, is a distinctly cold war text, inextricable from the historical moment in which it was written ("Drill and Distraction" 831). This connection to war, however, is more than contextual or biographical. War plays a central role in Kittler's theorization of media, as it does in the work French philosopher Paul Virilio. War, the German media theorist Norbert Bolz, suggests, is "the father of all media" (qtd. in Winthrop-Young, "Drill and Distraction" 828), and war is omnipresent in Kittler's account of media, especially of discourse network 1900, and the post-Second World War rise of computation. Kittler notes that Remington turned to the manufacture of typewriters after a decline in gun sales after the Civil War, and calls the typewriter a "discourse machine gun" (*Gramophone* 14).

Noting the shared histories of the Gatling gun and Étienne-Jules Marey's "chronophotographic rifle" (a precursor to movie cameras), Kittler writes, "The history of the movie camera thus coincides with the history of automatic weapons" (*Gramophone* 124). This coincidence recurs in later technologies, like the synchronized gear used in film cameras that was first used in First World War fighter aircraft to fire a machine gun in between the spinning the blades of the propeller.[7] Marey's chronophotographic

---

[7]Kittler (*Gramophone* 125) quotes Virilio who describes "people like Roland Garros (d. 1918), whose machine-gun could be safely synchronized to fire through the propeller" (18). This is not quite right. The problem is how to fire a gun from an aircraft. One could set machine guns outside the propeller, but this made targeting more difficult. Placing the gun where a pilot could conveniently target it, however, meant that gun would be shooting *at* or *through* the spinning propeller. Garros had added protective deflector plates, to reduce the impact of bullets fired that happened to hit the propeller. It was only later that the Dutch Anthony Fokker developed an interrupter mechanism which, in effect, synchronized the firing of the gun to the spinning of the propeller. Fokker used cams to allow the propeller to, in effect, fire the gun. With such a device, a pilot could use a front-facing machine gun without any risk of damage to the propeller. It is this latter development, a gear-based synchronization, far more than Garros's, that would seem to unite the film camera and the combat aircraft.

FIGURE 5.1 *"The Photographic Gun," from E. J. Marey,* Movement *(1895), courtesy of HathiTrust,* https://babel.hathitrust.org/cgi/pt?id=gri.ark:/13960/t3904rf58.

gun seems to dramatically illustrate this coincidence of perception and violence (see Figure 5.1). The two, for Kittler and Virilio, are necessarily inseparable. Or, as Jim Morrison (yes, of The Doors) writes—in a poem that Kittler, with his typical enthusiasm for the rock music of the 1960s, quotes—"The sniper's rifle is an extension of his eye. He kills with injurious vision" (Morrison qtd. in Kittler, *Gramophone* 284n35). Elsaesser similarly notes that the carbon arc lamps used for film projectors were first developed for use as anti-aircraft search lights (195).[8] Even Kittler's slogan, "Media determine our situation" (xxxix), is not simply a flat statement of media determinism, but a martial declaration. As Matthew Kirschenbaum points out, Kittler's term "*situation*" (in German *Lage*) alludes to the terminology of the Prussian war game or *Kriegspiel* (285). Walter Benjamin's suggestion that "there is no document of civilization which is not at the same time a document of barbarism" (*Illuminations* 256) here receives a media materialist rewriting: there is no technology that is not already a military technology. Or, as Kittler more pithily puts it, the entertainment industry is "an abuse of military equipment" (*Gramophone* 97).

A skeptic may wonder how firm this connection between war and media history really is. Doesn't the deep, underlying connection between media and war that Kittler and Virilio describe cherry pick its evidence? As Winthrop-Young writes, "Are not the origin and decisive early growth of modern media technologies such as the telephone unrelated to war or military expertise? Does not the cultural history of the telephone ... prove that social contingencies outweigh military application?" ("Drill and Distraction" 833). More broadly, might an example like Marey's chronophotographic rifle testify not to some shared link between media and military histories, but to a process of industrialization subtending both media and military technologies? Rather than an essential connection between war and media, the admittedly striking image of Marey's chronophotographic rifle might evidence a history of increased precision and technologization that both media and military technology draw on. Such a history would include techniques for

---

[8]Hertha Ayrton refined the first electric light technology (carbon arc lights) to produce more stable arc. This stabilized arc allowed for the development of both searchlights and improved film projection (Byers and Williams 16–18).

precision machining, a history of *engineering* as a way of knowing the world, and what a more Marxian reading might describe as changes in the means of production.

Winthrop-Young answers such skepticism by suggesting that the term *war* itself, like the term *discipline* in Foucault, captures a wider range of experience than "mobilization" or "actual combat" alone. It describes a technologically altered condition which "transcends its restricted meaning and now refers to a set of basic operational procedures that are as indispensable to combat situations and military engagements as they are to the routines of everyday of moderns society" ("Drill and Distraction" 837). Kittler's claim, despite his fondness for anecdotal examples, is not an empirical one about the origins of media, but about the structure of media themselves and their evolution. The novel and extreme demands of modern warfare present unique cognitive and perceptual challenges, but challenges that are answered in ways that have ramifications well beyond *war* in the restricted sense. "Modern media," Winthrop-Young continues, "drill, reshape, and mobilize the human body, its sensory apparatus, and its nervous system to make it more compatible with the requirements of modern electronic warfare" ("Drill and Distraction" 838). Behind the modernity thesis (discussed in Chapter 1), in short, is war.

To illustrate, we might consider the history of flight and aircraft cockpits. Duffy, in *The Speed Handbook* (2009), explores the new pleasures created by the car. In images of the car, the driver is figured as a sort of hero. The car was a prosthetic technology that empowered the driver. "The logic of the car and its driver, however, as opposed to that of the train and its passengers, was that the human subject would prove equal to—and, more, exert power over—the machine" (181). In the car,

> The new science of ergonomics developed around car design; the curves of seats and dashboards followed the body's curves, while the car body's own curves mimicked those of the most beautifully stylized human bodies ... the car was scaled to the human body, suggesting in its human scale that it might be a partner to it, deferring to human height, reach, and comfort. It implied that its mechanical power worked in tandem with the bodies' locomotion.
>
> (192)

Rather than the car—with its pleasures of speed, and heroic rhetoric—it is the martial experience that interests Kittler and Virilio. The demands that flight makes on a pilot seem less thrilling, in their account, and more traumatizing. When open to the air, in early aircraft, pilots used the iconic aviator goggles to protect their eyes from debris the force of wind. The conditions of such flight were so intense that it was not uncommon for pilots to stuff their ears with cotton, to reduce the deafening roar of the wind and the thundering of the airplane engine (Maurer 66). Flight helmets of the 1930s began to include radio or other communication devices. Ultimately, more complex, electronic technology would be added. The demands of modern flight require not simply better (or worse), senses, but utterly different, *inhuman* perception.

Technology, even in the crude form of goggles and cotton wadding, "rebalance" the sensorium in McLuhan's terms. Ryan Bishop and John Philips in *Modernist Avant-Garde Aesthetics and Contemporary Military Technology: Technicities of Perception* (2010) describe technologies as intervening in a "gap" in perception between the perceiver and the perceived. Goggles, for instance, occupy this gap, but so too do more advanced technologies, like radar, electronic guidance, and heads-up displays that provide guidance and targeting information (Bishop and Phillips 27). This augmentation and reshaping of the human sensorium is itself determined by the agonistic character of warfare. The contest in war becomes who can see further and see faster. Or, as Virilio puts it, "*the history of battle is primarily the history of radically changing fields of perception*" (Virilio 7, original emphasis). The agon of war, and the competition for technology to better perceive the enemy (and, in turn, countermeasures to escape/decoy such accelerated perception), emerges as the real motor of technological change, which in turn reshapes the sensorium. This may sound like a militarized account of McLuhan's view of media as prostheses, but it discards the humanist assumptions of McLuhan's media theory entirely. It is war and technology which are the chief agents here:

> The media don't emerge from the human body, rather you have, for example, the book, and the military generals in considering how they can subvert the book or the written word, come up with the telegraph, namely, the telegraph wire; and then to offset the military telegraph, they come up with the wireless radio, which Hitler builds into his tanks. In England Alan Turing or Churchill

ponder a way to beat Germany's radio war, and they arrive at the computer to crack the radio signals—and the German goose is cooked, that's the end of the war. A history like this doesn't need individual bodies or a subject that expands in and through the media—such a history can do without the subjective agency of a historical actor.

(Kittler, "Technologies" 738)

Here the needs of the military—generals planning wars and governments cracking codes—are the ultimate drivers of history. The human individual is simply along for the ride, reduced to part of the apparatus. To return to the cockpit, consider this description of the pilot's role:

> the pilot tend[s] to be an expensive liability (not only in cost but also in weight and complexity of cockpit systems) and it is not from sentimentality that, for the last hundred years or so, aircrew have been central to, and the focus of, the aircraft system. It is because they can do the required job better than any other option.
>
> (Rood 3)

The complexity of the cockpit as an interface between the pilot and the plane is described here as less an extension of the pilot than a reduction of the pilot to a particularly complex (and costly) part of the aircraft.

The role of war shifts the determining (one might fairly say *determinist*) element of Kittler's thinking from media themselves to the military uses of such technology. Kittler's history, in fact, solves the problem of Foucault's unmotivated historiography by showing how, at the level of media, *war* is what has motivated the large-scale epistemic shifts that Foucault charts. Played in a sufficiently paranoid key, this account of the relationship between technology and media, to use a commonly invoked example, makes video games look like a process for training a new generation of soldiers and pilots.

The centrality of war inflects Kittler's media theory not only in its tendency to trace (with remarkable tenacity) the origin of media technologies to the military, but in how it imagines the relationship between media forms. The relationship among media—between the book and film, or radio and the gramophone—is often described in metaphors of ecology (a "media ecology") or economy (the "monopoly" of the book). Such metaphors capture the way that media and their uses evolve together in complicated ways. The centrality of war in Kittler's media theory is evident in his tendency to imagine media's relationship as one of agonistic competition. The book is not joined by, or augmented by the gramophone or film; it is in competition with them. While such a model may, as we have seen, tend to ignore continuities between media, the general model has proved valuable within modernist studies. Jonathon Foltz discounts a crude model in which, for instance, filmmakers and novelists were competing with one another in zero-sum game for audiences. But media do compete with one another in a wider sense. Competition between media, Foltz writes, is "a perennial condition of aesthetic practice without any meaningful alternative, where winning is never an option and only transformation is constant ... The novel ought, then, to be considered as only one kind of cultural technology among others, engaged in a long, adaptive passage through the imagined negations provoked by adjacent media" (13). My own work on modernist obscenity, in *Filthy Material: Modernism and the Media of Obscenity* (2019), draws on such a model to suggest that modernist debates about obscenity were, in a Kittlerian metaphor, proxy wars between the book as a medium and its modern alternatives. Even as John Lurz's *The Death of the Novel* contests elements of Kittler's model of media history (3–5), his own examination of how modernist novels exploited the medium-specific elements of the book continues to imagine the book's properties in contradistinction to other media. Such a model of media history and relationship can prove enormously useful to modernist studies, even without Kittler's deterministic insistence on the singular importance of war.

The Death of Literature

The place of literature is strangely ambiguous in Kittler's work. Even as he develops his history of media through readings of canonical literary texts, Kittler denies those texts any special status beyond the insight they offer into the history of media. As Larson Powell notes, in "Media as Technology and Culture" (2014), "Kittler's popularity was paradoxically dependent on the hermeneutical and humanities traditions it ostentatiously negated" (409). The range of texts that he addresses is also rather untraditional. Alongside analyses of Goethe and Rilke we find equally attentive readings of Pink Floyd and the Rolling Stones. The strict distinctions between art and its others, so essential to the Frankfurt School and to Clement Greenberg, are not meaningful to Kittler. "Literary texts," Kittler explains, "can thus be read as a methodological, but only a methodological, center of *Discourse Networks*" (*Discourse* 371).[9] That is, the category of literature is not interesting in itself, but only as an excrescence of media history. It has chiefly methodological importance—the traditional domains of the literary and the aesthetic register the effects of changes in the discourse network, and so are useful for the insight they offer into this more fundamental reality.

Modernism, in this history, marks the end of "literature," at least as it existed during the period Kittler calls Romanticism. Its demise is particularly clear in Kittler's discussion of the phonograph. Arguing for poetry's essentially oral character, in terms similar to Milman Parry (discussed in Chapter 3), Kittler invokes Nietzsche to argue that traditional (and perhaps especially Romantic) poetry "with its beats, rhythms (and, in modern European languages, rhymes)" is fundamentally a technological solution to a problem of human memory. "Unrecognized by philosophical aesthetics, the storage capacity of memory was to be increased and the signal-to-noise ratio of channels improved" (*Gramophone* 80). Poetry's rhyme and meter were chiefly, Kittler argues, aids to memory. Sound recording, however, changes everything. With the phonograph, "Technology triumphs over mnemotechnology. And the death bell tolls for poetry" (80). The result of this technological "triumph," Kittler suggests, is a bifurcation between avant-gardist poetry and popular recorded music. His distinction here replays, without the sense of elitist judgment, the very similar distinctions between avant-garde and kitsch (described by Greenberg), or between modernism and

---

[9]Perhaps despite himself Kittler's own fondness for quoting rock bands, like Pink Floyd, as offering trenchant accounts of media (e.g., *Gramophone* 36), grants rock music a sort of vanguardist pride of place. Such music plays the role in *Gramophone, Film, Typewriter*, that high modernist art and music plays for Adorno.

the culture industry (described by Adorno and Horkheimer). Freed from the work of mnemotechnics, poetry no longer needs devices like meter, rhyme, and conventional rhythm. Under these revised technological conditions, poets face a choice. They can follow the example of Mallarmé into poetic experiments with print as a medium and "inaugurate a cult of and for letter fetishists, in which case poetry becomes a form of typographically optimized blackness on exorbitantly expensive white paper." Or, poets can embrace the new technology and become "nameless songwriters ... on records," lyricists for what Adorno and Horkheimer would call the culture industry (*Gramophone* 80). The coherence of poetry was secured by its monopoly over both the *voice* and even over particular themes—romance chief among them. "With the invention of technical sound storage, the effects that poetry had on its audience migrate to the new lyrics of hit parades and charts .... Lowbrow and highbrow culture, professional technology and professional poetry: the founding age of modern media left us with those two options" (82). This key modernist theme—the dissociation of the sensibility described by T. S. Eliot; the great divide between modernism and mass culture—here receives a media technological explanation. To the question, "What happened to poetry in the twentieth century?" Kittler answers simply: The phonograph.

The central role of the phonograph, or gramophone,[10] in Kittler's media history stems from the way it records sound without *meaning* in the conventional linguistic/hermeneutic sense. It is this property that Kittler isolates as essential, rather than the way it separates a voice from a body, or preserves sound over time, or reconfigures the contexts of listening. The gramophone, like recorded sound generally, indeed, does all those things, but for Kittler its importance is a consequence of offering a mode of inscription outside writing in the conventional sense. The phonograph is "a machine that records noises regardless of so-called meaning" (*Gramophone* 85). In semiotic terms, the phonograph represents sound *indexically*

---

[10]While Kittler uses the word gramophone (*grammophon* in German), the terms phonograph and gramophone are often used interchangeably, and both operate through a stylus's inscription on a recording material (tinfoil, wax, shellac, vinyl). Typically a gramophone uses flat circular records (like record players still in use today), while a phonograph, which is the earlier sound recording technology (the one used in *Dracula*), used cylinders to record sound.

rather than *symbolically*. Kittler describes this as the replacement of *meaning* by *noise*. The all-too human meaning that traditional hermeneutics sought to recover from text is replaced by a mechanism. Kittler quotes the German poet Rainer Maria Rilke's 1919 essay "Primal Sound," in which Rilke describes the experience of making a crude phonograph as a student in school. It was not the crude reproduction of sound that Rilke found fascinating, but the strange marks that the needle of the homemade gramophone left on the cylinder—a sort of primitive writing. He describes later seeing very similar marks on a human skull, at the fibrous joints from the growth of the skull's coronal sutures. The similarity leads Rilke to a morbid thought: "What if one changed the needle and directed it on its return journey along a tracing which was not derived from the graphic translation of sound but existed of itself naturally—well, to put it plainly along the coronal suture, for example?" (qtd. in Kittler, *Gramophone* 40–1). What, that is, if instead of a phonograph cylinder, one played a human skull? What sound would it make? The significance of this strange fantasy of cranial playback is, for Kittler, the way it unmoors signification from writing and therefore from meaning. "Ever since the invention of the phonograph," he writes, "there has been writing without a subject" (44). Rilke's odd daydream operates the same way, without any human intended meaning (while conveniently connecting media technological signification to human death). The post-structuralist dissolution of the subject begins in modernism, inaugurated by the phonograph's automated operation.

Here too, however, Kittler's insistence on absolute breaks—from a Romantic, humanist model of book-bound hermeneutic meaning, to modernist, technologically recorded noise—ignores continuities. Lisa Gitelman's account of the phonograph, also notes the peculiar, writing-like inscriptions made by the phonograph. Gitelman finds here, however, a *continuity* between writing technologies. The phonograph in particular was initially understood alongside the various competing systems of shorthand writing, which were, like the phonograph when it first appeared, imagined as a sort of direct transcription of sound. Rather than the sharp tectonic break in the Foucauldian *episteme* that Kittler imagines, Gitelman describes a history where "[p]rint and nonprint media evolve in mutual inextricability" (*Scripts* 13). What would eventually emerge as a mass market for recorded music, in a technology that was used primarily for passive consumption, was originally imagined as an adjunct to writing. This imbrication of writing and phonography is evident even in the word *phonography* (sound writing), which, before it referred to mechanically recorded sound, was what Isaac Pitman called his shorthand system—the first such system, Pitman claimed, "based explicitly on the phonetics of English" (Gitelman, *Scripts* 24).

But for Kittler, the break is fundamental and absolute. Juan Suárez, in *Pop Modernism* (2007), detects this break at work in Eliot's *The Waste Land*. In his reading of Eliot's poem, he follows Kittler's lead and abandons the pretense of revealing some meaning. Suárez offers "no further interpretations of the text but the unveiling of modes of inscription on which its meaning depends" (Suárez 123). A gramophone appears in *The Waste Land*, after the unsettling encounter between the typist and the clerk in "The Fire Sermon." Tiresias, who has observed the encounter, reports,

> She turns and looks a moment in the glass,
> Hardly aware of her departed lover;
> Her brain allows one half-formed thought to pass:
> "Well now that's done: and I'm glad it's over."
> When lovely woman stoops to folly and
> Paces about her room again, alone,
> She smoothes her hair with automatic hand,
> And puts a record on the gramophone.
>
> (l.249–256)

The gramophone operates to thematically illustrate the emptiness of modern life. It joins canned food ("food laid out in tins," l. 223), popular music ("that Shakespeherian Rag," l.128), and acne-plagued office workers ("the young man carbuncular," l.231) as yet one more element of a degraded, mechanical modernity. Suárez, though, sees the operation of the gramophone in the poem operating at a more fundamental level. The poem is populated by ghostly, zombie-like voices of the past in the form of allusions and images of death and unburied corpses. These images and allusions stage a return of the past, Suárez contends, that echoes the gramophone itself. "The return of the dead may be attributed to the poem's mythic substratum but also to the nebulous embodiments and the equivocal forms of absence-presence allowed by modern media" (Suárez 128). The automaticity of the gramophone's materiality becomes for Suárez a key image of modernism.

> What such diverse figures as Sigmund Freud, F. T. Marinetti, Tristan Tzara, Marcel Proust, Gertrude Stein, Ernest Hemingway, André Breton, James Joyce, John Dos Passos, and Marcel Duchamp, to name a few, endlessly recorded in their writing is precisely language unbound—nonsense, wordplay, unconscious rhymes and rhythms, strings of association, snatches of conversation caught on the run, glossolalia. Rather than create, they took dictation, their ears wide open to the world's unsuppressible cacophony.
>
> (128–9)

As Kittler contends, the gramophone captures not simply language or meaning, but whatever cultural noise passes before it—a sort of recording emulated by modernist art and literature. The fragmentary, polyvocal, and even nonlinguistic sounds of the poem echo the indiscriminate recording of the phonograph as described by Kittler. *The Waste Land* operates like a gramophone.

Perhaps the most sophisticated interpretation of modernism from a Kittlerian perspective is Julian Murphet's. His *Multimedia Modernism: Literature and the Anglo-American Avant-garde* (2009) embraces the media determinism that is so often lodged as a critique against Kittler and others. He avoids claiming that changes in media themselves determine art, noting instead that artists of the avant-garde behave as though this were so (*Multimedia* 2). Media determinism is thus less a transhistorical fact about technology than a historically specific reaction to media change. Murphet invites us "to learn to see the medium itself seizing hold of the individual in order to tell the cryptic and allegorical tale of its relations, some friendly, some less amicable, with other media." This story of the conflict between media—both between the old and new media (the book vs the phonograph), and amongst media—Murphet suggests, is "the secret story of modernism itself, of which the avant-garde is simply the most perspicacious scribe" (*Multimedia* 3). Murphet translates the Kittleriean theme of an agon among media, and of the arts as transcription of media history to a narrative focused on the avant-garde. He detects in the Anglo-American avant-garde a mode of aesthetic representation in which shifts in media appear to register themselves.

Murphet's ascription of agency to media is distinctly Kittlerian. He rejects "a familiar three-stage hypothesis according to which new technologies alter the public imagination, which in turn transforms the raw material and formal strategies of artists and writers" (Murphet 9–10). By centering, in some proportion, consciousness or society as mediating technological change, such a model remains fundamentally humanist (or at least sociological). In modernism, Murphet contends, one witnesses something more radical. "The opacity of the modernist text, its recourse to as yet unsystematized informational registers, is not some 'inward turn' to the depths of a putative 'modern subject,' but on the contrary, a raising of the matter of literature to a surface of touch and conversion with other media" (Murphet 4). Modernist writers were, in short, engaged in "a concerted becoming-media of the arts" (Murphet 5).

We see this becoming-media of the arts, Murphet suggests, in the work of Gertrude Stein. In a lecture Stein once remarked that what she was "doing what the cinema was doing" (294). Her first American publication, in fact, was in a special issue of *Camera Work*, "A Photographic Quarterly," filled with images of post-impressionist art, including many by Picasso and Matisse. Stein's challenging prose-poem portraits of Matisse and Picasso offer what Alfred Steiglitz, in introducing the issue, calls a "Rosetta Stone." Her prose poems use "a medium in the technical manipulation of which we are all at least tyros," that is, language, to translate the innovations of post-impressionist painting across media. Steiglitz justifies the relevance and importance of Stein's prose poems in a periodical dedicated to photography by explaining that they "bear, to current interpretive criticism, a relation exactly analogous to that born [sic] by the work of the men of whom they treat to the painting and sculpture of the older schools" (4). Stein's poems, Stieglitz suggests, explain post-impressionism by performing the same aesthetic reorientation in a different medium.

Yet, as Murphet notes, subtending and enabling this exchange between painting and literature on the pages of a "photographic quarterly" is still another medium. The work of translating modernism across media is performed by the halftone printing that made the *Camera Work* special issue possible. Beginning in the latter half of the nineteenth century, half-tone printing used a series of dots to print images; it was a cheap and effective way of reproducing photographs and so was essential to *Camera Work*. This photomechanical technology which enabled *Camera Work*, as Michael North has also noted (*Camera* 60), allowed Stein's poem and Picasso's painting to appear on the same page of Steiglitz's journal. This colocation is as crucial to Murphet as the phonograph is to Kittler. It undoes the traditional *beaux-arts* conventions of the arts. Both Cubism and Stein's poems are revealed as "correlative instances of a reactive and intuitive abstraction that emerges as an inter-medial mutual adjustment" (Murphet 74). The page reproduced by halftone frees both painting and poem, image and word. In *Camera Work*, as in the wider media ecology of modernism, "word and image are identically subordinated, at a stroke, to a third and hitherto unexampled social power: namely, the photomechanical power of reproduction and its reliance on abstract grids" (Murphet 76). A Kittlerian anti-humanism is not far behind, for this narrative shifts the writer from an imaginative representer of the world, a creative writer, to a recording device: "these portraits owe nothing to imagination, but have been levelled to the flatness of their own materiality—'language as letters,' whose writer comes to resemble little more than a recording functionary" (Murphet 79). Stein claimed to be "doing what the cinema was doing" (294). In Murphet's interpretation, that means recording.

Kittler's work has a vexed relationship to contemporary approaches to media within modernist studies. While figures like Vissmann, Suárez, and Murphet continue a recognizably Kittlerian framework, more often critics take inspiration from the media archaeological focus on archival history than Kittler's deterministic insistence on the priority of war and media materialities as historical agents. Kittler's media theory is a decidedly "strong" theory at a moment when the New Modernist Studies has gravitated toward what Paul Saint-Amour, in a 2018 essay, has called "weak theory" ("Weak Theory"). Weak theory forgoes strong, unifying, deterministic claims in favor of description. Murphet, perhaps unsurprisingly, describes such "weak theory" as decadent,[11] but in fact most approaches to modernism and its media are a sort of weak media theory. Far more than any of the theorizations of media discussed here, the general tendency of approaches to media within modernist studies is less theoretical and more historical. Divorced from Kittler's strident anti-humanism and determinism, media archaeology's patient, textured contextualism is entirely at home in the New Modernist Studies.

---

[11] See his short essay "Decadence."

Conclusion: Digital Modernism

As at the turn of the last century, today there seems general consensus that *something* has happened at the level of media. If André Bazin asked *What is Cinema?*, the question "What is the digital?" hovers over the present. What are its contours and consequences? What are its politics? Just as one could see in cinema, among other things, a narrative mode, a visual poetry, or a hieroglyphic language, it is not entirely clear what exactly "the digital" is. Is it defined by the idea of computation and computability developed by, perhaps, Alan Turing? Are its origins in the analytical engine designed by Charles Babbage and Ada Lovelace in the first half of the nineteenth century? With Gottfried Wilhelm Leibniz's articulation of a binary representation of mathematics at the start of the eighteenth century? Perhaps the key fact of our moment is not computability per se, but the *ubiquity* of communications and connection? Does it originate, then, in the telegraph, described by Tom Standage in *The Victorian Internet* (1998)? Or perhaps the most salient attribute of the present is the fact of near constant recording, a shift in human memory that has been perhaps unrivaled since the invention of writing itself, as suggested by Vilém Flusser in *Does Writing Have a Future?* (1987)

All the questions that attended the emergence of film at the turn of the last century have returned in what feels like a *new* new media age. Marshall McLuhan, heralded for his apparently prophetic ability to see into the future, had anticipated it as an "electric age" and a "global village." While he was thinking chiefly of broadcasting and television, the internet, in many ways, is more of a "global village" than television ever was. The internet seems to repeat the tension between Walter Benjamin, on one hand, and Theodor Adorno and Max Horkheimer on the other. The excitement and potential that Benjamin saw in film was revived (often in a libertarian key) in proclamations by the internet's earliest proponents, like John Perry Barlow in "A Declaration of the Independence of Cyberspace" (1996). Simultaneously, however, the increasing sophistication of internet tracking and surveillance, driven by advertising, suggests that even Adorno and Horkheimer's most paranoid-sounding concerns about "administered life" may have been too modest. Friedrich Kittler saw the defining fact of the present technological moment not in global networking, the democratization of media, or the ubiquity of computers as technologies of surveillance and manipulation. Instead, it was in binary data, which promises a single "medium" (realized materially in devices as different as compact discs, fiber optic networks, volatile "flash" memory, and spinning magnetic platters) to dissolve all of culture in a stream of bits. A brief moment of dance from an old TV show is picked up by a popular video game, which spawns a series of "how to" videos on platforms from YouTube to TikTok, and then rematerializes (as I myself have witnessed) in elementary and preschools.[1] This mobility of culture is enabled by a single digital substrate, through which culture passes from one monetized platform to another. While it is a very different set of technologies, this moment, like the modernist period, seems like a media modernity, a moment of radical newness at the level of technologies of cultural communications, storage, and representation. As Tom Gunning writes, the two halves of the twentieth century "hail each other like long lost twins" ("Re-Newing Old Technologies" 51).

This book has explored the ways that modernism might be understood in relationship to its own media moment. Yet even our sensitivity to the shaping role media played in the modernist period might itself be understood as a reflection of our own moment. For instance, Emily Bloom describes her work on modernist radio as offering a model for our own digital moment.

---

[1] I am referring most immediately to the way that the video game Fornite has led to the circulation of brief dances, included in the game under the provocative nominalization *emote*. For details see Adi Robertson's "The 'Carlton Dance' Couldn't Be Copyrighted for a Fortnite Lawsuit."

As we stand on another precipice in this digital age, it is an important moment to revisit writers who struggled with similar conflicts and reshaped literary traditions to address a changing world. Rather than bemoaning the 'death of print' or embracing techno-determinism, these writers found a third path: channeling literary history into innovative broadcasts and leaving upon traditional forms, from the poem to the novel to the stage play, a distinctive radiogenic trace.

(Bloom 25–6)

As many of the scholars and critics discussed here note, our present interest in modernism's relationship to its media reflects not only a judgment about the modernist period but the condition of our own. Julian Murphet writes, "It is, then, in the consolidated context of the epochal advent of the computer that the assumption of a mediatory code of media systems to interrogate the conditions of possibility of modernist formal innovation attains a full dialectical intelligibility" (*Multimedia* 11). That is, it is only under our own technological conditions (chiefly, those of the computer) that we have become sufficiently sensitive to the ways modernist form reflects its own moment of technological change.

New Media's Modernism

Some critics have seen in modernism itself an uncanny anticipation of our own media moment. Paul Stephens, in *The Poetics of Information Overload: From Gertrude Stein to Conceptual Writing* (2015), describes modernism as a response to a feeling of "information overload" akin to our own. Following Sven Speiker, who describes "early-twentieth-century modernism as a reaction formation to the storage crisis that came in the wake of [James] Beninger's revolution, a giant paper jam based on the exponential increase in stored data" (qtd. in Stephens 8–9), Stephens traces a lineage of avant-garde poetry that responds to this condition. The tradition Stephens follows is akin to that described by Marjorie Perloff in *Radical Artifice: Writing Poetry in the Age of Media* (1991). Just as McLuhan suspected, it is avant-garde poets, from Gertrude Stein through Charles Olson to Lyn Hejinian, Bruce Andrews, and more contemporary avant-garde poets like Kenneth Goldsmith, who are especially attuned to the effects of media change. For Stephens they are sensitive to the challenge of information overload in particular. Ezra Pound, in *How to Read* (1931), defined "Great literature" as "language charged with meaning to the utmost possible degree" (23) and later describes literature as "the most condensed form of communication" (53). This positions literature as the antidote to what he describes in *Guide Kulchur* (1938) as "the heteroclite mass of undigested information hurled at him daily and monthly" (23; qtd. in Love 89). While Kittler declares that technological modernity essentially brings "poetry" to an end (*Gramophone* 80), Stephens identifies a particular strain of avant-garde poetry as uniquely suited to those same conditions: "many of the central aesthetic and political questions with regard to information overload are addressed or anticipated within twentieth-century avant-garde writing" (Stephens xi). Stephens sees modernist poems themselves as an attempt to overcome this information overload. "Could," Stephens asks, "*The Cantos* and *The Waste Land* be considered epics of sampling or of data compression?" (11).

In "Cybernetic Modernism and the Feedback Loop: Ezra Pound's Poetics of Transmission" (2016), Heather Love explores a parallel reading of Pound in order to connect his poetry to the midcentury discourse of cybernetics. First defined by Norbert Wiener, cybernetics was to be a science of communications, with *feedback* as a key component. Perceiving a fundamental similarity between control processes in both computing machines and in "living tissue," Wiener proposes cybernetics to describe "the entire field of control and communication theory, whether in the machine or in the animal" (11). It is evident even in something as simple as picking up a pencil. Picking up a pencil involves moving a whole series of muscles; but that is not what we think about when we pick up a pencil. Indeed most people don't know which particular muscles are involved. Instead, Wiener explains, we simply do it: "what we will is to *pick the pencil up*. Once we have determined on this, our motion proceeds in such a way that we may say roughly that the amount by which the pencil is not yet picked up is decreased at each stage. This part of the action is not in full consciousness." Doing so requires, however, "a report to the nervous system, conscious or unconscious, of the amount by which we have failed to pick up the pencil at each instant" (7). This is the importance of *feedback* and communication to any complex system—whether picking up a pencil or (to select another of Wiener's examples) aircraft-targeting systems. Feedback plays a crucial role in cybernetics because it allows processes of control to adapt and adjust. Pound's poetry, Love suggests, with its repetitions, creates feedback loops akin to those described by Wiener. Yet, she insists, Pound's readers operate very differently than the cybernetic machines described by Wiener. "Through the poetry, Pound certainly enacts a cybernetic communication strategy. Its wildly looping linguistic feedback, however, presents an aesthetically excessive alternative to the regulated, statistical pattern seeking of Wiener's prediction machines" (106). Modernist fragmentation here offers an aestheticized alternative to cybernetic rationalization. In Love's reading, "Modernist authors—and modernist culture more broadly—contributed early and important ideas to the twentieth century's evolving conceptions of information and data and also to its emergent understanding of technology's social implications and subjective dimensions. By explicating these connections, we can showcase modernism's status as a formative movement in the looping cultural lineage of cybernetic thought" (Love 107).

Like Pound's, the work of Gertrude Stein has proven rich for such comparisons between the media conditions of the early twentieth century and our own. Stephens sees in Stein's poetry a resistance to the conditions of information overload produced by Taylorist industrial labor production. "Stein's use of repetition makes the reader extremely self-conscious of the rhythmic nature of language, and runs generally counter to the Taylorist notion of a discrete normative duration" (Stephens 55). The repetitious syntax of a book like *The Making of Americans* works to create a continuous present, and so "the state of continuous partial attention is celebrated, and produces not stress or crisis, but rather pleasure and possibly contemplative absorption" (Stephens 50). Elements like repetition have often led readers to find Stein's work "unreadable," but Stephens suggests such repetition makes Stein's work uniquely responsive to the problem of information overload.

Natalia Cecire, in "Ways of Not Reading Gertrude Stein" (2015), similarly reads Stein's work in reference to labor—not, however, the Taylorist labor of production that Stephens highlights, but to the ignored, and specifically feminine, labor of social reproduction and domestic life. Such labor is evident, Cecire argues, in both *The*

Autobiography of Alice B Toklas and in Stein's poem "Sacred Emily" (where the Steinian slogan "a rose is a rose is a rose" first appears). If Stein's literary work reproduces the repetitiousness of domestic work historically performed by women (the so-called reproductive labor of childcare, cooking, and cleaning), Cecire suggests, then the tendency of critics to treat it as somehow "unreadable" reveals the gendered logic of other claims about *unreadability* in the present. In particular, claims about the unreadability of large databases of texts, including literary texts, that are purportedly made tractable not by *reading* but by "distant reading"—using computers, text analysis, and "data mining."[2] Stein's modernism reveals the gendered character of what counts as worth reading in ways that continue to be relevant. "Stein's unreadability," Cecire writes, "anticipates the conditions of distant reading" (295). Moreover, this is not simply a matter of stylistic similarity between approaches to Stein's difficult body of work and digital approaches to large databases of text; it reflects the history of women's labor more generally—from the domestic labor that is highlighted, Cecire suggests, by Stein in "Sacred Emily" and *The Autobiography of Alice B Toklas* to the labor of typing, the work of early "computers"—like "typewriter," as Cecire notes, the term "computer" could refer both to the person who operated the device (typically a woman) and the device itself— or contemporary book digitization.

James Purdon's *Modernist Informatics: Literature, Information, and the State* (2016) likewise sees in modernist literature an anticipation of our own information age. Rather than cybernetics or distant reading, however, Purdon locates modernism within a longer history of informatics. While the emergence of "informatics," as the science of communications technology, is typically located in the 1960s (the OED lists the first use of the term in 1967), Purdon follows the historian James Beniger in describing a "control revolution" with origins much earlier in the century. Rather than the quasi-Kitterlian focus on the computing technologies of the Second World War, associated with cybernetics and Vannevar Bush among others, Beniger's "control revolution," described in a 1986

---

[2] Tanya Clement, for instance, discusses her work distant reading stein in "The Story of One: Narrative and Composition in Gertrude Stein's *The Making of Americans*" (2012).

book of that title, locates the emergence of the information society in industrial forces, akin to those described by Jonathan Crary and Mary Ann Doane, and ultimately grounded in the economy. For Beniger, whose work seems increasingly relevant to attempts to trace the prehistory of digital technology in the modernist period, the rise of informatics and the "information society" have their origin in the increased speed enabled by advancements in industrial production. The railway offers a key example. As is well known, the speed of trains required standardized time zones to avoid accidents and ensure safe, efficient rail travel. For Beniger the key to rail travel is a sort of preprocessing which transforms the world into information by simplifying it. The establishment of five standardized North American time zones in 1883, and twenty-four global standardized zones in 1884, simplified the continuous passage of time into discrete areas. "What was formerly a problem of information overload and hence control for railroads and other organizations that sustained the social system at its most macro level was solved by simply ignoring much of the information, namely that solar time is different at each node of a transportation or communication system" (Beniger 15). Standardization, or what Beniger calls "preprocessing," overcomes information overload by imposing a uniformity that discards the richness and complexity of more traditional sorts of knowledge. In the face of overload, information management requires a deliberate impoverishment and a simplification of complexities.

Like other recent work in modernist studies, Purdon turns to the institutions that shaped media and its relationship to modernism, and the chief institution in Purdon's analysis is governmental. He reveals how information "has emerged as both the basis of modern political power and one of its primary objects of attention and control" (Purdon 7). His work then traces the tension such processes of simplification leave in the work of writers who were intimately familiar with the emerging information society, whether through the Mass-Observation project, through First World War bureaucracy (as Ford Madox Ford was), or through the experience of Black Out during the Second World War (as Elizabeth Bowen was). "The productive challenge posed to literature by the genres of information," Purdon argues, "was a significant factor in the cultural shaping of modernist narrative" (Purdon 5). He describes, for instance, the postal address system as a preprocessing of information complexity. This system becomes central to the plot of Joseph Conrad's *The Secret Agent* (1907). In that novel the piece of evidence that enables the police to connect the evil Mr. Verloc to the bombing of the Greenwich Observatory is a postal address. This key clue, Purdon notes, is "not a Holmesian spatter of mud or tobacco ash, but a written address label" (28). One reads not, like the genius Holmes, a meaning intrinsic to the thing, but a sign that has already been processed as data. Even something as simple as a postal address represents a Beningerian imposition of an information grid over a messier, more complex reality. For Purdon, Conrad's novel ultimately asks "Might the gratuitous, the material, the messy, mean anything? Or are we condemned, like Inspector Heat, to read only for that which points us away from what is in front of us to a system of which we already feel ourselves to be the masters?" (37). Purdon finds a similar sort of preprocessing in the marketing of Conrad's work, where the systems of mass consumption Beniger describes shaped the reception of literary works. In the uncertainty of how to understand *The Secret Agent*'s odd genre—as a sort of impressionist spy thriller—one sees as well the way that emergent information regimes shape modernism.

Ultimately, Purdon discovers in modernist informatics a prehistory of our own moment. He uncovers "informatic systems in the period between steam and cybernetics, when the statistical analyses of nineteenth-century public offices gradually became the informatic protocols of twentieth-century ministries, and the attention of government shifted from the analysis of populations and quantities to the control of access and channels" (Purdon 7). Between steam and computing power, modernism captures the moment when "information" crystallizes into an object, but an object that is as yet unavailable to the manipulations that digital technology will make possible. "This particular form of modernism flourished in a historical window between the development of technologies and techniques for controlling information flows, and the recognition that in the future such flows would ultimately come to govern not only the operation of the state, but individual identity as well" (188). Such a vision recalls N. Katherine Hayles's description of Henry James's novella *In the Cage* (1898) in "Escape and Constraint: Three Fictions Dream of Moving from Energy to Information" (2002), as a "prequel to the story of information in the twentieth century" (242). And both Purdon and Hayles see the more complete consequences of informationalization as evident in decidedly postmodern works of fiction. Rather than seeing, as Jessica Pressman and others do, a continuity between new media art and the modernism of the start of twentieth century, Purdon and Hayles highlight a contrast. Hayles finds the nascent vision of information in James's modernist novella completed in the total informationalization evident in science fiction works by Philip K. Dick and Alice Sheldon (writing under the pen name James Tiptree Jr). Purdon similarly sees his account of modernism as something like an archaeology of the "new responses to the conditions and pathologies of microprocessing and digitization, from the fiction of Thomas Pynchon and William Gibson to more recent work in live coding performance, in the use of digital effects and artifacts (pixellation, for instance) in non-digital media, and in the emergence of 'glitch' art" (Purdon 189).

It is to that more recent work that Purdon describes that we now, in closing, turn our attention. If our moment represents a second moment of media modernization, might there be a contemporary cultural or aesthetic modernism of our own moment? Can we hear in contemporary culture an echo of aesthetic modernism, harmonically resonating with that earlier moment, attuned by a single shared condition of medial change?

The New Aesthetic and New Media Modernism

If modernism represents a response to its media moment, might there be a modernism of our own moment? That would certainly be one way of understanding the loose grouping of works gathered under the name the "New Aesthetic." Originally a Tumblr blog organized by the British artist James Bridle, the New Aesthetic collects a wide range of materials, both artistic and vernacular, that in some way capture the *new* aesthetics of the our present. These works include advertisements, architecture, and art that reflect the way the world appears through the lens of the digital. Some of the images invite us to see the world the way computers do; "Seeing Like Digital Devices" was the subtitle of the panel that brought the New Aesthetic into prominence. Such digital devices now seem to offer a nearly ubiquitous adjunct to our perceptions: drone photography, surveillance cameras, facial recognition, the odd layering of satellite imagery, and other information produced by Google Maps, for instance. These images reflect a new technological reality. "It is impossible for me ... " Bridle writes in "The New Aesthetic and Its Politics" (2013),

> not to look at these images and immediately start to think about not what they look like, but how they came to be and what they become: the processes of capture, storage, and distribution; the actions of filters, codecs, algorithms, processes, databases, and transfer protocols; the weight of datacenters, servers, satellites, cables, routers, switches, modems, infrastructures physical and virtual; and the biases and articulations of disposition and intent encoded in all of these things, and our comprehension of them.

Bridle's Tumblr blog, still active at the time of writing,[3] collects precisely these new media inspirations, sometimes by simply drawing attention to them. The New Aesthetic might include art which problematizes precisely the interaction between the digital world and the "real" world. This is certainly one way of understanding Kelly Goeller's street art installation "Pixel Pour" (and "Pixel Pour 2.0"). Goeller places what appears to be pixellated water flowing from actual vent pipes. The result suggests the digital breaking into the "real" world. Appropriately, it is from the infrastructure that we typically ignore, or do not understand—vent pipes which emerge from city sidewalks, whose purpose is often unclear or simply ignored—that the digital seems to pour into this world. Pixelification more broadly—the appearance of the blocky patterns that make up the images on digital screens—is one of the stylistic hallmarks of the New Aesthetic. Bridle's collection shows it appearing in as widely disparate places as artworks, throw pillows, and military camouflage. In highlighting the ubiquity of such design elements, the New Aesthetic exposes the degree to which digital media shape culture even off the screen.

The New Aesthetic takes some banal element of digital culture (e.g., the pixel) and defamiliarizes it; it makes thick and opaque

---

[3] Available at: https://new-aesthetic.tumblr.com/

those elements that too easily glide into our experience of a digitally remediated world. What modernist poetry did to language, or modernist fiction did to the experience of daily life, or modernist painting did to the experience of looking, so the New Aesthetic does to our own ubiquitous digital environment. In "An Essay on the New Aesthetic" (2012), Bruce Sterling consistently frames it with reference to the avant-gardes of a previous century—to Baudelaire, to Cubism and Surrealism, to Marcel Duchamp and André Breton. Sterling smartly notes that in allying itself so firmly with a modernist, or early twentieth-century avant-garde, the New Aesthetic leaps over the more typical way of understanding such aesthetic engagements with contemporary technology—as essentially *postmodern*. In part that is because the postmodern itself has now aged, and an older, modernist lineage ironically seems a surer way of making it new.

> Most of the people in its network are too young to have been involved in postmodernity. The twentieth century's Modernist Project is like their Greco-Roman antiquity. They want something of their own to happen, to be built, and to be seen on their networks. If that has little or nothing to do with their dusty analog heritage, so much the better for them.

And so, "The New Aesthetic is one thing among a kind: it's like early photography for French Impressionists, or like silent film for Russian Constructivists, or like abstract-dynamics for Italian Futurists" (Sterling).

James Bridle's own series of "Drone Shadows" draw the outline of military drones, or "unmanned combat aerial vehicles," in public areas. These works make visible the often invisible presence of drones, intruding and materializing a digital technology (enabled by autonomous aircraft and a globalized telecommunications network). Just like "Pixel Pour," the "Drone Shadows" materialize what is often immaterialized by digital technology. But by placing their chalk outlines (redolent of a crime scene) to locales not typically subject to drone surveillance and strikes, they also expose the uneven distribution of violence enabled by this technology. As in the work of Teju Cole discussed below, and explored by scholars including J. D. Schnepf, Nathan Hensley, and Priya Satia, the *drone* has

FIGURE C.1 *James Bridle,* Drone Shadow 004, *Courtesy of the Artist.*

emerged as a uniquely powerful emblem of the power of the digital, and so a rich site for a new media modernism.

If the New Aesthetic is one manifestation of a "new media modernism," it is certainly not the only one. Nor is it even necessarily the most markedly *modernist*. Jessica Pressman's *Digital Modernism: Making it New in New Media* (2014) is the most sustained study of the relationship between contemporary new media and modernism. She links the high literary modernism of the early twentieth century with key works of new media literature. She examines, for instance, the ways that Judd Morrisey's *The Jew's Daughter* (2000) remediates *Ulysses* through its own, medium-specific exploration of digital textuality.[4] Morrisey's digital work presents a single column of text, which looks initially like a page from a book. On the page, however, a word or phrase appears in blue, like a hyperlink on a webpage. Hovering over this "link" with the mouse alters the text; it suddenly changes, sometimes subtly, sometimes more dramatically. On this newly rearranged page, another word appears in blue,

---

[4]Morrisey's text is available at http://www.thejewsdaughter.com.

which, when hovered over, similarly repeats the process. In this way, one "reads," or navigates the text. "*The Jew's Daughter* looks like a hypertext but refuses to act like one, and this refusal is central to its digital modernist aesthetic" (Pressman 107). By appearing to alter a single text, rather than linking to others, Morrisey's shifting text demands a reader attend carefully to each change—there is no "back" navigation. One struggles to understand Morrisey's text, which refuses the most fundamental affordance of the book as a medium—its fixity. It thus demands a mode of attention and reading that Pressman does not hesitate to call *close reading*. The modernist lineage of this mode of close reading is confirmed at the level of the content in the ways that *The Jew's Daughter* draws on and remediates *Ulysses* (Morrisey's work takes its title from the song Stephen sings Bloom in the "Ithaca" episode of Joyce's novel). For Pressman, this lineage not only reveals the crucial role that modernism has played as a resource for new media artists and writers. It also reveals something crucial about modernism itself. In this case, it shows that the "Ithaca" episode of *Ulysses* was already structured as a sort of database—a set of information accessed through a process of queries and responses. Ultimately, Pressman provocatively compares stream of consciousness narration to hypertext as fundamentally similar "technologies" for depicting the "associative nature of cognition" (118).

The newness of Pressman's digital modernism exists in tension, however, with the newness of the New Modernist Studies more broadly. If Pressman looks at "Making It New in New Media," she does so by examining new media from the perspective of a now rather old canon of modernism. As Shawna Ross, in an incisive review, notes, the canon of modernism that informs the new media works she explores is the unexpanded canon of the old modernist studies (14); it is the modernism of Pound and Joyce above all, with appearances from Gertrude Stein, Bob Brown, and others. Pressman's digital modernism seeks to "make new" modernism itself, just as the modernism of Pound or Joyce "made new" Homer. Close reading, sometimes relegated to secondary status, returns to centrality in Pressman's account, by offering a key strategy of resistance to the new media environment. And at the very heart of Pressman's definition of modernism is *difficulty*. Pressman, with good reason, suggests that the high/low distinctions typical of Clement Greenberg are complicated by an environment where corporate media platforms and a variegated media ecology "complicate[] any simple designations of high/low, modernism/postmodernism, counterculture/status quo, and so forth" (7). Yet Pressman's account nevertheless sounds a rather Greenbergian note. She celebrates a digital modernism that critiques "a society that privileges images, navigation, and interactivity over complex narrative and close reading." If, particularly in older accounts, modernism tended to be anything *but* celebratory of its contemporaneous *modernity* (think of *The Waste Land* above all), the digital modernist works Pressman describes similarly "challenge contemporary culture and its reigning aesthetic values" (2).

Pressman's account of digital modernism contrasts with other attempts to bring modernism into dialogue with new media. Pressman's focus on electronic literature explicitly seeks to separate digital modernism from, for instance, video games: "digital modernism rebels against this cultural situation and the affective mode exemplary of it—interactivity—by returning to an older aesthetic of difficulty and the avant-garde stance it invokes" (Pressman 9). In this way, as Mark McGurl notes in *The Program Era* (2009), "electronic literature remediates the values and practices of textual modernism (the fragmentation, difficulty, and general 'literariness' ...), replaying the venerable modernism/mass culture dialectic in its status war with a non-literary commercial variant, the video game" (43). Others, though, see a continuity. Dustin Anderson, in "Hemingway's Console: Memory and Ethics in the Modernist Video Game" (2018), sees a thematic continuity between the treatment of guilt in games like *Call of Duty 2* and Hemingway's *For Whom the Bell Tolls* (254). The depiction of memory of Joyce's *Finnegans Wake*, Anderson suggests, is enacted by Ubisoft's *Assassin's Creed* (259). Andrew Ferguson, in "Mirror World, Minus World: Glitching Nabokov's Pale Fire" (2013), offers a compelling comparison of video games and modernism, arguing that the experience of playing video games (his key example is the eight-bit classic *Super Mario Brothers*) is fundamentally akin to the experience of reading Vladimir Nabokov's *Pale Fire* (1962). Ferguson traces the ways that *glitching* and other concepts from video gaming recall a mode of modernist reading. The model offered by digital games thus becomes a way of retroactively understanding the unique challenges of modernist narrative. Ferguson augments Roland Barthes's famous division of *readerly* and *writerly* texts by describing a *playerly* text, and so links a tradition of modernist narrative experimentation (exemplified by Nabokov) to new media.

While not focused on games, Lisa Siraganian, in "Modernist Poetics After Twitter, Inc." (2016), similarly finds a modernism specific to the new media platforms. She sees in the work of a number of a poets on Twitter—including Mark Leidner, on whom she focuses—a recovery of modernism, what she calls "neo rearguard modernism" (204). Leidner describes finding poetic *form* in a wide range of contemporary new media genres: "IM chats, status updates, tweets, improvisational jokes, ad-hoc movie reviews, blog post, Instagram photomontages, and so on" (qtd. in Siraganian 210). In a reinvention of the medium akin to that described by Krauss or Cavell, Leidner's poetry seeks to make art out of social media forms. "Leidner sometimes struggles to subjugate that origin to his poetic vision," Siraganian explains, "more so than Bishop attempting to dominate the sestina or the villanelle. But the struggle is the point; the difficulties and failures of framing and forming art in Twitter only make his aesthetic successes sweeter" (212). For Siraganian, such media poetics are not about Twitter as a *medium* characterized by its constraint (first 140, now 280 characters), or its mode of distribution, but about Twitter as an emblem and product of a broader neoliberal culture: "the business models of social media platforms such as Twitter matter because these economic realities are inextricably and profoundly connected to the operations and characteristics of the medium itself" (207). By insisting on a conventionally modernist (and even *high* modernist) use of a mass media form, Siraganian detects a critical force in tweets.

While Siraganian does not discuss them, Teju Cole's "Seven Short Stories About Drones" (2013) similarly bring together Twitter as medium with a modernist literary tradition. Cole's seven short stories are *very* short—each is short enough to fit in a single 140-character tweet. Each retells a recognizable opening from a major novel, which is then abruptly cut short by the violence of a drone strike. The first, for instance, introduces drone violence to Woolf's *Mrs. Dalloway*: "Mrs Dalloway said she would buy the flowers herself. Pity. A signature strike leveled the florist's" (Cole). While the remaining works alluded to include Chinua Achebe's *Things Fall Apart* (1958) and Herman Melville's *Moby Dick* (1851), the center of gravity is clearly modernist: James Joyce's *Ulysses* (1922), Franz Kafka's *The Metamorphosis* (1915), Ralph Ellison's

The Invisible Man (1952), and Albert Camus's *The Stranger* (1942). By cutting off each of these novels at their very first sentence, Cole's "Seven Short Stories" joins a modernist literary inheritance with a new media technology (Twitter) in order to offer a critique of drone strikes and American state violence. In "Seven Short Stories About Drones" the brevity of the tweet, as a form, comes to threaten the richness and fullness of the modernist novel. The violence of a drone strike is figured by the brevity of the tweet. Yet, as with Siraganian's reading of Leidner's poetry, the modernist tweet serves to point to something beyond either literature or medium—to neoliberalism for Siraganian, or to the post-9/11 security state for Cole.

Modernism's enmeshment with the media of its moment makes it an especially powerful mirror for ours. We see this in the critics who find in modernist literature an anticipation of problems of information overload or interconnectivity that feel utterly contemporary. That same enmeshment also makes modernism a powerful tool for intervening and reimagining our moment, as we see in the contemporary writers and artists who return to modernist aesthetic strategies, and even particular modernist works, in order to address the present. The accounts of media and its modernism that we have surveyed may therefore prompt us to reask the questions those theorizations raised: to continue to wonder about what, if anything, media determines. What forces does it channel? What histories does it enable? Whom does it empower? The New Modernist Studies' expansion of modernism as a category may help to ensure that our answers to those questions remain useful.

WORKS CITED

Adorno, Theodor et al. *Aesthetics and Politics*. London: NLB, 1977.
Adorno, Theodor W. *Aesthetic Theory*. Trans. Robert Hullot-Kentor. London: Continuum, 2002.
Adorno, Theodor W. "Art and the Arts." *Can One Live After Auschwitz? A Philosophical Reader*. Ed. Rolf Tiedemann. Trans. Rodney Livingstone. Stanford, CA: Stanford University Press, 2003, 368–87.
Adorno, Theodor W. *Current of Music Elements of a Radio Theory*. Ed. Robert Hullot-Kentor. Polity, 2009.
Adorno, Theodor W. "The Curves of the Needle." *October* 55 (1990): 49–55.
Adorno, Theodor W. *Essays on Music*. Ed. Richard Leppert, Berkeley: University of California Press, 2002.
Adorno, Theodor W. "On Jazz." Trans. Jamie Owen Daniel. *Discourse* 12.1 (1989): 45–69.
Adorno, Theodor W. *Minima Moralia: Reflections on a Damaged Life*. Trans. E. F. N. Jephcott. London: Verso, 2005.
Adorno, Theodor W. "Schema of Mass Culture." *The Culture Industry: Selected Essays on Mass Culture*. Ed. J. M. Bernstein. London: Routledge, 2001, 61–97.
Adorno, Theodor W. "A Social Critique of Radio Music." *The Kenyon Review* 18.3/4 (1996): 229–35.
Adorno, Theodor W. "Transparencies on Film." *New German Critique* 24/25 (1981): 199–205.
Adorno, Theodor W., and Max Horkheimer. *Dialectic of Enlightenment: Philosophical Fragments*. Ed. Gunzelin Schmid Noerr. Trans. Edmund Jephcott. Stanford, CA: Stanford University Press, 2002.
Anderson, Dustin. "Hemingway's Console: Memory and Ethics in the Modernist Video Game." *Popular Modernism and Its Legacies: From Pop Literature to Video Games*. Ed. Scott Ortolano. New York: Bloomsbury Academic, 2018, 247–61.
Anderson, Joseph, and Barbara Anderson. "The Myth of Persistence of Vision Revisited." *Journal of Film and Video* 45.1 (1993): 3–12.

Apollinaire, Guillaume. *Calligrammes; poèmes de la paix et da la guerre, 1913-1916*. Mercure de France, 1918. *Internet Archive*, http://archive.org/details/calligrammespo00apol.

Armstrong, Nancy. *Fiction in the Age of Photography: The Legacy of British Realism*. Cambridge, MA: Harvard University Press, 1999.

Armstrong, Tim. *Modernism, Technology, and the Body: A Cultural Study*. Cambridge: Cambridge University Press, 1998.

Aronowitz, Stanley. *Dead Artists, Live Theories, and Other Cultural Problems*. New York: Routledge, 1994.

Barlow, John Perry. "A Declaration of the Independence of Cyberspace." *Electronic Frontier Foundation*, January 20, 2016. https://www.eff.org/cyberspace-independence.

Barthes, Roland. "The Death of the Author." *Image, Music, Text*. Trans. Stephen Heath. New York: Hill and Wang, 1977, 142–8.

Baudelaire, Charles. *The Painter of Modern Life: And Other Essays*. Ed Jonathan Mayne. London: Phaidon, 1965.

Baumbach, Nico. "Nature Caught in the Act: On the Transformation of an Idea of Art in Early Cinema." *Cinematicity in Media History*. Ed. Jeffrey Geiger and Karin Littau. Edinburgh University Press, 2013, 107–16.

Bazin, André. "The Technique of *Citizen Kane*." *Perspectives on Citizen Kane*. Ed. Ronald Gottesman. New York: Prentice Hall International, 1996, 229–37.

Bazin, André. *What Is Cinema?* Trans. Hugh Gray. Berkeley: University of California Press, 1967.

Beecroft, Alexander. "Blindness and Literacy in the Lives of Homer." *The Classical Quarterly* 61.1 (May 2011): 1–18.

Beeston, Alix. *In and Out of Sight: Modernist Writing and the Photographic Unseen*. New York: Oxford University Press, 2018.

Beniger, James. *The Control Revolution: Technological and Economic Origins of the Information Society*. Cambridge, MA: Harvard University Press, 1986.

Benjamin, Walter. "Author as Producer." *The Work of Art in the Age of Its Technological Reproducibility and Other Writings on Media*. Trans. Edmund Jephcott. Cambridge, MA: Belknap Press of Harvard University Press, 2008, 79–95.

Benjamin, Walter. "Newspaper." *The Work of Art in the Age of Its Technological Reproducibility and Other Writings on Media*. Trans. Rodney Livingstone Cambridge, MA: Belknap Press of Harvard University Press, 2008, 360–1.

Benjamin, Walter. "Theses on the Philosophy of History." *Illuminations*, Ed. Hannah Arendt, Trans. Harry Zohn. New York: Schocken Books, 1986, 253–64.

Benjamin, Walter. "The Work of Art in the Age of Its Technological Reproducibility." *The Work of Art in the Age of Its Technological Reproducibility, and Other Writings on Media*. Ed. Michael William Jennings, Brigid Doherty, and Thomas Y. Levin. Trans. E. F. N. Jephcott. Cambridge, MA: Belknap Press of Harvard University Press, 2008, 19–55.

Berman, Marshall. *All That Is Solid Melts into Air: The Experience of Modernity*. New York: Simon and Schuster, 1982.

Bernstein, J. M. "Introduction." *The Culture Industry: Selected Essays on Mass Culture*, by Theodor Adorno. London: Routledge, 2001, 1–28.

Bernstein, J. M. "Late Style, First Art: The Fates and Politics of Modernism." *MLN* 133.3 (June 2018): 604–36.

Bishop, Ryan, and John Phillips. *Modernist Avant-Garde Aesthetics and Contemporary Military Technology: Technicities of Perception*. Edinburgh University Press, 2010.

Blondheim, Menahem. "'The Significance of Communication' According to Harold Adams Innis." *The Toronto School of Communication Theory: Interpretations, Extensions, Applications*. Eds. Rita Watson and Menahem Blondheim. Jerusalem: Hebrew University Magnes Press, 2007, 53–81.

Blondheim, Menahem, and Rita Watson. "Innis, McLuhan and the Toronto School." *The Toronto School of Communication Theory: Interpretations, Extensions, Applications*. Jerusalem: Hebrew University Magnes Press, 2007, 7–26.

Bloom, Emily C. *The Wireless Past: Anglo-Irish Writers and the BBC, 1931-1968*. Oxford: Oxford University Press, 2016.

Bolter, J. David, and Richard Grusin. *Remediation: Understanding New Media*. Cambridge, MA: MIT Press, 1999.

Bordwell, David. "The Idea of Montage in Soviet Art and Film." *Cinema Journal* 11.2 (1972): 9–17.

Bordwell, David. *On the History of Film Style*. Cambridge, MA: Harvard University Press, 1997.

Bradbury, Malcolm, and James MacFarlane. "Name and Nature of Modernism." *Modernism 1890-1930*. London: Penguin, 1991, 19–55.

Bridle, James. "The New Aesthetic and Its Politics." *Booktwo.Org*. June 12, 2013. https://booktwo.org/notebook/new-aesthetic-politics/.

Brown, Bob. *The Readies*. Baltimore, MD: Roving Eye Press, 2014.

Burke, Kenneth. "Medium as 'Message'." *McLuhan: Pro and Con*. Ed. Raymond Rosenthal. Baltimore, MD: Penguin, 1968, 165–77.

Butler, Shane. *The Ancient Phonograph*. New York: Zone Books, 2015.

Buxton, William J. "The Rise of McLuhanism, The Loss of Innis-Sense: Rethinking the Origins of the Toronto School of Communication." *Canadian Journal of Communication* 37.4 (Dec. 2012). https://www.cjc-online.ca/index.php/journal/article/view/2658.

Byers, Nina, and Gary Williams. *Out of the Shadows: Contributions of Twentieth-Century Women to Physics*. Cambridge: Cambridge University Press, 2006.
Canudo, Ricciotto. "Birth of a Sixth Art." *French Film Theory and Criticism: 1907-1929*. Ed. Richard Abel. Princeton, NJ: Princeton University Press, 1993, 58–66.
Carey, James W. "Marshall McLuhan: Geneaology and Legacy." *The Toronto School of Communication Theory: Interpretations, Extensions, Applications*. Ed. Rita Watson and Menahem Blondheim. Toronto: University of Toronto Press, 2007, 82–97.
Carey, John. *The Intellectuals and the Masses: Pride and Prejudice among the Literary Intelligentsia, 1880-1939*. London: Faber and Faber, 1992.
Caughie, Pamela L. "Audible Identities: Passing and Sound Technologies." *Humanities Research* 16.1 (2010): 91–109.
Cavell, Stanley. *The World Viewed: Reflections on the Ontology of Film*. Cambridge, MA: Harvard University Press, 1979.
Cecire, Natalia. "Apple's Modernism, Google's Modernism: Some Reflections on Alphabet, Inc. and a Suggestion That Modernist Architect Adolf Loos Would Be Totally Into." (Aug. 11, 2015). Works Cited. http://natalia.cecire.org/research/apples-modernism-googles-modernism-some-reflections-on-alphabet-inc-and-a-suggestion-that-modernist-architect-adolf-loos-would-be-totally-into-soylent/.
Cecire, Natalia. "Ways of Not Reading Gertrude Stein." *ELH* 82.1 (2015): 281–312.
Chartier, Roger. *The Cultural Origins of the French Revolution*. Trans. Lydia G. Cochrane. Durham, NC: Duke University Press, 1991.
Chinitz, David. *T. S. Eliot and the Cultural Divide*. University of Chicago Press, 2003.
Clark, T. J. "Arguments about Modernism: A Reply to Michael Fried." *Pollock and After: The Critical Debate*. New York: Harper & Row, 1985, 81–8.
Clark, T. J. "Clement Greenberg's Theory of Art." *Critical Inquiry* 9.1 (1982): 139–56.
Clement, Tanya. "The Story of One: Narrative and Composition in Gertrude Stein's *The Making of Americans*." *Texas Studies in Literature and Language* 54.3 (2012): 426–48.
Cohen, Debra Rae, Michael Coyle, and Jane Lewty, eds., *Broadcasting Modernism*. Gainesville, FL: University Press of Florida, 2009.
Cohen, Debra Rae. "Intermediality and the Problem of the *Listener*." *Modernism/Modernity* 19.3 December (2012): 569–92.
Cohen, Milton A. *Hemingway's Laboratory: The Paris In Our Time*. Tuscaloosa: University of Alabama Press, 2005.
Cole, Teju. "Seven Short Stories about Drones." *The New Inquiry* (Jan.14, 2013). https://thenewinquiry.com/blog/seven-short-stories-about-drones/

Comentale, Edward P. *Sweet Air: Modernism, Regionalism, and American Popular Song*. Urbana, IL: University of Illinois Press, 2013.

Cook, Deborah. *The Culture Industry Revisited: Theodor W. Adorno on Mass Culture*. Lanham, MD: Rowman & Littlefield, 1996.

Cooper, John Xiros. "Modernism in the Age of Mass Culture and Consumption." *The Oxford Handbook of Modernisms* (Dec. 2010).

Crary, Jonathan. *Techniques of the Observer: On Vision and Modernity in the Nineteenth Century*. Cambridge, MA: MIT Press, 1990.

Daniel, Jamie Owen. "Introduction to Adorno's 'On Jazz'." *Discourse* 12.1 (1989): 39–44.

Danius, Sara. *The Senses of Modernism: Technology, Perception, and Aesthetics*. Ithaca, NY: Cornell University Press, 2002.

Danto, Arthur C. *After the End of Art: Contemporary Art and the Pale of History*. Princeton, NJ: Princeton University Press, 1997.

Decherney, Peter. "Copyright Dupes: Piracy and New Media in Edison v. Lubin (1903)." *Film History: An International Journal* 19 (2007): 109–24.

Deming, Robert H., ed. *James Joyce: The Critical Heritage. Vol. 1: 1907-27*. New York: Barnes & Noble, 1970.

Dettmar, Kevin J. H., and Stephen Watt, eds. *Marketing Modernisms: Self-Promotion, Canonization, Rereading*. Ann Arbor, MI: University of Michigan Press, 1996.

DiBattista, Maria. "This Is Not a Movie: *Ulysses* and Cinema." *Modernism/modernity* 13.2 (2006): 219–35.

Dinsman, Melissa. *Modernism at the Microphone: Radio, Propaganda, and Literary Aesthetics During World War II*. London: Bloomsbury Academic, 2015.

Doane, Mary Ann. *The Emergence of Cinematic Time: Modernity, Contingency, the Archive*. Cambridge, MA: Harvard University Press, 2002.

Duffy, Enda. *The Speed Handbook: Velocity, Pleasure, Modernism*. Durham, NC: Duke University Press, 2009.

Eagleton, Terry. *Literary Theory: An Introduction*. Minneapolis, MN: University of Minnesota Press, 2008.

Eagleton, Terry. *Walter Benjamin or, Towards a Revolutionary Criticism*. London: Verso, 1981.

Eisenstein, Elizabeth. *The Printing Press as an Agent of Change*. Cambridge: Cambridge University Press, 1980.

Eisenstein, Elizabeth. *The Printing Revolution in Early Modern Europe*. Cambridge: Cambridge University Press, 2012.

Eliot, T. S. "Marie Lloyd." *Selected Prose of T.S. Eliot*. Ed. Frank Kermode. New York: Harcourt Brace Jovanovich, 1988, 172–4.

Ellmann, Richard. *James Joyce*. Oxford: Oxford University Press, 1983.
Elmer, David. "The Milman Parry Collection of Oral Literature." *Oral Literature* 28.2 (2013): 341–54.
Elsaesser, Thomas. "Media Archaeology as Symptom." *New Review of Film and Television Studies* 14.2 (2016): 181–215.
Emerson, Lori. *Reading Writing Interfaces: From the Digital to the Bookbound*. Minneapolis: University of Minnesota Press, 2014.
Ernst, Wolfgang. "Media Archaeography: Method and Machine Versus History and Narrative of Media." *Media Archaeology: Approaches, Applications, and Implications*. Ed. Erkki Huhtamo and Jussi Parikka. Berkeley: University of California Press, 2011. 239–55.
Farrell, Thomas J. "The West Versus the Rest: Getting Our Cultural Bearings from Walter J. Ong." *Explorations in Media Ecology* 7.4 (2008): 271–81.
Felski, Rita. "Modernist Studies and Cultural Studies: Reflections on Method." *Modernism/Modernity* 10.3 (2003): 501–17.
Ferguson, Andrew. "Mirror World, Minus World: Glitching Nabokov's Pale Fire." *Textual Cultures* 8.1 (2013): 101–16.
Flaubert, Gustave. *The Letters of Gustave Flaubert*. Ed. Francis Steegmuller. Cambridge, MA: Harvard University Press, 1980.
Fleissner, Jennifer L. "Dictation Anxiety: The Stenographer's Stake in Dracula." *Nineteenth-Century Contexts* 22.3 (2000): 417–55.
Foltz, Jonathan. *The Novel after Film: Modernism and the Decline of Autonomy*. New York: Oxford University Press, 2018.
Foucault, Michel. *Language, Counter-Memory, Practice: Selected Essays and Interviews*. Trans. Donald F. Bouchard, and Sherry Simon. Ithaca, NY: Cornell University Press, 1977.
Foucault, Michel. *The Order of Things: An Archaeology of the Human Sciences*. New York: Vintage Books, 1994.
Fowler, Robert. "The Homeric Question." *The Cambridge Companion to Homer*. Ed. Robert Fowler. Cambridge: Cambridge University Press, 2004. 220–32.
Francina, Francis. "Institutions, Culture, and America's 'Cold War Years': The Making of Greenberg's 'Modernist Painting.'" *Oxford Art Journal* 26.1 (2003): 69–97.
Freeman, Judi. "Léger's *Ballet Mécanique*." *Dada and Surrealist Film*, Ed. Rudolf E. Kuenzli. New York: Willis, Locker, and Owens, 1987. 28–45.
Fried, Michael. *Art and Objecthood: Essays and Reviews*. University of Chicago Press, 1998.
Fried, Michael. "How Modernism Works: A Response to T. J. Clark." *Critical Inquiry* 9.1 (1982): 217–34. Print.
Fried, Michael. *Manet's Modernism, or, The Face of Painting in the 1860s*. University of Chicago Press, 1996.

Friedman, Susan Stanford. *Planetary Modernisms: Provocations on Modernity across Time*. New York: Columbia University Press, 2015.
Frisby, David. *Fragments of Modernity: Theories of Modernity in the Work of Simmel, Kracauer and Benjamin*. Cambridge, MA: MIT Press, 1988.
Frye, Northrop. "Across the River and Out of the Trees." *University of Toronto Quarterly* 50.1 (1980): 1–14.
Gance, Abel. "A Sixth Art." *French Film Theory and Criticism: 1907-1929*. Ed. Richard Abel. Princeton, NJ: Princeton University Press, 1993. 66–7.
Gencarelli, Thomas F. "Neil Postman and the Rise of Media Ecology." *Perspectives on Culture, Technology and Communication: The Media Ecology Tradition*. Ed. Casey Man Kong Lum. Cresskill, NJ: Hampton Press, 2006. 201–58.
Gitelman, Lisa. *Always Already New: Media, History and the Data of Culture*. Cambridge, MA: MIT Press, 2006.
Gitelman, Lisa. *Scripts, Grooves, and Writing Machines: Representing Technology in the Edison Era*. Stanford, CA: Stanford University Press, 1999.
Gitelman, Lisa. "Souvenir Foils: On the Status of Print at the Origin of Recorded Sound." *New Media, 1740-1915*. Eds. Gitelman and Pingree. Cambridge, MA: MIT Press, 2013. 157–73.
Gitelman, Lisa, and Geoffrey B Pingree, eds. *New Media, 1740-1915*. Cambridge, MA: MIT Press, 2003.
Gordon, W. Terrence. *Marshall McLuhan: Escape into Understanding: A Biography*. New York: Basic Books, 1997.
Green, D. H. "Orality and Reading: The State of Research in Medieval Studies." *Speculum* 65.2 (1990): 267–80.
Greenberg, Clement. "Avant-Garde and Kitsch." *Art and Culture: Critical Essays*. New York: Beacon Press, 1965, 3–21.
Greenberg, Clement. *The Collected Essays and Criticism*. Ed. John O'Brian, University of Chicago Press, 1986.
Greenberg, Clement. "Towards a Newer Laocoon." *Pollock and After: The Critical Debate*. Ed. Francis Frascina. New York: Harper & Row, 1985. 35–46.
Guillory, John. "Genesis of the Media Concept." *Critical Inquiry* 36.2 (2010): 321–62.
Gunning, Tom. "The Cinema of Attraction[s]: Early Film, Its Spectator and the Avant-Garde." *The Cinema of Attractions Reloaded*. Ed. Wanda Strauven. Amsterdam University Press, 2006. 381–8.
Gunning, Tom. "Re-Newing Old Technologies: Astonishment, Second Nature, and the Uncanny in Technology from the Previous Turn-of-the-Century." *Rethinking Media Change: The Aesthetics of Transition*. Ed. Brad Seawell, Henry Jenkins, and David Thorburn. Cambridge, MA: The MIT Press, 2003. 39–60.

Habermas, Jürgen, "The Entwinement of Myth and Enlightenment: Re-Reading Dialectic of Enlightenment." *New German Critique* 26 (1982): 13–30.

Hansen, Miriam. "The Mass Production of the Senses: Classical Cinema as Vernacular Modernism." *Modernism/modernity* 6.2 (1999): 59–77.

Havelock, Eric. *Preface to Plato*. Cambridge, MA: Belknap Press of Harvard University Press, 1963.

Hayles, N. Katherine. "Escape and Constraint: Three Fictions Dream of Moving from Energy to Information." *From Energy to Information: Representation in Science and Technology, Art, and Literature*. Eds. Bruce Clarke and Linda Dalrymple Henderson. Stanford, CA: Stanford University Press, 2002. 235–54.

Hayles, N. Katherine. *How We Became Posthuman: Virtual Bodies in Cybernetics, Literature, and Informatics*. Chicago, IL: University of Chicago Press, 1999.

Hayles, N. Katherine. "Print Is Flat, Code Is Deep: The Importance of Media-Specific Analysis." *Poetics Today* 25.1 (2004): 67–90.

Hayles, Katherine, and Jessica Pressman, ed. *Comparative Textual Media: Transforming the Humanities in the Postprint Era*. Minneapolis, MN: University of Minnesota Press, 2013.

Hensley, Nathan K. "Drone Form: Mediation at the End of Empire." *Novel* 51.2 (2018): 226–49.

Heyer, Paul. *Harold Innis*. Lanham, MD: Rowman & Littlefield, 2003.

Holtby, Winifred. *Virginia Woolf: A Critical Memoir*. Chicago: Cassandra Editions, 1978.

Hornby, Louise. *Still Modernism: Photography, Literature, Film*. New York: Oxford University Press, 2017.

Hovanec, Caroline. "Another Nature Speaks to the Camera: Natural History and Film Theory." *Modernism/modernity* 26.2 (2019): 243–65.

Huhtamo, Erkki. "From Kaleidoscomaniac to Cybernerd: Notes toward an Archaeology of the Media." *History of Sociological Impact of New Technologies* 30.3 (1997): 221–4.

Huhtamo, Erkki, and Jussi Parikka, eds. *Media Archaeology: Approaches, Applications, and Implications*. Berkeley: University of California Press, 2011.

Hullot-Kentor, Robert. *Things Beyond Resemblance: Collected Essays on Theodor W. Adorno*. New York: Columbia University Press, 2008.

Huyssen, Andreas. *After the Great Divide: Modernism, Mass Culture, Postmodernism*. Bloomington, IN: Indiana University Press, 1986.

Innis, Harold. *The Bias of Communication*. 2nd ed. University of Toronto Press, 1964.

Isherwood, Christopher. *The Berlin Stories*. New York: New Directions, 2008.

Jacobi, Carol, Hope Kingsley, and Elizabeth Jacklin. *Painting with Light: Art and Photography from the Pre-Raphaelites to the Modern Age*. London: Tate Publishing, 2016.
Jameson, Fredric. *Late Marxism: Adorno, or, The Persistence of the Dialectic*. London: Verso, 2007.
Jameson, Fredric. *The Prison-House of Language: A Critical Account of Structuralism and Russian Formalism*. Princeton, NJ: Princeton University Press, 1972.
Jameson, Fredric. *A Singular Modernity: Essay on the Ontology of the Present*. London: Verso, 2002.
Jay, Martin. *Adorno*. Cambridge, MA: Harvard University Press, 1984.
Jenemann, David. *Adorno in America*. Minneapolis, MN: University of Minnesota Press, 2007.
Jenkins, Henry. *Convergence Culture: Where Old and New Media Collide*. New York: New York University Press, 2006.
Johns, Adrian. "How to Acknowledge a Revolution." *The American Historical Review* 107.1 (2002): 106–25.
Johns, Adrian. *The Nature of the Book: Print and Knowledge in the Making*. University of Chicago Press, 1998.
Johns, Adrian. "How to Acknowledge a Revolution." *The American Historical Review* 107.1 (2002): 106–25.
Johnson, B. S. "Introduction to *Aren't You Rather Young to Be Writing Your Memoirs?*" *The Novel Today: Contemporary Writers on Modern Fiction*. Ed. Malcolm Bradbury. London: Fontana, 1977. 151–68.
Joyce, James. *A Portrait of the Artist as a Young Man*. Ed. Chester Anderson. New York: Viking Press, 1964.
Joyce, James. *Ulysses*. New York: Random House, 1990.
Kalliney, Peter J. *Commonwealth of Letters: British Literary Culture and the Emergence of Postcolonial Aesthetics*. New York: Oxford University Press, 2013.
Kane, Brian. "Phenomenology, Physiognomy, and the 'Radio Voice'." *New German Critique* 43 (2016): 91–112.
Kane, Brian. *Sound Unseen: Acousmatic Sound in Theory and Practice*. New York: Oxford University Press, 2014.
Kant, Immanuel. "An Answer to the Question: What Is Enlightenment?" *Practical Philosophy*, Ed. Mary J. Gregor. Cambridge: Cambridge University Press, 1996. 11–22.
Kant, Immanuel. *Critique of Judgment*. Trans. Werner S. Pluhar. Indianapolis, IN: Hackett Pub. Co, 1987.
Keane, Damien. *Ireland and the Problem of Information: Irish Writing, Radio, Late Modernist Communication*. University Park, PA: Pennsylvania State University Press, 2014.
Kenner, Hugh. "Marshall McLuhan, R.I.P." *Mazes: Essays*. San Francisco: North Point Press, 1989. 295–7.

Kenner, Hugh. *The Mechanic Muse*. Oxford: Oxford University Press, 1987.
Kerckhove, Derrick De. "McLuhan and the 'Toronto School of Communication.'" *Canadian Journal of Communication* 14.4 (1989). https://cjc-online.ca/index.php/journal/article/view/533
Kirschenbaum, Matthew. "Kriegsspiel." *Debugging Game History: A Critical Lexicon*. Ed. Raiford Guins, Henry Lowood, and A. C. Deger. Cambridge, MA: MIT Press, 2016. 279–86.
Kittler, Friedrich. *Discourse Networks 1800/1900*. Trans. Michael Metter and Chris Cullens. Stanford, CA: Stanford University Press, 1990.
Kittler, Friedrich. *Gramophone, Film, Typewriter*. Ed. Geoffrey Winthrop-Young. Trans. Michael Wutz. Stanford, CA: Stanford University Press, 1999.
Kittler, Friedrich. "Technologies of Writing: Interview with Friedrich A. Kittler." *New Literary History* 27.4 (1996): 731–42.
Kracauer, Siegfried. *From Caligari to Hitler: A Psychological History of the German Film*. New York: Noonday Press, 1960.
Kracauer, Siegfried. "Mass Ornament." *The Mass Ornament: Weimar Essays*, Ed. Thomas Y. Levin. Cambridge, MA: Harvard University Press, 1995, 75–88.
Krauss, Rosalind. "Photographic Conditions of Surrealism." *The Originality of the Avant-Garde and Other Modernist Myths*. Cambridge, MA: MIT Press, 1985. 87–130.
Krauss, Rosalind. *Perpetual Inventory*. Cambridge, MA: MIT Press, 2010.
Krupnick, Mark. "Marshall McLuhan Revisited: Media Guru as Catholic Modernist." *Modernism/modernity* 5.3 (1998): 107–22.
Leavis, F. R. *Culture and Environment: The Training of Critical Awareness*. London: Chatto & Windus, 1962.
Lebeau, Vicky. *Psychoanalysis and Cinema: The Play of Shadows*. London: Wallflower, 2001.
Léger, Fernand. "*La Roue*: Its Plastic Quality." *French Film Theory and Criticism: 1907-1929*, Ed. Richard Abel. Princeton, NJ: Princeton University Press, 1993. 271–4.
Levenson, Michael H. *A Genealogy of Modernism: A Study of English Literary Doctrine, 1908-1922*. Cambridge: Cambridge University Press, 1984.
Lewis, Pericles. *The Cambridge Introduction to Modernism*. Cambridge: Cambridge University Press, 2007.
Love, Heather A. "Cybernetic Modernism and the Feedback Loop: Ezra Pound's Poetics of Transmission." *Modernism/modernity* 23.1 (2016): 89–111.
Lukács, Georg. "Reification and the Consciousness of the Proletariat." *History and Class Consciousness*. Trans. Rodney Livingstone. London: Merlin Press, 1971. 83–222.

MacCabe, Colin. *T.S. Eliot*. Devon, UK: Northcote House Publishers Ltd, 2006.
MacNeice, Louis. "Eliot and the Adolescent." *T. S. Eliot: A Symposium*. Ed. Richard March and Tambimuttu. Freeport, NY: Books for Libraries Press, 1968. 147–52.
Marcus, Laura. "How Newness Enters the World: The Birth of Cinema and the Origins of Man." *Literature and Visual Technologies: Writing After Cinema*. Ed. Julian Murphet, and Lydia Rainford. Houndmills, Basingstoke, Hampshire: Palgrave Macmillan, 2003. 29–45.
Marcus, Laura. *The Tenth Muse: Writing about Cinema in the Modernist Period*. Oxford: Oxford University Press, 2007.
Marcus, Laura. *Virginia Woolf*. Liverpool University Press, 1995.
Marinetti, F. T. "The Founding and Manifesto of Futurism." *Marinetti: Selected Writings*. New York: Farrar, Strauss and Giroux, 1971. 39–44.
Matthews, John. "Faulkner and the Culture Industry." *The Cambridge Companion to William Faulkner*. Ed. Philip M. Weinstein. Cambridge: Cambridge University Press, 1995. 51–74.
Maurer, Maurer. *Aviation in the U.S. Army, 1919-1939*. Washington, DC: Office of Air Force History, U.S. Air Force, 1987.
McCabe, Susan. *Cinematic Modernism: Modernist Poetry and Film*. Cambridge University Press, 2005.
McCourt, John. "Introduction: From the Real to the Reel and Back: Explorations into Joyce and Cinema." *Roll Away the Reel World: James Joyce and Cinema*. Ed. John McCourt, Cork University Press, 2010. 1–11.
McEnaney, Tom. *Acoustic Properties: Radio, Narrative, and the New Neighborhood of the Americas*. Evanston, IL: Northwestern University Press, 2017.
McGann, Jerome. *Black Riders: The Visible Language of Modernism*. Princeton, NJ: Princeton University Press, 1993.
McGurl, Mark. *The Program Era: Postwar Fiction and the Rise of Creative Writing*. Cambridge, MA: Harvard University Press, 2009.
McLuhan, Marshall. *Culture Is Our Business*. New York: McGraw-Hill, 1970.
McLuhan, Marshall. *The Gutenberg Galaxy: The Making of Typographic Man*. University of Toronto Press, 2011.
McLuhan, Marshall. "Joyce, Mallarmé, and the Press." *Interior Landscape: The Literary Critiism of Marshall McLuhan 1943-1962*. Ed. Eugene McNamara. New York: McGraw-Hill, 1969. 5–21.
McLuhan, Marshall. *Letters of Marshall McLuhan*. Toronto: Oxford University Press, 1987.
McLuhan, Marshall. *The Mechanical Bride: Folklore of Industrial Man*. Boston: Beacon Press, 1967.

McLuhan, Marshall. *The Medium Is the Massage*. New York: Bantam Books, 1967.
McLuhan, Marshall. "McLuhan's Laws of the Media." *Technology and Culture* 16.1 (1975): 74–8.
McLuhan, Marshall. "Probe as a Tease." 1967. http://www.marshallmcluhanspeaks.com/understanding-me/1967-probe-as-a-tease/.
McLuhan, Marshall. *Report on Project in Understanding New Media*. Washington, DC: U. S. Office of Education, 1960.
McLuhan, Marshall. *Understanding Media: The Extensions of Man*. Cambridge, MA: MIT Press, 1994.
Metcalf, Stephen. "Neoliberalism: The Idea That Swallowed the World." *The Guardian*, August 18, 2017. https://www.theguardian.com/news/2017/aug/18/neoliberalism-the-idea-that-changed-the-world.
Miller, Tyrus. *Modernism and the Frankfurt School*. Edinburgh University Press, 2014.
Misa, Thomas J. "How Machines Make History, and How Historians (And Others) Help Them to Do So." *Science, Technology, & Human Values* 13.3/4 (1988): 308–31.
Mitchell, W. J. T. *Picture Theory: Essays on Verbal and Visual Representation*. University of Chicago Press, 1994.
Mitchell, W. J. T. "Representation." *Critical Terms for Literary Study*. Ed. Frank Lentricchia, and Thomas McLaughlin. 2nd ed. University of Chicago Press, 1995. 11–22.
Mitchell, W. J. T., and Mark Hansen. "Introduction." *Critical Terms for Media Studies*. University of Chicago Press, 2010. vii–xxii.
Morgan, Daniel. "Bazin's Modernism." *Paragraph* 36.1 (2013): 10–30.
Mullaney, Thomas. *The Chinese Typewriter: A History*. Cambridge, MA: MIT Press, 2017.
Murphet, Julian. *Multimedia Modernism: Literature and the Anglo-American Avant-Garde*. Cambridge: Cambridge University Press, 2009. Print.
Murphet, Julian. "New Media Modernism." *The Cambridge Companion to the American Modernist Novel*. Ed. Joshua Miller. Cambridge: Cambridge University Press, 2015. 210–26.
Musser, Charles. *Before the Nickelodeon: Edwin S. Porter and the Edison Manufacturing Company*. Berkeley, CA: University of California Press, 1991.
Musser, Charles. *The Emergence of Cinema: The American Screen to 1907*. New York: Scribner, 1990.
National, ABC Radio. "Marshall McLuhan Debates His Ideas on Australian TV in 1977." The McLuhan Project. http://www.abc.net.au/rn/legacy/features/mcluhan/videos.htm.

Niebur, Louis. *Special Sound: The Creation and Legacy of the BBC Radiophonic Workshop*. New York: Oxford University Press, 2010.
Nieland, Justus. "Infrastructures of Being: Modernism as Media Theory." *Modernism/modernity* 23.1 (2016): 233–42.
North, Michael. *Camera Works: Photography and the Twentieth-Century Word*. New York: Oxford University Press, 2005.
North, Michael. *The Dialect of Modernism: Race, Language, and Twentieth-Century Literature*. New York: Oxford University Press, 1994.
Olson, Charles. "Projective/Verse." *The Norton Anthology of Modern and Contemporary Poetry*. Ed Jahan Ramazani et al., 3rd ed, New York: W. W. Norton & Company, 2003. 1053–61.
Olson, David. "Whatever Happened to the Toronto School?" *The Toronto School of Communication Theory: Interpretations, Extensions, Applications*. Eds. Rita Watson and Menahem Blondheim. University of Toronto Press, 2007. 354–60.
Ong, Walter J. *Orality and Literacy*. London: Routledge, 2013.
Orr, John. *Cinema and Modernity*. Cambridge, UK: Polity Press, 1993.
Paraskeva, Anthony. *Samuel Beckett and Cinema*. London: Bloomsbury Academic, 2017.
Parikka, Jussi. *What Is Media Archaeology?* Cambridge, UK: Polity Press, 2012.
Peters, John Durham. *The Marvelous Clouds: Toward a Philosophy of Elemental Media*. University of Chicago Press, 2015.
Pippin, Robert. "Authenticity in Painting: Remarks on Michael Fried's Art History." *Critical Inquiry* 31.3 (2005): 575–98.
Pound, Ezra [B. H. Dias]. "Art Notes: Kinema, Kinesis, Hepworth, Etc." *New Age* 23.22 (Sept. 1918): 352. Modernist Journals Project. http://modjourn.org/render.php?id=116537017046875&view=mjp_object
Pound, Ezra. *ABC of Reading*. New York: New Directions, 1960.
Pound, Ezra. *Literary Essays of Ezra Pound*. Norfolk, CT: New Directions, 1954.
Pound, Ezra. "A Retrospect." *Pavannes and Divisions*, New York: Knopf, 1918. 95–111. Internet Archive, http://archive.org/details/cu31924021664408.
Powell, Larson. "Media as Technology and Culture." *German Studies Review* 37.2 (2014): 405–16.
Pressman, Jessica. *Digital Modernism: Making It New in New Media*. New York: Oxford University Press, 2014.
Purdon, James. *Modernist Informatics: Literature, Information, and the State*. New York: Oxford University Press, 2016.
Richards, I. A. "Literature, Oral-Aural and Optical." *Complementarities: Uncollected Essays*. Ed. John Paul Russo. Cambridge, MA: Harvard University Press, 1976. 201–8.

Robertson, Adi. "The 'Carlton Dance' Couldn't Be Copyrighted for a Fortnite Lawsuit." *The Verge*, February 15, 2019. https://www.theverge.com/2019/2/15/18226180/copyright-office-alfonso-ribeiro-carlton-fresh-prince-dance-rejected-fortnite-nba-2k-lawsuit.

Rood, Graham. "A Brief History of Flying Clothing." *Journal of Aeronautical History* (2014): 3–54. https://www.aerosociety.com/media/4847/a-brief-history-of-flying-clothing.pdf.

Ross, Shawna. "Close Rereading: A Review of Jessica Pressman, *Digital Modernism: Making It New in New Media*." *Digital Humanities Quarterly* 9.1 (2015).

Saint-Amour, Paul. "Weak Theory, Weak Modernism." *Modernism/Modernity*, September 2018. https://modernismmodernity.org/articles/weak-theory-weak-modernism.

Satia, Priya. "Drones: A History from the British Middle East." *Humanity: An International Journal of Human Rights, Humanitarianism, and Development* 5.1 (2014): 1–31.

Sayers, Jentery. "Prototyping the Past." *Visible Language* 49.3 (2015): 157–77.

Schaeffer, Pierre. "Acousmatics." *Audio Culture: Readings in Modern Music*. Ed. Christoph Cox and Daniel Warner. New York: Bloomsbury Academic, 2017. 95–101.

Schleifer, Ronald, and Benjamin Levy. "'The Condition of Music': Modernism and Music in the New Twentieth Century." *The Cambridge History of Modernism*. Ed. Vincent B. Sherry. Cambridge: Cambridge University Press, 2016. 289–306.

Schnepf, J. D. "Domestic Aerial Photography in the Era of Drone Warfare." *MFS Modern Fiction Studies* 63.2 June (2017): 270–87.

Schonig, Jordan. "Contingent Motion: Rethinking the 'Wind in the Trees' in Early Cinema and CGI." *Discourse* 40.1 (2018): 30–61.

Schopenhauer, Arthur. *The World as Will and Representation*. Ed. Judith Norman et al., Cambridge: Cambridge University Press, 2010.

Shail, Andrew. *The Cinema and the Origins of Literary Modernism*. New York: Routledge, 2012.

Shklovsky, Viktor. "Art as Technique." *Literary Theory: An Anthology*. Eds. Julie Rivkin and Michael Ryan. London: Blackwell, 2004. 15–21.

Singer, Ben. *Melodrama and Modernity: Early Sensational Cinema and Its Contexts*. New York: Columbia University Press, 2001.

Siraganian, Lisa. "Modernist Poetics After Twitter, Inc." *The Contemporaneity of Modernism: Literature, Media, Culture*. Ed. Michael D'Arcy, and Mathias Nilges. New York: Routledge, Taylor & Francis Group, 2016. 203–15.

Sitney, P. Adams. *Modernist Montage: The Obscurity of Vision in Cinema and Literature*. New York: Columbia University Press, 1990.

Solomon, Stefan. *William Faulkner in Hollywood: Screenwriting for the Studios*. Athens, GA: The University of Georgia Press, 2017.
Sontag, Susan. "Against Interpretation." *A Susan Sontag Reader*. New York: Farrar, Straus, Giroux, 1985. 95–104.
Spiegel, Alan. *Fiction and the Camera Eye: Visual Consciousness in Film and the Modern Novel*. Charlottesville: University Press of Virginia, 1976.
Standage, Tom. *The Victorian Internet: The Remarkable Story of the Telegraph and the Nineteenth Century's Online Pioneers*. London: Weidenfeld & Nicolson, 1998.
Stieglitz, Alfred. "Editorial." *Camera Work*, August 1912: 4–5. Modernist Journals Project. https://modjourn.org/issue/bdr565920/.
Stein, Gertrude. "Portraits and Repetition." *Writings, 1932-1946*. Ed. Harriet Chessman and Catherine Stimpson. New York: Library of America, 1998. 287–312.
Stephens, Paul. *The Poetics of Information Overload: From Gertrude Stein to Conceptual Writing*. Minneapolis, MN: University of Minnesota Press, 2015.
Sterling, Bruce. "An Essay on the New Aesthetic." *Wired*, April 2012. https://www.wired.com/2012/04/an-essay-on-the-new-aesthetic/.
Sterne, Jonathan. *The Audible Past: Cultural Origins of Sound Reproduction*. Durham: Duke University Press, 2003.
Sterne, Jonathan. "Theology of Sound: A Critique of Orality." *Canadian Journal of Communication* 36 (2011): 207–25.
Stewart, Garrett. *Between Film and Screen: Modernism's Photo Synthesis*. University of Chicago Press, 1999.
Stille, Alexander. "Marshall McLuhan Is Back From the Dustbin of History; With the Internet, His Ideas Again Seem Ahead of Their Time." *The New York Times*, October 14, 2000. https://www.nytimes.com/2000/10/14/arts/marshall-mcluhan-back-dustbin-history-with-internet-his-ideas-again-seem-ahead.html.
Stoker, Bram. *Dracula*. Ed. Roger Luckhurst. New York: Oxford University Press, 2011.
Suárez, Juan Antonio. *Pop Modernism: Noise and the Reinvention of the Everyday*. Urbana, IL: University of Illinois Press, 2007.
Taylor, Richard. "Ideology as Mass Entertainment: Boris Shumyatsky and Soviet Cinema in the 1930s." *Inside the Film Factory: New Approaches to Russian and Soviet Cinema*. Ed. Richard Taylor, and Ian Christie, London: Routledge, 1991. 193–216.
Theall, Donald, and Joan Theall. "Marshall McLuhan and James Joyce: Beyond Media." *Canadian Journal of Communication* 14.4 (1989): 46–66.
Trotter, David. *Cinema and Modernism*. Malden, MA: Blackwell Pub, 2007.

Vertraten, Peter. "A Modernist 'Attempt at Cinema': The 'Impurity' of *Pierrot Le Fou*." *Modernism Today*. Ed. Sjef Houppermans et al. New York: Rodopi, 2013. 219–35.
Virilio, Paul. *War and Cinema: The Logistics of Perception*. London: Verso, 1989.
Vismann, Cornelia. *Files: Law and Media Technology*. Trans. Geoffrey Winthrop-Young. Stanford, CA: Stanford University Press, 2008.
Watson, Rita, and Menahem Blondheim, eds. *The Toronto School of Communication Theory: Interpretations, Extensions, Applications*. Jerusalem: Hebrew University Magnes Press, 2007.
Watt, Ian. *Conrad in the Nineteenth Century*. Berkeley, CA: University of California Press, 1979.
Watt, Ian. *The Rise of the Novel: Studies in Defoe, Richardson and Fielding*. Harmondsworth: Penguin, 1963.
Weber, Max. *The Protestant Ethic and the Spirit of Capitalism*. Trans. Talcott Parsons. London: Allen & Unwin, 1976.
Weheliye, Alexander G. *Phonographies: Grooves in Sonic Afro-Modernity*. Durham, NC: Duke University Press, 2005.
Wellbery, David. "Foreword." *Discourse Networks 1800/1900*. Stanford, CA: Stanford University Press, 1990. vii–xxxiii.
Wershler-Henry, Darren S. *The Iron Whim: A Fragmented History of Typewriting*. Durham, NC: Cornell University Press, 2007.
Whittington, Ian. *Writing the Radio War: Literature, Politics and the BBC, 1939-1945*. Edinburgh University Press, 2018.
Wicke, Jennifer. *Advertising Fictions: Literature, Advertisement & Social Reading*. New York: Columbia University Press, 1988.
Wicke, Jennifer. "Reading Modernism, After Hugh Kenner (1923–2003): Hugh Kenner's Pound of Flesh." *Modernism/modernity* 12.3 (2005): 493–7.
Wicke, Jennifer. "Vampiric Typewriting: Dracula and Its Media." *ELH* 59.2 (1992): 467–93.
Wiener, Norbert. *Cybernetics: Or, Control and Communication in the Animal and the Machine*. New York: John Wiley & Sons, Inc., 1948.
Williams, Keith B. "Time and Motion Studies: Joycean Cinematicity in *A Portrait of the Artist as a Young Man*." *Cinematicity in Media History*. Ed. Jeffrey Geiger, and Karin Littau. Edinburgh University Press, 2013. 88–106.
Williams, Raymond. *Keywords: A Vocabulary of Culture and Society*. New York: Oxford University Press, 1983.
Williams, Raymond. *The Politics of Modernism: Against the New Conformists*. London: Verso, 1989.
Williams, Raymond. *Television: Technology and Cultural Form*. London: Fontana, 1974.

Willmott, Glenn. *McLuhan, Or, Modernism in Reverse*. University of Toronto, 1996.
Wimsatt, W. K. *The Verbal Icon*. University of Kentucky Press, 1954.
Wolfe, Tom. "Suppose He Is What He Sounds Like, the Most Important Thinker Since Newton, Darwin, Freud, Einstein, and Pavlov." *McLuhan: Hot and Cold*, Ed. Gerald Emanuel Stearn. New York: Dial Press, 1967. 15–34.
Wollaeger, Mark. *Modernism, Media, and Propaganda: British Narrative from 1900 to 1945*. Princeton, NJ: Princeton University Press, 2008.
Woolf, Virginia. "The Cinema." *The Captain's Death Bed : And Other Essays*. London: Hogarth Press, 1950. 166–171.
Woolf, Virginia. *The Common Reader*. New York: Harcourt, Brace & World, 1953.
Woolf, Virginia. *The Diary of Virginia Woolf. Vol. 3: 1925-1930*. Ed. Anne O. Bell. New York: Harcourt Brace Jovanovich, 1981.
Woolsey, John "Opinion, in United States of America v. One Book Called 'Ulysses.'" *Ulysses*. New York: Random House, 1990. ix–xiv.
Zielinski, Siegfried. *Deep Time of the Media: Toward an Archaeology of Hearing and Seeing by Technical Means*. Trans. Gloria Custance. Cambridge, MA: MIT Press, 2006.

INDEX

Boldface locators indicate figures; locators followed by "n." indicate endnotes

Achebe, Chinua, *Things Fall Apart* 225
Adorno, Theodor 24–5, 75, 140–1, 149, 195, 203 n.9, 204. *See also* culture industry
 "administered life" 212
 Aesthetic Theory 160
 "The Curves of the Needle" 168 n.17
 dialectical history 141 n.2, 147, 161–2, 176
 Dialectic of Enlightenment 24, 147, 150, 160, 162–3, 165–6, 167 n.15, 168, 174
 mass culture 147–8, 159, 163, 167
 Minima Moralia 159
 modernism 172–80
 "Music and Mass Culture" 174
 myth 160–2
 Negative Dialectics 162 n.12
 "On Jazz" 159 n.10, 177
 "The Radio Symphony: An Experiment in Theory" 149 n.4
 radio voice 170–1, 177, 179–80
 "A Social Critique of Music" 149
 "Transparencies on Film" 168 n.17
Alexander III, Tsar 36
"Analysts" (Homeric Question) 114

Anderson, Dustin, "Hemingway's Console: Memory and Ethics in the Modernist Video Game" 224
Andrews, Bruce 213
Annie Hall 106 n.1
Antheil, George 33
anti-aircraft search lights 198
Apollinaire, Guillaume, *"Il Pleut"* 126, **127**, 128–9
archaeological approach 24
Armstrong, Nancy, *Fiction in the Age of Photography* 19–21, 62
Armstrong, Tim, *Modernism, Technology, and the Body* 124
Arnheim, Rudolf 27
Arnold, Matthew 149
Aronowitz, Stanley, *Dead Artists, Live Theories* 51
arts 9–10, 18, 24, 27, 38, 47, 56, 80, 100, 149, 173, 183
 autonomy 84–7, 154, 157, 175
 beaux-arts 209
 birth of new 29–32
 as category 95
 and culture 4, 10, 73, 79, 158
 and culture industry 75
 installations and performances 96
 and kitsch 77–9, 89
 minimalist art and 94
 of modernization 2–3

and/or objects 87–94
"promise of happiness" 164
to technology 103–4
aura 153–8, 160
authenticity and modernism 88, 92, 99, 104
autonomy and politics (art) 84–7, 154, 157, 175
"Avant-Garde and Kitsch" (Greenberg) 73–9, 83–4, 86, 102, 174, 203
Avatar 195
Ayrton, Hertha, electric light technology 198 n.8

Babbage, Charles 1 n.1, 211
Bacon, Francis 163
Ballet Mécanique 33–4, 45
Barlow, John Perry, "A Declaration of the Independence of Cyberspace" 212
Barnes, Djuna 187
Barthes, Roland 224
    "The Death of the Author" 194
    Mythologies 108
Baudelaire, Charles, crowd experience 143
Bazin, André 27 n.1, 39, 44
    "In Defense of Mixed Cinema" 5
    "The Evolution of the Language of Cinema" 39 n.4
    understanding of *Citizen Kane* 40–1, 43, 45
    What is Cinema? 19, 39, 211
BBC 168–9, 179
Beardsley, Monroe C. 87
Beckett, Samuel 172, 175–6
    Film 33
    Malone Dies 83
    Molloy 83
    The Unnameable 83
Beecroft, Alexander 133 n.17

Beeston, Alix, *In and Out of Sight* 21–2
Beethoven, Ludwig van 148, 164, 168, 172–3
Beniger, James 213
    "control revolution" 216–17
    preprocessing 217
Benjamin, Walter 24–5, 35, 43, 66, 70, 79, 97, 141, 149, 177, 184, 212
    aestheticization of politics 157
    "Angel of History" 141 n.2, 185
    aura 153–8, 160
    "Author as Producer" 150–3, 153 n.5
    dialectical approach 151
    modernity thesis 66 n.16
    "Newspaper" 153 n.5
    post-capitalist society 159
    "Theses on the Philosophy of History" 141 n.2, 185
    "The Work of Art in the Age of Its Technological Reproducibility" 65, 149, 152–3, 156, 158
Bennett, Arnold, "Modern Fiction" 28
Bergson, Henri 121
Bernstein, J. M. 73, 175
Bicycle Thieves 41
Bishop, Ryan 200
Bloch, Ernst 142 n.3
Blondheim, Menahem 113, 118 n.12, 119
Bloom, Emily
    modernist radio 212–13
    The Wireless Past: Anglo-Irish Writers and the BBC, 1931–1968 178
Bloom, Leopold, *Ulysses* 31
Bolter, Jay David 9. *See also* remediation
    logic of hypermediacy 71–2
    Remediation 71

Bolz, Norbert 196
Borderline 33
Bordwell, David 36, 38, 66 n.16
  Film Art 37
  On the History of Film Style 37, 64
  modernity thesis 64–70
Bourdieu, Pierre, *Distinction* 77
Bowen, Elizabeth 190
Bradbury, Malcolm, *Modernism: A Guide to European Literature 1880–1930* 2–4
Bradnum, Frederick, "Private Dreams and Public Nighmares" 169
Braque, Georges 15, 73 n.1, 74
Breton, André 207, 221
  dualism of perception/representation 20–1
Bridle, James 219
  "Drone Shadows" 221, **222**
  "The New Aesthetic and Its Politics" 220
  Tumblr blog 219–20
Brooks, Cleanth
  Understanding Poetry 110 n.5
  The Well-Wrought Urn 86
Brown, Bob 223
  "readies" 3, 3 n.3
Bürger, Peter 172
Burke, Kenneth 122
Bush, Christopher, *Ideographic Modernism* 135–6
Bush, Vannevar 216
Butler, Shane, *The Ancient Phonograph* 186

Call of Duty 2 224
calligrammes (Apollinaire) 126, **127**, 128
Camus, Albert, *L'Etranger* 40, 226
Canudo, Ricciotto 27
  "The Birth of a Sixth Art" 65

capitalism 2–3, 14, 14 n.8, 24, 36, 70, 145–6, 149, 154, 159–60, 163, 173, 178, 181
capitalist production process 145
Carey, James W. 12
Carey, John, *The Intellectuals and the Masses: Pride and Prejudice among the Literary Intelligentsia, 1880–1939* 144
Caughie, Pamela 177
Cavell, Stanley 23, 52, 71, 73, 92, 101, 140, 225
  admiration for Hollywood movies 102
  search for new automatisms 98–103
  skepticism 88–9
  The World Viewed: Reflections on the Ontology of Film 42 n.6, 98, 101–2
Cecire, Natalia
  unreadability 216
  "Ways of Not Reading Gertrude Stein" 215
Cerasulo, Tom, *Authors Out Here* 46
Chaplin, Charlie, *Modern Times* 66
Chartier, Roger, *The Cultural Origins of the French Revolution* 11 n.7
Cheng, Vincent, *Joyce, Race, and Empire* 83
Chinitz, David, *T. S. Eliot and the Cultural Divide* 74, 77
cinema. *See* film/cinema
cinematograph 29, 65
  as invention without a future 30
  scenography and 50
Civil Rights movement 13–14
Clark, T. J. 103–4
  "Eliotic Trotskyism" 84

class struggle 151, 191
"classical cinema" 38, 41–2
Clement, Tanya 216 n.2
Close Up 52, 66
Cohen, Debra Rae
  Broadcasting Modernism 176
  "Intermediality and the Problem of the *Listener*" 179
Cohen, Milton, *Hemingway's Laboratory* 51
Cole, Teju 221
  "Seven Short Stories About Drones" 225–6
Coleman, James, slide tape works 97
Comentale, Edward, *Sweet Air: Modernism, Regionalism, and American Popular Song* 77
communication technologies 4, 73, 100, 104, 143, 216
Communist Manifesto (1848) 75
comparative textual media 17
"The Complete Works" (bpNichol) 130
composite photography 21
computing technology 1, 1 n.1, 184, 188, 195, 212–13, 216, 219
concrete poetry, tradition 128–30
Conrad, Joseph 34, 50, 63, 190
  The Secret Agent 218
"continuity editing" 38–9, 41, 156
Cook, Deborah 158 n.9
Cooper, John Xiros, "Modernism in the Age of Mass Culture and Consumption" 74, 77–8
Courbert, Gustave 81
Coyle, Michael, *Broadcasting Modernism* 176
Crary, Jonathan 69 n.18, 70, 185 n.4, 194, 217

condition of modernity 68
observation, reconceptualization 67
Techniques of the Observer: On Vision and Modernity in the Nineteenth Century 66–9
crooning of crooners 171 n.18
Crosby, Bing 171 n.18
cross-cutting 38, 48, 59
cultural groupings 2
culture industry 75, 140, 147, 158 n.9, 163–72, 181, 204
  "factory-like" situation 167 n.15
  media and 165–6, 168
  modernism and 172–4
Cummings, E. E. 128, 131
cybernetics 214–16, 218

Dallas, George Mifflin 32
dance 27 n.1, 212
Daniel, Jamie 159 n.10
Danielewski, Mark, *House of Leaves* 61
Danius, Sara, *The Senses of Modernism: Technology, Perception, and Aesthetics* 124–5
Danto, Arthur, "The Artworld" 95
De Kerckhove, Derrick 112 n.7
Decherney, Peter 32
Dedalus, Stephen (*Portrait of the Artist as a Young Man*) 75
Deming, Robert H. 48
Derrida, Jacques 189
  écriture 7
determinism, media 10–14, 132, 141–2, 182–3, 198, 207, 209
  problem of 10–15, 87
  seductive fallacy of 15
Dettmar, Kevin, *Marketing Modernisms* 74

DiBattista, Maria
  realms 60
  "This Is Not a Movie: *Ulysses* and Cinema" 59–60
Dick, Philip K. 219
Dickens, Charles 173
digital modernism 211, 221, 223–4
Dinsman, Melissa, *Modernism at the Microphone: Radio, Propaganda, and Literary Aesthetics During World War II* 176
distant reading 216, 216 n.2
Doane, Mary Anne 67 n.17, 69 n.18, 70, 217
  contingency 69
  The Emergence of Cinematic Time 52, 65, 68–9
  rationalization of time 68–70
Döblin, Alfred 148
Donald, Judd, *Untitled* 93
Duchamp, Marcel 95, 207, 221
Duffy, Enda, *The Speed Handbook* 65, 199

Eagleton, Terry 154 n.7, 192
  technologism 156 n.8
Edison, Thomas 29–30, 185
  Christening and Launching Kaiser Wilhelm's Yacht "Meteor" 32
  paper prints 32
Edison v. Lubin 32
Eisenstein, Elizabeth, *The Printing Press as an Agent of Change* 11 n.7
Eisenstein, Sergei 23, 36, 45, 47, 60 n.14
  Battleship Potemkin 37, 143–4
  Hollywood film 37
  October 36
  Strike 36–7, 37

electric media 13, 15, 124
Eliot, George 173
Eliot, T. S. 2, 23, 57 n.13, 74, 77, 105–6, 110, 121, 131, 144, 176, 204
  "Marie Lloyd" 28, 28 n.3
  "Metaphysical Poets" 109
  The Waste Land 54–8, 206–7, 214
Ellison, Ralph, *The Invisible Man* 225–6
Ellmann, Richard 60 n.14
Elsaesser, Thomas 198
  "Media Archaeology as Symptom" 195
Emerson, Lori 128, 130–1, 133, 184
  Reading Writing Interfaces 129
Ernst, Wolfgang 184

fabrication technologies 186–7
Farrell, Thomas J. 135 n.18
fascism 146, 156–8, 159 n.10, 171–2, 178
Faulkner, William 41
  "Turnabout" 46
Felski, Rita, "Modernist Studies and Cultural Studies" 66
Ferguson, Andrew, "Mirror World, Minus World: Glitching Nabokov's Pale Fire" 224
film/cinema 3, 22, 27, 27 n.1, 69–70, 73, 87, 143–5, 153, 155–6, 158–9, 167, 188, 195, 211. See also specific films
  avant-garde 40, 45, 66
  exhibition of 29
  histories of 38
  indexicality of 54, 142
  and literary modernism 56, 58
  and literature 23, 48–64

as medium 28, 30, 32, 38, 42–3, 56, 58, 62, 101, 145, 147, 156
and modernism 52, 54, 56, 58, 60, 64, 67, 101
modernist writing and 48–9
newness of modernism 28, 46
nickelodeons 30
problem of modernist 32–46
and prose style 59
techniques 40, 78
as "vernacular" modernism 43, 65
film modernism 22, 34–5, 39, 42. *See also* modernist film
fine arts 9, 18, 30, 87
first-wave feminism 4
Fitzgerald, F. Scott 22, 46
flashbacks 40–1
Flash (web animation technology) 97
Flaubert, Gustave 76 n.4
Flaubertian realism 50
Fleissner, Jennifer 193
Flusser, Vilém, *Does Writing Have a Future?* 211
Fokker, Anthony 196 n.7
Foltz, Jonathan 202
  The Novel After Film 48, 64
Ford, Ford Madox 63, 190, 217
Fornite 212 n.1
Forster, E. M., *Howards End* 154
Foucault, Michel 69 n.18, 193–4, 199, 201
  historicism 79, 189–91
  The Order Things 194
Fowler, Robert 114
Francina, Francis 85 n.6
Frankenthaler, Helen 94
Frankfurt School 24, 40, 74, 79, 102, 104, 139–40, 142 n.3, 144, 147, 150, 180, 203
  dialectical history 181, 183, 185

dichotomies 141
fascism and capitalism 178
materialist history 140
media 140, 142–3, 167, 177
modernism 104, 142–3, 177
preoccupations 176
free market 100, 162
Freeman, Judi 34
French New Wave 23, 41–2
Freud, Sigmund 2–3, 147, 207
  Civilization and its Discontents 143
  Group Pyschology and the Analysis of the Ego 143
  melancholy 54
  "reaction formation" 175
Fried, Michael 23, 71, 81, 87, 89, 98–9, 152
  absorption and theatricality 88, 90, 92, 101, 104
  "Art and Objecthood" 92–3, 96, 101, 104
  The Face of Painting in the 1860s 90
  literalist art 92
  Manet's Modernism 90–1
  minimalist art 93–4, 96
  politics of conviction 103–4
Friedman, Susan Stanford, *Plantery Modernism* 10
Frisby, David, *Fragments of Modernity* 144
Frye, Northrop 107
Futurists 2, 221

Galsworthy, John, "Modern Fiction" 28
Gance, Abel 27
  La Roue 33–4
Garros, Roland 196 n.7
Gaskell, Peter 143
Gates, Henry Louis, *The Signifying Monkey* 134

Gatling gun 196
Gencarelli, Thomas 17 n.10
Gibson, William 219
Gilbert, Sandra, *The Madwoman in the Attic* 192–3
Gilbert, Stuart 60 n.14
Gitelman, Lisa 14, 16, 119, 141, 205
  Always Already New: Media, History, and the Data of Culture 8
  New Media, 1740–1915 17
  Scripts, Grooves, and Writing Machines 177, 185, 206
  souvenir foils 185 n.4
glitch art 219
Godard, Jean Luc, *Breathless* 41, 45
Goeller, Kelly, "Pixel Pour" 220–1
Goldsmith, Kenneth 214
Goody, Jack 112 n.7
  The Consequences of Literacy 5 n.4
Gordon, W. Terrence 112
gramophone 155, 166, 188, 201–2, 204–7, 204 n.10
Gravity 195
Green, D. H. 116
Greenberg, Clement 25, 60, 71, 81, 88, 91, 93, 97, 102, 108, 122, 139, 141, 168, 175, 175 n.19, 185, 188, 223
  autonomy 86–7, 152, 175
  "Avant-Garde and Kitsch" 73–9, 83–4, 86, 104, 174, 203
  and the Cold War 85
  definition of medium 72, 80, 87
  "kitsch" 23, 74, 100, 121, 144, 174
  language of quest 73 n.1
  "literature" 80, 83
  "Marxian stance" 85
  medium purity 23–4, 73, 79, 82–3, 175
  medium specificity 80, 98, 103
  modernism 23, 73, 83, 87, 92, 94, 122
  "Modernist Painting" 84–5, 85 n.6, 99–100
  opacity 71, 83
  reduction and purification, process 87, 91, 93–5, 100, 140
  telos 95, 99
  "Towards a Newer Laocoon" 80–2, 84
Greene, Graham 190
Griffith, D. W. 34, 38–9, 52
  cross-cutting 48
  Intolerance 35, 37, 56
Grusin, Richard 10. *See also* remediation
  logic of hypermediacy 72
  Remediation 71
Gubar, Susan, *The Madwoman in the Attic* 192–3
Guillory, John 10
  "Genesis of the Media Concept" 9
Gunning, Tom 57, 62, 212
  "The Cinema of Attractions" 44–5
  narrative integration, cinema of 62–3

Habermas, Jürgen 160, 161 n.11
Hansen, Mark 15
  Critical Terms for Media Studies 7
  ontological condition of humanization 8
Hansen, Miriam 57
  classicism and modernism 38
  "The Mass Production of the Senses" 43

vernacular modernism 43, 65
Havelock, Eric 112–13, 112 n.6, 132
  A Preface to Plato 112 n.6, 116–17
Hayles, N. Katherine 167, 218–19
  Comparative Textual Media 17
  How We Became Posthuman 195
  medium specific analysis 167, 167 n.14
  "Print is Flat, Code is Deep" 17
Hazlitt, William 15
Hegel, Friedrich 136, 161–3
  Lectures on Aesthetics 27
Heidegger, Martin, *Being and Time* 88
Heisenberg 2–3. *See also* uncertainty principle (Heisenberg)
Hejinian, Lyn 213
Hemingway, Ernest 53, 207
  flat prose style 50–1
  To Have and Have Not 46
  For Whom the Bell Tolls 39, 224
Hensley, Nathan 221
Herbert, George
  "The Altar" 128
  "Easter Wings" 128
Heyer, Paul 118 n.12
Higgins, Dick 128
historicism 79, 141, 141 n.2, 189, 191
  and dialectics 141 n.2
Hollywood star system 156
Holtby, Winnifred 49, 58
Homer 112, 117, 120, 126, 132–3, 133 n.17, 157, 223
  "Homeric Question" 113–14, 117
  The Iliad 113, 115–16
  The Odyssey 113, 115

Horkheimer, Max 75, 140, 142, 149, 170, 173, 178, 195, 204. *See also* culture industry
  "administered life" 212
  dialectical history 141 n.2, 147, 161–2, 176
  Dialectic of Enlightenment 24, 147, 150, 160, 162–3, 165–6, 167 n.15, 168, 174, 191
  mass culture 167
  myth 160–1
Hornby, Louise, *Still Modernism* 21–2, 54
Howard, William K., *The Power and the Glory* 40
Huhtamo, Erkki, *topoi* 186
Hullot-Kentor, Robert 169, 171
humanism 182
  and its discontents 133–7
  prosthesis and 122–5
Humphrey, Robert 49
Huntington, Samuel 135 n.18
Hutchinson, A. S. M., *If Winter Comes* 74
Huxley, Aldous
  After Many a Summer Dies the Swan 47
  Brave New World 47
Huyssen, Andreas 74, 79
  After the Great Divide 74–5, 175

Imagists 2
imperialism, consequences 4
indexicality of film 54, 142
industrialization 3, 14, 69, 88
informatics (communications technology) 216–18
information society 217
information technology 188
  modernist fiction and 190

Innis, Harold 79, 112–13, 117, 118 n.11, 121, 123, 135, 139
 The Bias of Communication 118–19
 manufacture of papyrus 118–19, 118 n.12
 orality and writing 120
 "A Plea for Time" 120–1
Institute for Social Research 140, 142 n.3
interrupter mechanism 196 n.7
Interstellar 195
Isherwood, Christopher, *Goodbye to Berlin* 50

James, Henry, *In the Cage* 218
Jameson, Fredric 86–7, 102–3, 165, 173, 191
 A Singular Modernity 43, 85
 "torn halves" 158 n.9
Janowitz, Hans 146
Jay, Martin 164
Jenemann, David, *Adorno in America* 168
Jenkins, Henry, transmedia storytelling 167 n.15
Jewish Mysticism 79
Johns, Adrian, *The Nature of the Book: Print and Knowledge in the Making* 11 n.7
Johnson, B. S. 60–1
 Christie Malry's Own Double-Entry 61
 precise use of language 61
 The Unfortunates 61
Joyce, James 15, 23, 42, 61, 63, 105–6, 121, 148, 187, 207
 Anna Livia Plurabelle 60 n.14
 Finnegans Wake 83, 124, 224
 modernism 60, 63
 Portrait of the Artist as Young Man 45, 48, 48 n.9, 75
 Ulysses 5, 20, 47–50, 56–60, 60 n.14, 77, 83, 124–5, 222–3, 225
Volta Cinema 47 n.8

Kafka, Franz 175, 190
 "In the Penal Colony" 195
 The Metamorphosis 225
Kalliney, Peter, *Commonwealth of Letters: British Literary Culture and the Emergence of Postcolonial Aesthetics* 179
Kane, Brian 41, 171
Kant, Immanuel 53 n.10, 72, 164
 "An Answer to the Question: What Is Enlightenment?" 160–1
Keane, Damien, *Ireland and the Problem of Information: Irish Writing, Radio, Late Modernist Communication* 178
Kenner, Hugh 12, 23, 128–9, 131
 "McLuhan Redux" 123 n.14
 The Mechanic Muse 10
 The Pound Era 23
Kentridge, William 97
kinetoscope 29–31
Kirschenbaum, Matthew 198
Kittler, Friedrich 11, 24–5, 79, 125, 166, 181–2, 185–7, 185 n.4, 198–9, 200, 204 n.10, 206–7, 212, 214
 decentered subject 194–5
 "discourse networks" 182, 187–93, 196, 203
 Gramophone, Film, Typewriter 196, 196 n.7, 198, 203 n.9, 205
 inhumanism 193–5
 "Media determine our situation" (slogan) 198

media theory 181, 201–2, 209
    pedagogy and imagination
        191–2
    post-structuralism 189,
        193–4
    Romanticism 203
Klee, Paul 15, 73 n.1, 185
Kracauer, Siegfried 144
    *From Caligari to Hitler: A
        Psychological History of the
        German Film* 146
    "The Mass Ornament" 145
    modern mythology 147
Krajewski, Markus, *Paper
    Machines: About Cards
    and Catalogs, 1548–1929*
    189–90
Krauss, Rosalind 21, 23, 71, 94,
        98, 140, 225
    *The Originality of the Avant-
        Garde and Other Modernist
        Myths* 20–1
    Perpetual Inventory 94, 97
    post-medium art 96, 103
    readymade strategy (medium)
        95
    syntax/spacing of reality 21
Krupnick, Mark 108, 110
Kuleshov, Lev 35–6

Lacan, Jacques 189
Lady Chatterley's Lover 20
Latham, Sean, *Modernism:
    Evolution of an Idea* 6
Latour, Bruno, "Actor-Network-
    Theory" 14 n.8
Lazarfeld, Paul, Princeton Radio
    Research Project 168
Le Bon, Gustave, *The Crowd* 143
Leavis, F. R. 105
    Culture and Environment 144
    *Mass Civilization and Minority
        Culture* 144

Lebeau, Vicky 147
Léger, Fernand 33–4. *See also
    Ballet Mécanique*
Leibniz, Gottfried Wilhelm 211
Leidner, Mark 225–6
Lenin, Vladimir 35
Léon, Paul 60 n.14
Leppert, Richard, "Music and
    Mass Culture" 174
Le Prince, Louis 29
Lessing, Gotthold, *Laocoon:
    An Essay on the Limits
    of Poetry and Painting* 60,
    80–1, 82 n.5, 122
Levenson, Michael H. 55
Lewis, Wyndham 106, 112
    Time and Western Man 121
Lewty, Jane, *Broadcasting
    Modernism* 176
The Listener 179
literalist art 92
literarization 152–3
literary realism 19
Locke, John 160
Lord, Albert 115
    The Singer of Tales 117
Louis, Morris 99
Lounsbury, Myron, *The Origins
    of American Film Criticism*
    27 n.2
Love, Heather, "Cybernetic
    Modernism and the
    Feedback Loop: Ezra
    Pound's Poetics of
    Transmission" 214–15
Lovelace, Ada 1 n.1, 211
Löwenthal, Leo 142 n.3
Lukács, Georg 141, 153
    "Reification and the
        Consciousness of the
        Proletariat" 147–8, 152
Lumière, August and Louis 29
    cinematograph 30

Lumières exhibition (1895) 29, 31
Repas de Bébe 52
Lurz, John, *The Death of the Novel* 202

MacCabe, Colin 55, 58
MacFarlane, James, *Modernism: A Guide to European Literature 1880–1930* 2–4
MacNeice, Louis 176
"Eliot and the Adolescent" 55–6
Mallarmé, Stéphane 123, 204
Un Coup de Dés 124, 128
Malraux, André, *La Condition humaine* 40
Manet, Edouard 68, 81, 91–2, 94, 101
Le Déjeuner sur l'herbe 81, **89**, 90, 92
Olympia 81, 92
Marcus, Laura 27 n.2, 51–2, 66
The Tenth Muse 27, 48
Marey, Étienne-Jules 29
chronophotographic rifle 196, 198
The Photographic Gun **197**
Marinetti, F. T. 45, 207
"The Founding and Manifesto of Futurism" 28, 157
Marshall, Berman, *All That is Solid Melts Into Air: The Experience of Modernity* 75 n.3
Marson, Una 179
Marx, Karl 2, 10, 140 n.1, 147, 161–3
Marxism 11 n.6, 79, 86, 156 n.8, 162
mass audience 139
mass communications technology 104, 169

mass culture 74, 86, 103, 110, 124, 147–8, 159, 163, 167, 175, 177, 180, 204, 224
masses 143–4, 147, 153, 156–7, 163, 165–6
massification 139
and commodification 143–50
mass markets 143, 205
mass media 24, 43, 140, 144–5, 147, 225
mass movements 143
Mass-Observation project 217
mass production 143–5
mass reproduction
of printed texts 150
technologies 24, 148–9, 153, 177
materiality 4, 9, 12, 24, 72–3, 79, 83, 87, 122, 140, 181, 189, 209
Matthews, John, "William Faulkner and the Culture Industry" 46
Maurer, Maurer 200
Mayer, Carl 146
McCabe, Susan 55–6, 57 n.13, 60
Cinematic Modernism 3 n.2, 48
McCourt, John, *Roll Away the Reel World* 47 n.8
McEnaney, Tom, *Acoustic Properties: Radio, Narrative, and the New Neighborhood of the Americas* 179
McGann, Jerome 82
McGurl, Mark, *The Program Era* 224
McKay, Claude 134
McLuhan, Marshall 4, 11–12, 15, 17, 23, 25, 105, 112 n.6, 118, 141, 150, 153, 166, 181–2, 194–5, 211, 213

Civil Rights movement 13–14
Culture is our Business 123 n.14
electric age and global village 120, 125–6, 211
The Gutenberg Galaxy 11 n.7, 106, 109, 117, 118 n.10
humanism and discontents 133–7
"Joyce and Mallarmé and the Press" 123–4
"Laws of Media" 132 n.16
The Letters of Marshall McLuhan 118 n.11
literary and cultural studies 107
The Mechanical Bride 108–12, 109 n.3
media as prosthetic augmentation 195, 200
The Medium is the Massage. 112–13, 116, 118 n.11, 133
mediumistic geneaology 122
modernist style 107–12
New Critical formalism 106
print 150
probes/mosaics 108–9
prosthesis, humanism 122–5
sense ratios 123
theory of media 79, 122, 200
typewriter 125–6, 128–32
Understanding Media 11, 13, 106, 110 n.5, 117, 122–3, 126, 132, 134, 178
mechanical reproduction 140, 142, 148–50, 153, 155, 160, 171, 178
media 6–7, 73, 139, 181, 195, 212
definition of 8
as "extensions of man" 133
history of 107, 112–22
specificity of 16–25
media archaeology 24, 183–7, 189, 191
media determinism. *See* determinism, media
media ecology 17 n.10, 46, 63, 187, 201, 209, 224
media environment 3, 6, 73, 107, 109, 114–15, 187, 223
media-specific analysis 17, 167
media technology 3–4, 12–13, 17, 113, 120, 123, 125–6, 139, 149–50, 166, 181–2, 184 n.3, 186, 188, 192, 194, 201, 226
medium 6–7, 9, 19, 21, 23, 72, 87, 188–9, 202, 223
as category 7, 23, 95
film as 28, 30, 32, 38, 42–3, 56, 58, 62, 101, 145, 147, 156
problem of determinism 10–15, 87
retreat to 79–84
Twitter as 225
Méliès, Georges 31, 52
Four Troublesome Heads 44
Melville, Herman 190
Moby Dick 225
Metz, Christian 38, 44
microphone 171 n.18
Miller, Tyrus 154, 172
Modernism and the Frankfurt School 148
minimalist art 92–4
Misa, Thomas 140 n.1
Mitchell, W. J. T. 15, 84
Critical Terms for Media Studies 7
ontological condition of humanization 8
mnemotechnology 203
mode of perception 65
mode of production 7, 10, 163, 166, 169, 191
modern information technologies 136

modernism 1–2, 10, 70, 106, 172–80, 183 n.1, 188, 191, 203, 226
  art of modernization 2–3
  as cultural defense 3
  definitions of 6–10
  as literature of technology 3
  and media environment 3, 6, 73, 107
  and popular/mass culture 73–4, 175, 204
  video games and 224
modernist art 71–2, 82, 94, 97–9, 101, 104, 106, 108, 172–3, 207
  acknowledgement 87, 99
  autonomy of 175
  history of 173
  and kitsch 77
  as media prophecy 106
  metaphysical meaning 173
modernist film 32, 101
  problem of 32–46
modernity 2, 4, 21, 43, 65–6, 68–9, 71, 75 n.3, 76, 89, 134, 141–2, 224
  "unfinished project" 161 n.11
modernity thesis (Bordwell) 64–70, 199
Mona Lisa 153, 155
montage 35–7, 40, 54, 78
Morris, William 82
Morrisey, Judd, *The Jew's Daughter* 222–3
Morrison, Jim 198
Mullaney, Thomas, *The Chinese Typewriter: A History* 136–7
Mulvey, Laura 44
Mumford, Lewis 140 n.1
  Culture of Cities 5
Murphet, Julian 53, 58, 209, 213

Multimedia Modernism: Literature and the Anglo-American Avant-garde 207–8
"New Media Modernism" 50–1
Murphy, Dudley 33–4. *See also Ballet Mécanique*
music 81–2, 121, 164–5, 184 n.3, 203
Musser, Charles
  The Emergence of Cinema 185–6
  Before the Nickoledeon 38
mutoscope 29–31, 185
Muybridge, Eadweard 29

Nabokov, *Pale Fire* 224
Nashe, Thomas 123
new media modernism 213–19
  new aesthetic and 219–26
New Modernist Studies 62, 66, 72–4, 83, 85, 107, 140, 176–8, 180, 193, 209
Nichols, Walter 85
Niebur, Louis, *Special Sound: The Creation and Legacy of the BBC Radiophonic Workshop* 169
Nieland, Justus 5–6
North, Michael 208
  Camera Works 20–1, 208–9
  The Dialect of Modernism 134

Oakley, Annie 31
October Revolution 36
Olson, Charles 213
  "Projective Verse" 131–2
Olson, David 112
Ong, Walter 24, 113, 115, 116 n.9, 117, 126, 128, 130–3, 135 n.18, 153, 185

"oral noetic world" 118
Orality and Literacy 113, 135
writing restructures consciousness 123
oral formulaic theory 115
orality 113, 116–17, 116 n.9, 120, 131, 133–5, 159
Oram, Daphne, "Private Dreams and Public Nighmares" 169
Orientalism 135
Orr, John 42 n.6, 44
  Cinema and Modernity 42
Ortega y Gasset, José 144
Oxford English Dictionary 7, 129

painting 43, 53, 68, 72, 82–3, 88, 90–2, 98–100, 103, 148, 154–5, 208
Paraskeva, Anthony, *Samuel Beckett and Cinema* 47
Parikka, Jussi 183 n.1
Parker, Dorothy 46
Parry, Milman 79, 113–16, 115 n.8, 203
  "Homeric Question" 116–18
Passos, John Dos 22, 41, 148, 207
  Manhattan Transfer 40
  U.S.A 48
Pater, Walter 81
  The Renaissance: Studies in Art and Poetry 82
  "The School of Giorgione" 82 n.5
Peirce, C. S. 54 n.12
Perloff, Marjorie, *Radical Artifice: Writing Poetry in the Age of Media* 213
persistence of vision 67, 67 n.17
Peters, John Durham 106 n.1
  The Marvelous Clouds 12–13
phenakistiscope 29, 67
Philips, John 200
phonautograph 185 n.4

phonograph/phonography 9, 17 n.11, 177, 186, 203–6, 204 n.10, 209
phonographic recording 30, 53, 148, 171 n.18, 207
photograph/photography 17, 33, 52–4, 67–8, 121, 153, 155–6, 188, 208, 220–1
  books and collections 16 n.9
  as medium 22
  modernism 21
  and painting 18–19
  and realism 19–20
  as stillness 21–2
photography effect 68
photomechanical technology 208–9
Photo-Secession movement 17–18
Picasso, Pablo 15, 43, 73 n.1, 78, 208
pictorialism **18**, 19
Pingree, Geoffery, *New Media, 1740–1915* 17
Pinker, Steven 161 n.11
Pink Floyd 203, 203 n.9
Pippin, Robert 92
  "Authenticity in Painting: Some Remarks on Michael Fried's Art History" 88
Pitman, Isaac, shorthand system 206
pixelification 220
playerly text 224–5
Poe, Edgar Allan 4, 110
  "A Descent into the Maelstrom" 110–11
Pollock, Jackson 74, 94, 98
  automatism 98–9
Porter, Edwin S. 38
Postman, Neil 17, 17 n.10
post-medium condition 94–7, 103
postmodernity 100, 219, 221

Pound, Ezra 3, 23, 27–8, 33, 105–6, 123, 128, 135–6, 176, 215, 223
  The Cantos 214
  Guide Kulchur 214
  "Homage to Sextus Propertius" 129
  How to Read 214
  'Make it New' 42
  "The Return" 129
  "The Seafarer" 129
Powell, Larson, "Media as Technology and Culture" 202
Pressman, Jessica 219, 224
  Comparative Textual Media 17
  Digital Modernism: Making it New in New Media 97, 222–4
printing press 11, 15, 119, 123, 131
Protestant Reformation 15
Proust, Marcel 207
public media 2
Purdon, James 217–19
  Modernist Informatics: Literature, Information, and the State 190, 216, 218
purification, process 87, 91, 93–5, 100, 140
Pynchon, Thomas 219

Queneau, Raymond, *Cent mille milliards de poèmes* 130

radio 1–2, 4, 11, 73, 121, 124, 149, 149 n.4, 167–8, 200–1
  Adorno on 170–1, 177, 179–80
  as aesthetic medium 176
  ambient availability 170
  fascistic dimension of 170–1
  medium specificity 168
  modernist 169, 176, 178–80, 212–13
  Nazi use of 171
  politics of 179
  relationship to nation 178
Radio Free Europe 179
Ray, Man 32
  Emak Bakia 33, 45
realism 15, 19–20, 44–5, 50, 63–4, 68, 83
Reith, John 149, 155
"relations of production" 151
remediation 10
Richards, I. A. 105–6, 110, 112 n.6
Richardson, Dorothy 65–6
  "Continuous Performance" 52
Richardson, Samuel 5
Riefenstahl, Leni, *The Triumph of the Will* 157
Rilke, Rainer Maria 203
  "Primal Sound" 205
Rockettes 144
Rockwell, Norman 83
  Saturday Evening Post covers 74, 77
Rodker, John, *Adolphe 1920* 31
Rogers, Gayle, *Modernism: Evolution of an Idea* 6
Rolling Stones 203
Romantic period 192
Romanticism 81, 188, 203
"Rosetta Stone" 208
Ross, Shawna 223
Rothko, Mark 77
Rousseau, Jean Jacques 160
Russian Revolution 35–6

Saint-Amour, Paul 209
Sand, George 76 n.4
Sandow, Eugen 31
Satia, Priya 221
Saussure, Ferdinand de 108

Sayers, Dorothy 176
Sayers, Jentery 187 n.5
  "Kits for Culture" 187 n.5
  "prototyping the past" 186–7, 187 n.6
Schaeffer, Pierre 168
  acousmatic sound 169
  Treatise on Musical Objects 169
Schneider, Alan, *Film* 33
Schnepf, J. D. 221
Schoenberg, Arnold 172
Schonig, Jordan 52, 53 n.10
Schopenhauer, Arthur, *The World as Will and Representation* 81
Scrutiny 144
secondary orality 120, 185
serial photography 21
series of conventions 38
Shail, Andrew 49, 64, 101
  The Cinema and the Origins of Literary Modernism 48, 58, 62
  film culture 62
  rematerialization of literary language 63
Sheldon, Alice 219
Sherwood, Robert 27 n.2
Shklovsky, Viktor 34
short films, exhibition 29–32
Simmel, Georg, "Metropolis and Mental Life" 65
Sinclair, Upton 148
Singer, Ben, *Melodrama and Modernity* 66, 66 n.16
Siraganian, Lisa, "Modernist Poetics After Twitter, Inc." 225–6
Sitney, P. Adams, *Modernist Montage: The Obscurity of Vision in Cinema and Literature* 36

Skladanowsky, Max 29
smartphone 9
Smith, Adam 160
Smith, Tony 95
Society of Independent Artists (exhibition) 95
Solomon, Stefan, *William Faulkner in Hollywood* 46
Sontag, Susan, "Against Interpretation" 86
Soviet cinema 35, 37
Speiker, Sven 213
Spengler, Oswald, *The Decline of the West* 121
Spiegel, Alan 52, 58
  Fiction and the Cinema Eye: Visual Consciousness in Film and the Modern Novel 49–50
Standage, Tom, *The Victorian Internet* 211
steampunk 183 n.1
Steiglitz, Alfred 208–9
Stein, Gertrude 22, 59, 187, 207–9, 213, 215, 223
  The Making of Americans 83, 215, 216 n.2
  "Sacred Emily" 216
Stephens, Paul, *The Poetics of Information Overload: From Gertrude Stein to Conceptual Writing* 213–15
stereoscope 68
Sterling, Bruce, "An essay on the New Aesthetic" 221
Sterne, Jonathan 119, 141, 166, 184 n.3
  The Audible Past: Cultural Origins of Sound Reproduction 8
  "Theology of Sound" 135
Sterne, Laurence, *Tristram Shandy* 44, 128

Stewart, Garrett 58
Stieglitz, Alfred
  Camera Work 18
  photography 19
Stille, Alexander 107
Suárez, Juan 209
  Pop Modernism 206
superstructure 10–11, 166
symptomatic technology 14

Taylor, Richard 36
technological determinism. *See* determinism, media
technological developments 1, 10
technology 1–2, 8, 10, 12, 14 n.8, 65, 68, 136, 139, 149, 155, 182, 184, 187, 195, 200, 212, 223
  art to 103–4
  literature of 3
  of mass reproduction 148–9, 153
  as tool 7
  war and 200
telegraph/telegraphy 1, 3, 9, 51, 105–6, 136, 200, 211
teleology 185
telephone 3, 12, 16, 126, 150, 177, 198
Tennyson, Alfred, "Enoch Arden" 39
"ten-reel drama" 57 n.13
thaumatropes 67
Theall, Donald, "Marshall McLuhan and James Joyce" 108 n.2
Theall, Joan, "Marshall McLuhan and James Joyce" 108 n.2
Thomas, Dylan 176
Thomas Garner 40
Thompson, Jerry 41
Thompson, Kristin, *Film Art* 37
The Tiller Girls 144–5
Tin Pan Alley (song) 74

Tiresias 206
Toomer, Jean 22
Toronto School 5 n.4, 23–4, 104, 106, 112–13, 118, 133, 139–40, 150, 179, 182, 185, 195
  alphabet, role of 136
  humanism of 134, 137
  media ecological thinking 113
  media history 183
  orality in 134–5
Toynbee, Arnold, *Study of History* 133–4
traditional arts 9, 43, 71, 96, 104
transistor radio 16
transmedia 167, 167 n.15
Trotter, David 52, 53 n.11, 57 n.13, 58, 62, 101
  Cinema and Modernism 28 n.3, 48, 55–8
  neutral perception 58
Trouvé, Gustave 186
Turing, Alan 185, 211
  "halting problem" 1 n.1
Twitter as medium 225
typewriter 16, 125–6, 128–32, 136–7, 188, 192–3, 216
  as discourse machine gun 196
  as oral medium 133
Tzara, Tristan 207

Ubisoft, *Assassin's Creed* 224
ultracinematographic style 5, 40
uncertainty principle (Heisenberg) 2
"Unitarians" (Homeric Question) 114
University of Victoria Maker Lab 187 n.5

Verstaten, Peter, "terminological deadlock" 28
Virilio, Paul 196, 196 n.7, 198, 200
Vismann, Cornelia 209

Files: Law and Media Technology 190
visual technologies 29, 67
vortographs 3
voyeurism 44
"vulgar determinism" 11
"vulgar Marxism" 10

war and media 196, 198–202, 209
Wark, McKenzie 11 n.6
Warren, Robert Penn, *Understanding Poetry* 110 n.5
Watson, Rita 113
Watt, Ian
  Conrad in the Nineteenth Century 63
  The Consequences of Literacy 5 n.4
  The Rise of the Novel 4–5
Watt, Stephen, *Marketing Modernisms* 74
weak theory 209
Weber, Max
  modernity 141
  The Protestant Ethic and the Spirit of Capitalism 141–2
Weheliye, Alexander, *Phonographies: Grooves in Sonic Afro-Modernity* 134
Weine, Robert, *The Cabinet of Dr. Caligari* 32, 146
Welles, Orson 23
  Citizen Kane 40–1
  The War of the Worlds 177
Wells, H. G. 3
  "Modern Fiction" 28
West, Nathanael 46–7
White, Clarence H., *Spring* **18**, 19
Whittington, Ian, *Writing the Radio War: Literature, Politics, and the BBC, 1939–1945* 178–9

Dr. Who (television show) 169
Wicke, Jennifer 23
  Advertising Fictions 74
Wiener, Norbert 214–15
Williams, Keith 48 n.9
Williams, Raymond 4–6, 14 n.8
  Keywords 143, 162
  modernism 1–2
  Television: Technology and Cultural Form 14
Willmott, Glenn 107, 108 n.2, 110
  McLuhan, or Modernism in Reverse 109 n.4
Wimsatt, W. K. 87
Winthrop-Young, Geoffery 195–6, 198–9
Wittgenstein, Ludwig 98
Wolfe, Tom 106–7
Wollaeger, Mark, *Modernism, Media, and Propaganda* 17 n.10
Woolf, Virginia 23, 28, 63–4
  "The Cinema" 39, 53, 53 n.11
  Mrs. Dalloway 225
  indexicality 54
  Jacob's Room 49
  To the Lighthouse 49, 51–2, 54
  "Time Passes" 52
  The Waves 16
Woolsey, John 49
Wutz, Michael 191

Young-Hae Chang Heavy Industries 97

Zielinski, Siegfried, *Deep Time of the Media* 186
zoetrope 29, 185
Zola, Emile 148
zoöpraxiscope 29
zootope 185 n.4
Zuse, Konrad 1 n.1